The Instruments of Music

ROBERT DONINGTON

The Instruments
of Music

METHUEN & CO LTD
11 NEW FETTER LANE, LONDON EC4

First published by Methuen & Co Ltd in hardback
September 22 1949
Second edition, revised 1951
Third edition, revised and enlarged 1970
© Robert Donington 1970
SBN 416 17210 5

Second edition first published as a University Paperback 1962
Third edition, revised and enlarged 1970
SBN 416 18450 2

Printed in Great Britain by
T. and A. Constable Ltd, Edinburgh

Distributed in the USA
by Barnes & Noble Inc

TO HELEN

who saw the start of this,
and got me back
on to my proper path

Contents

PART ONE
HOW SOUND WORKS

PART TWO
HOW MUSICAL INSTRUMENTS WORK

PART THREE
MUSICAL INSTRUMENTS DESCRIBED

Plates

Between pages 22 and 23

Figures

Acknowledgements

I once more gratefully acknowledge the generous assistance, over one edition or another of this book, of the following persons, without, of course, implying that they are to be held responsible in any way for what finally got into it: Helen Anderson; Anthony C. Baines; Philip A. T. Bate; Gerald S. Bedbrook; N. A. Bessaraboff (Nicholas Bodley); W. F. H. Blandford; L. E. A. Bourn; Adam Carse; R. Thurston Dart; Hugh Gough; W. A. Guthrie; Eric Halfpenny; Gerald R. Hayes; F. Hillier; John Hough; Edgar Hunt; Lyndesay G. Langwill; Ll. S. Lloyd; R. Morley Pegge; Michael Prynne; F. Geoffrey Rendall; A. Thompson-Allen; Maurice Vincent; Egon Wellesz.

Most of the above are or were members of the Galpin Society, which is now the indispensable organization of those working on the instruments of music, whether as musicians, historians, collectors, teachers, classifiers or craftsmen. The Galpin Society Journal is invaluable, and the symposium *Musical Instruments*, admirably edited by Anthony Baines for the Society, will be found mentioned in my Reading List.

I must further renew my grateful acknowledgements to the Films Division of the Central Office of Information (Great Britain) and the Ministry of Education, jointly, for supplying me with the photos of Plates 24–35, and permission to reproduce them; to the publishers (The Macmillan Co, New York) and executors of Dayton C. Miller for permission to reproduce Figs. 1–16 from his book *Sound Waves* (for which see my Reading List); to the Boston Fine Arts Museum and N. A. Bessaraboff for permission to reproduce Figs. 19–22 and 24–25 from his book *Ancient European Musical Instruments* (for which see my Reading List); to Sir Robert Witt for the special favour of loaning me the photos for Plates 1–19 at a time when it would have been difficult to secure such material from the Continental galleries; to Thomas Harris, O.B.E., for a similar kindness with regard to Plates 20–21; and to the Radio Times Hulton Picture Library for Plate 36.

David Lasocki very kindly and helpfully discussed with me some of the recent developments in the technique of the flute and the recorder. I had a most excellent letter of criticism and information from that astounding Baroque (and modern) style trumpeter, Edward H. Tarr. My valued colleague at the University of Iowa, the composer Richard Hervig, went over my passages concerning the new music and the new instruments of music. I am grateful to all of these; and yet more am I grateful to the Contemporary Music Center here, under the general supervision of Richard Hervig and the brilliant musical directorship of the outstanding young composer William Hibbard.

Hugh Boyle finally read through my complete proofs, making many valuable suggestions of which it was mostly possible to incorporate the substance.

Both my English and my American typists, Mrs Dolores Ryan and Miss Jerry Nyall, deserve a special word of thanks for their rare skill and patient helpfulness.

ROBERT DONINGTON

The University of Iowa
Summer, 1969

INTRODUCTION

New music for a new age

The years since first I wrote this book have brought much strange new music, which would not have seemed to be music at all to a previous generation, and which even to many of the present generation scarcely seems to be music. But, of course, it is music. The complaint is one heard in every generation, and it is no more true now than ever it was. It is traditional for the young to grow up by asserting themselves against tradition.

In this book, many instruments of music are described which have a long traditional background. Some of them have been used, essentially in their present form, from the late Renaissance or earlier. Others have come into use, or have undergone substantial change, since that distant threshold of the modern age. Others, again, have gone out of use, perhaps for centuries, but have been or are being brought back into use because we find them best for music, originally composed for them, which we want to bring back into use.

All these traditional instruments are treated in this present, greatly revised and expanded, edition essentially as they were treated in the earlier editions. They are given equal treatment on purely acoustic considerations. Whether they are old and familiar, or not so old, or newly returning from an old but long forgotten past, makes no difference. If they are in substantial use at all in the current music-making of our main Western tradition, their place here is where they belong by virtue of their structure, their acoustic principles and their manner of performance.

There is no special treatment. What is currently familiar gets in, what is not currently familiar stays out. This is not a specialized treatise in any direction. It is a general introduction.

But now there are further instruments of music, currently familiar, which are not traditional. To some extent, this was already the case when first this book was written. Due place was found for them, on the same basic principles of structure, working method and method of handling. The use of electrical impulses as a source (not merely as an amplification or as a reproduction) of sound vibration was and remains the chief novelty involved. But the growth and development of such methods during the intervening years have changed the balance almost out of all recognition. It is here that my present revision and expansion needed to go so very far beyond anything that I had previously attempted.

All portions of the book, traditional or untraditional, have been revised, from these prefatory observations at the beginning, through the body of the book to the Bibliography and the Index at the end.

There is much new knowledge of old instruments to be taken into account, and I have tried to do so. There is, again, continuous new research in the basic study of acoustics, on the physiology of hearing, and other scientific subjects concerning which I have always felt it worth sharing with the reader an elementary understanding; I have made an effort to keep up to date, though the reader must not expect there the precision and immediacy of a front-line scientific report, which is not within my province, my capacities or my purpose here. There is much change, too, in the broad habits and manners of our current music-making, and in that I am on home territory and able to give a more professional report.

But over and above all this, there is the new music itself, and there are the new instruments of music so particularly associated with the new music. No mere revision would have been sufficient there. I have written very numerous new passages, long and short, by which to bring in whatever seems of outstanding importance; and once again, I have done this on the same plan of placing each novelty where it best seems to belong in consideration of its working principles.

If it is an instrument of music, no matter how revolutionary, and if it has come or is coming into habitual Western use, it has a place in my book, and into that place I have tried to put it. So rapid is the rate of development that I can hardly hope to have kept quite up with the times, still less to stay with them as the new growth continues; but the reader may at least fairly hope to be told, in general terms, that here there is a fascinating new line of development opening up, and another there.

Nothing is to be slighted merely because it cuts across the traditional lines. Nothing, on the other hand, is to be carried beyond the relatively elementary treatment, for general readers and for students intent on building up their general foundations, which is the purpose of the present book. Finally, at the end of the book, there is a long chapter of general observations on the New Music, which chapter itself is new.

How new is the newest?

I am bound to say that I think the older generation has more excuse than usual for having difficulties with the new music of the younger generation. I mean no insult to either side when I suggest that the generation gap, always an obstacle to be overcome, is wider now than in the past, as I think both sides would probably agree.

No artist of importance (as opposed to hangers-on) goes new for the sake of going new. He goes new because he cannot help expressing, as artists do, needs quite deep within the unconscious, and often running quite contrary to our conscious tendencies.

The irony is that much new music is brought consciously under very strict mathematical control, in reaction against which other new music is trusted supposedly to chance. But a little way beneath the surface, both these departures from tradition look singularly alike. They look singularly like rebellions against the perils of personal responsibility, by getting mathematics to decide, or chance (if it is chance) to decide what it is more traditional for the artist in person to decide.

Outward appearances notwithstanding, modern art tends to be as irrational as it is irreverent, and at bottom more of the heart than of the head. The unconscious seems to be very successfully getting its own back for the obsessive reliance on materialist science and intellectualized reason which is so dangerously unbalanced a feature of our times. This is certainly disconcerting; but it may well be beneficial. Almost certainly it is beneficial.

Our times are, by common consent, more than usually disturbed. They are more than usually out of balance, and in need of compensating tendencies from the side of the unconscious. That is quite traditionally a function of the rebel contingent, including rebel artists, whose role is never so unprecedented as both parties, old and new, suppose, but is a normal part of the grand dialectic of human history. Nevertheless, because our present imbalance is more than usual, the newness of our new art may really be more than that of other times.

At other times, other transitions were also in progress; but never, surely, with the explosive speed and violence of scientific invention and social turmoil we are now experiencing, hopefully on the way through to something stabler as well as richer.

Our new music is much more radically new, for example, than that *Ars Nova*, that New Art, by which de Vitry and Machaut expanded the organization of rhythm in the fourteenth century beyond the *Ars Antiqua*, the Old Art, of Leonin and Perotin in the twelfth: and notice, too, how much swifter our time-scale is today, changing by decades rather than by centuries. We are, again, much newer than those *Nuove Musiche*, those Italian New Musics which led to public opera and chamber cantata across the borders of the sixteenth and seventeenth centuries, new thing under the sun though opera undoubtedly was. But still it relied on the basic raw material of tonality, as did Beethoven and Wagner, Debussy and Schoenberg.

There is tonality wherever there are tones to pull our expectations this way or that. There can be modality, which is tonality organized by modes. There can be key tonality, which traditionally incorporates the major and minor modes, and may be combined with other modal tendencies (including the whole tone scale, itself a kind of mode). There can be bitonality and polytonality and pantonality (two keys; many keys; or all keys at once so that none prevail, as in serial tonality).

Schoenberg did not like his serial tonality to be called atonality, and rightly; for the tonal pull is as strong as ever, though not allowed to settle into a key. But in our new music, there may be no stable tones to exercise a steady pull, but only shifting glissandos. There may be no tones at all, but only sounds indefinite in pitch. Where there are no tones, there can be no tonality.

Definite pitches in continuous motion are fluid tonality; indefinite pitch is atonality. These are not unprecedented elements in music. There have been glissandos before; there has been noise as well as tone; there have always been rhythm and dynamics and tone-colourings, and such factors other than pitch have been used as structural materials. But never with the enormous predominance so often encountered in the new music of our day.

The new music is still music

Yet this does not imply, as some conservatives feel, that music has ceased to be music. Any organization of sounds which is coherent and purposeful can be music.

Not everything audible is in itself music. But anything audible can become music. Even the dripping of a tap, or the wheels of a train passing over the rails, can become an imaginary music for the hearer, though in this case the coherence is projected mentally and not purposefully presented.

One idea in some modern music is to catch casual sounds, and impose a purpose on them which they do not themselves possess. This can now readily be done, with or without deliberate distortions in any degree, by electronic methods; and such are the latest developments in Concrete Music.

The nearest equivalent in painting, some fifty years ago, was the original surrealist idea of seeing patterns in the grain of a wooden floor, for example, and allowing the mind to project images into them. The images are thrown up by the unconscious, to which the casual sounds, like the casual patterns, serve as convenient carriers. The stimulus does not really come from any outside accident; the stimulus comes from an inside pressure, which is always present, and which in the case of artists can be released creatively on the slightest provocation.

Some modern music (e.g. by Milton Babbitt) is produced by mathematical calculations of the utmost strictness; but they are, perhaps, no more nor less relevant than the patterns in the grain of the wood. They seem to serve with the same success (and in the same way) as hooks for unconscious projection.

Again, material for such calculations may be chosen just because it is in itself irrelevant (e.g. by John Cage), in full and deliberate awareness of its potentiality for releasing unplanned consequences.

But what the conscious does not plan, the unconscious all the more effectually takes over. This is only an extension of the usual artistic combination of largely conscious craftsmanship with largely unconscious contents.

The proportion of conscious and unconscious elements in art, as in other activities and opinions, varies very greatly; and in most works of art, the part played by conscious purpose and conscious craftsmanship is more or less prominent and important.

Every so often, in the history of art, it seems to become necessary to some artists to rebel with more than usual intransigence against what is conscious and traditional. Dadaism, Cubism, Surrealism, Serialism or Aleatorism can all be seen as attempts to overturn established conventions, and to let in fresh impulses from the irrational underside of human nature.

Yet it would seem that consciousness cannot abdicate too far or too long, this side of madness; for to be human is to be conscious, as the other animals are not; and the wildest art is still a bringing up into consciousness, from whatever depths. Finding order where chaos was, or making order for oneself: that, too, is in human nature, and especially is it in the artist's nature.

The new music a mirror of our times

It may help us to understand and to accept the extremities of modern music if we think of them, on this level, as an unusually powerful release of material from the unconscious. There is at the same time a compulsion to go the limit, and an inhibition against letting anything emotional build up. But it does build up, if only in the illusory obsessiveness of the control or in the illusory abdication of control: both of which are open invitations to the unconscious to take over in force.

There is, in some modern music, the fragmentariness of a dream, and the seeming inconsequence. But often, too, there is the dreamer's intuition of patterns behind the fragments, and of hidden links between the disjointed happenings. Sometimes there is a nightmare quality. But nightmares too are meaningful, if we can take in their meaning. Other modern music is exceptionally structured.

There are rationalizations offered by composers for all this, so inadequate that they are obviously not the complete explanation. But there is also an irrational authoritativeness which commands a respect that the rationalizations do not. We are gripped, even if we could not for the life of us say why it is that we gripped. Such deep interest does not arise for nothing or out of nothing; and we have only to watch the new musicians at work to see how deeply they themselves are interested.

What of it if some composers need the reassuring illusion of mathematical control, afraid as perhaps they are of being controlled by their own strenuously repressed emotions? What of it if other composers need the releasing irresponsibility of aleatory chanciness, fearing as perhaps they do to take conscious responsibility for their own decisions: which amounts to letting the unconscious do more of the deciding for them? For the only chance that can result is a chance for the unconscious to have the last word; and whatever puts consciousness into creative relationship with unconsciousness is itself creative.

The very sounds of modern music are often evocative as a dream is evocative, and sometimes terrifying as a nightmare is terrifying. The ghosts gibber, the phantoms shriek, the poltergeists pound and batter at the seat of reason. But this is our world; and this is the music which is coming out of it. Admire the artist who dares to conjure these fearful forces, and to confront them with at least a measure of conscious order. It is demons unconfronted who might destroy our world.

An artist goes his way from inner necessity, and not from outer wilfulness. If we find much of our modern music violent, and untraditional, that may be because our times are violently on the change, and because tradition alone is not enough. It never is. But tradition does not usually have to adapt itself quite so fast and so far as it is now constrained to do. The way to the future of music is undoubtedly rather rough going just on this bit of the journey.

The music of the future?

We always think we can see the way the future is shaping up; and we very seldom can.

What we should nowadays regard as traditional music may yet remain both valid and valuable. Not, indeed, if it is only traditional, which means only a copy. There is no new creation in copying works of art: our own feelings and intuitions are the sole models for new creation. But artists can and do have feelings and intuitions about different aspects of experience, and can come up with different styles, even at one and the same time and place.

Our world is not at all a simple place, and least of all in our century of whirlwind changes, far exceeding the changes of many centuries past. There is not only room, there is probably great need, for a variety of styles.

Naïve traditionalists are a pathetic remnant, though this is no excuse for kicking them when they are down. But there are also composers in whom tradition is not naïve; for whom tonality is not a spent or even a weakened force; who are aware of modernity, but not immersed in it; whose music can only be valid if it does not follow the fashionable extremes. For if there is one thing worse than another to copy in the arts, with no inner conviction, it is the latest fashion.

But like it or dislike it, share in it or watch it with disinvolved respect, we cannot rid ourselves of all this highly untraditional originality which is going on so interestingly around us.

The new music of today is no passing eccentricity. It commands the enthusiasm of the younger generation, who do not find it in any way strange or in need of explanation. It is what by far the most lively and talented of the younger musicians, led by a devoted contingent of older pioneers, are setting their hands to in any number of fascinating variations. The best that the more traditionally inspired of us can ask (and even this we cannot be sure of getting) is a reasonable degree of mutual tolerance. Tradition itself is not obsolete, and cannot be. But as usual, the young men tend to think it is; and that, as usual, is a part of their weakness, and a part of their strength.

As for the music of the future, that will look after itself in due time and season, as the future always does. There has been a tremendous widening of musical resources. And a tremendous narrowing. The unbounded potentialities of traditional tonality, the long-cultivated fields and the fertile soil, are no small loss to set against the gains. But it would be an exaggeration to conclude that tonality has been destroyed. It is still there for anyone who cares to use it, and can find fresh and valid ways of doing so.

Tonality is a system so vast that one might almost compare it to a solar system. It has its own laws of gravity and of motion, of centripetal attraction and of centrifugal repulsion, of momentum and of inertia, of energy and of repose. These laws are as impartial as other laws of nature, and as immutable.

No areas of the tonal system have been rendered uninhabitable, though very many have been rendered unfashionable. They are, perhaps, unhealthy for the younger generation, who have self-protective instincts in such a matter. But fresh winds may blow there again, and the air may clear.

Or perhaps one may see it like an allergy. The young composers are, to take an extreme example, understandably allergic to Richard Strauss: his influence would hopelessly mislead their personalities. But that is their allergy, and their loss. Strauss' music is not unwholesome to most of my generation. He was one of the best and most honest of craftsmen, and the stream of his inspiration runs pure and deep.

And there comes the test of mutual tolerance. The younger generation finds it hard if not impossible to give Strauss his due. The older generation finds it hard though certainly not impossible to give the younger generation their due. But we had better do so. It is their future.

Will tonal music flourish in the future? Will it coexist with atonality? Will the two mainly merge in new combinations, as they do in so very many experiments today, and as perhaps we may be most inclined to prophesy? We do not know yet; we have not got there yet.

One thing, however, we can know. Shape up how it will, the new music has come to stay.

And with the new music, the new instruments, and the new uses of old instruments, inextricably bound up with the new music.

Instruments: the working tools of music

In this much revised and much expanded new edition of my old book, I have done my best to present recent developments with the same equal sympathy as the traditional instruments of classical and romantic music and the returning instruments of early music. For all the instruments of music are on an equal footing before the law when we come to the crucial question: are they good and faithful servants of their own purposes?

An instrument good for its purpose is a good instrument, and an instrument bad for its purpose is a bad instrument. There may be better purposes and worse purposes too, of course, and we all have our own judgements as to that. But any serious and sincere musical purpose of our own age and culture is of interest to us here.

In practice, instruments overlap too much for their placing to be altogether logical; but logical arrangement is the intention, and by the logic of their function and not of their history. This is not a history of musical instruments. It is an introduction to instruments as the working tools of music.

It is an introduction designed for people like myself, who have the curiosity to ask: how does music work? What are the physical properties of sound-vibration, from which we have fashioned and continue to fashion an art closer to our inner nature than to the world outside? An art which uses objective material for subjective purposes? An art of physical occurrences turned to psychological account? An art of manipulations and an art of moods?

And more concretely: what makes a violin sound different from a viol? A piano from a harpsichord? An oboe from a clarinet? In what ways do different instruments serve their different purposes, and why are they so distinctive in their proper functions? What are the orders, the species and the families of instruments? What are their chief representatives in current Western use? Their ranges, tunings, basic techniques and idioms? Their most prominent uses and potentialities, severally and jointly?

Not even the most concrete of these questions can be seen in context without the kind of prior explanation of principles which I shall be attempting here. In terms explained or self-explanatory for the unspecialized reader, I shall move from the general to the particular in the systematic order proper to a text-book. But whether read from simple curiosity, or made the basis of a course of study, I hope my book may give pleasure as well as profit. Pleasure is not the only value of music; but it would be a bad day if pleasure ceased to be its obvious motive.

PART ONE

HOW SOUND WORKS

PART ONE

HOW SOUND WORKS

CHAPTER I

THE RAW MATERIAL OF MUSIC

What is the raw material of music?

Sound is the raw material of music.

Paradoxically enough, although we always think of sounds as reaching us from the outside, sound is something which only exists in our minds. Strictly speaking, sound is the name for what happens to us mentally when certain physical events occur within range of our hearing faculties.

These physical events are sound-waves. The term sound-waves, however, is itself a little misleading. We are apt to think of the waves of the sea, which undulate up and down in various more or less complicated ways according to the conditions of wind and current. Sound-waves are also more or less complicated. But they do not undulate up and down. They contract and expand in and out.

A more scientific term is sound-vibrations. All more or less elastic substances are capable of springy contraction and expansion: that is what calling them elastic means. Some elastic substances are more springy than others. We can impart energy in the form of vibrations to a sufficiently springy substance, for example by hitting it. This compresses it; but some of the energy will recoil again, like a bouncing ball. These repercussions will not die out until the energy has been absorbed and no more is being supplied. When the repercussions are fairly long-lasting of their own accord and sound results, we call the substance resonant.

Rather surprisingly on first thoughts, air is an elastic substance capable of resonance. Since both we and other objects are normally surrounded by air, repercussions in suitable objects transmit themselves to this surrounding air, and if we are not too far away, these repercussions reach our ears. If we are too far away, the energy becomes dispersed before it reaches us.

Such repercussions are sound-vibrations. When *sound-vibrations*

3

reach our ears, we feel them through the response of our aural
nerves, and this response as our mind experiences it is *sound*.

Frequency and pitch

Any repercussions, within certain limits, may give us the sensation
of sound, and can therefore be described as sound-vibrations. The
primary limits are of frequency and of wave-length. These two
factors of frequency and of length are interconnected. The reason is
that under ordinary conditions the speed at which sound-vibrations
travel is always virtually the same: about twelve miles a minute.
Thus if the sound-vibrations are shorter they will have to be more
rapid to keep up this virtually uniform speed. If they are longer
they will have to be less rapid. We have only to think of two men,
one with short legs and the other with long legs, walking com-
panionably side by side. The short-legged man will have to take
more steps in a given time if he wants to keep level; and the long-
legged man, fewer steps.

When vibrations are too long and slow, and likewise, at the other
extreme, when vibrations are too short and rapid, our hearing
faculties are not capable of responding to them, and we have no
sensation of sound. In this event, and again in the event of too low a
level of energy reaching our ears, from our point of view there is no
sound, although there may be vibrations which some scientific
instrument may be quite capable of recording.

One way of describing this would be to say that although there are
vibrations we are not experiencing them as sound-vibrations. But
there is no scientific line of division which marks sound-vibrations
off from vibrations in general. The limits are set by our hearing
faculties; such limits vary quite widely between different individuals,
and still more widely between different animals.

Scientists distinguish vibrations by their *frequency*. This means the
frequency with which the vibration proceeds away from the point of
balance; returns to the point of balance; proceeds away from the
point of balance again, but in the opposite direction; and returns
to the point of balance again. This two-in-one or double vibration
completes one *cycle*: and the frequency is measured in vibration
cycles per second (v.c.p.s. or more briefly c.p.s.).

The higher the frequency, the higher the *pitch*; and the lower the
frequency, the lower the pitch. (But intensity can also lower pitch.)

The lowest pitch human ears can hear is about 20 c.p.s. (the lowest standard note of the piano is some 27 c.p.s.). The highest pitch human ears can hear is about 20,000 c.p.s. (not far above the squeak of a bat; but few older people can any longer hear a bat squeaking). A dog will hear, and obey, a whistle pitched too high for any human ears to hear at all.

The lowest notes of a very big organ are believed to be too low to be directly audible, though they can make an indirect contribution to the sound, and their ponderous vibrations can be felt in our bodies as a throbbing pulsation. Electronic apparatus can readily produce vibrations above the highest humanly audible pitch, which will not be heard but felt as uncomfortable or painful sensation. If this is too intense and prolonged, it may cause temporary or permanent impairment of the hearing. So may excessive volume.

The point here is that *frequency is the basic factor determining pitch*.

Noise and tone

All tone is sound, but not all sound is tone. Sound which is not tone includes all varieties of noise.

The sound-vibrations which result in noise are those of which the frequency never settles down to any regular periodicity, but is inherently erratic. We may get a vague sense of pitch, but too indeterminate to pick out as definite tone however momentarily.

The sound-vibrations which result in tone are those of which the frequency settles down at least momentarily to a regular periodicity. We get a definite sense of pitch even if it is continuously on the move, like the tone of a siren when it is gathering or losing speed: i.e., in music, a glissando.

Music has, for many centuries in the West until quite recently, used chiefly sounds of definite pitch, i.e., tones. Some traditional instruments, however, include both regular and irregular vibrations, in deliberately audible strengths: the beautiful and accurately pitched notes of the kettledrums are an outstanding example. Others include, preponderantly if not exclusively, irregular vibrations only, at least at audible strength: side-drums and bass drums are excellent examples of such primarily percussive sounds in traditional music.

But much recent music includes very many more instruments of partially, preponderantly or exclusively unpitched sound. The introduction into music of the whole range of sounds previously rejected as mere noise has become a notable feature of our times.

Apart from the deliberate use of noise in music, some unwanted noise is unavoidable: fingers thudding on fingerboards and keyboards; piano or harpsichord actions; key actions on wood-wind, etc. But in practice these are much fainter than the other extraneous noises of a concert room: chairs being moved; music-pages and programmes being turned; some people coughing and others whispering; and various noises from outside.

Some unwanted tone occurs: but unless this by some mishap becomes loud enough to hear as squeaks on strings, squawks on reeds or cracked notes on brass, its extent is negligible.

Here the point is that *irregular vibrations produce noise but regular vibrations produce tone*. But both are usable in music.

Pure tone and compound tone

Every musician likes to think that he is producing a pure tone. What he means by this is a tone in which only the desired vibrations are occurring, but these as freely as possible. In aiming at this he is right: it is the secret of good tone-production. But strictly he is using the wrong name for it; for good musical tone is always in some degree compound and not what a scientist could describe as pure (sometimes, and better, called simple tone).

In the strict and scientific sense, *pure tone* is tone produced by the vibration of the sounding substance in one entire piece and in no other way. This gives a tone of the frequency which we perceive as the note, and of no other frequency.

A tuning fork is specially designed to give (once the preliminary high-pitched jangle produced by striking it has died down) a substantially pure tone. Blowing gently across the top of a bottle will give a fairly pure tone. Sounding a tuning fork across a bottle partly filled with water until its note corresponds to the tuning fork will give a very pure tone. It sounds like a cool, cooing 'oo': a nice sound, but we should soon get tired of it. The B.B.C.'s tuning signal on the note $a' = 440$ (the present, internationally agreed standard of pitch) is broadcast as a pure tone, and will be received as such if the set is good enough and is kept at low volume to avoid distortion in the ear. It is not quite like any sound we hear in ordinary music.

The nearest sounds to a pure tone in ordinary music are low, soft notes on the flute and some organ stops. They are by no means entirely pure; but they are pure enough to make their own special effect of transparent innocence. They stand at the coolest extreme of musical sonorities, and very beautiful they are when imaginatively used. Even so, they must not be heard for too long at a time, since if they are, they will come to seem monotonous.

Monotonous is a very accurate word for it, since the whole point about pure tone is that it is literally 'one-toned'. The notes heard in ordinary music are never absolutely 'one-toned', and for the most part they are very far from that colourless quality. The notes heard in ordinary music are all more or less made up of *compound tone*. But in electronic music, pure tones can be used effectively.

If you can find a length of wire fencing neither too tight nor too slack for the purpose, twang it sharply and watch its visible vibrations at the same time as listening to the resulting sound. You will certainly see the whole length between the posts vibrating from side to side. These whole-length vibrations will be producing a tone which you will hear as a note.

If that were all, you would be hearing a pure tone. But it is not all. You may quite possibly be able to see that shorter lengths of the wire are also vibrating on their own account. These part-length vibrations are superimposed on the whole-length vibrations. Each different length of vibration will be producing an additional pure tone which is combining with the others. The combined product is a compound tone.

The pure tones which combine to produce a compound tone are called its partial tones or *partials*. In the ordinary course of events, we do not hear them as distinct notes each in its own right. We only hear the lowest partial as a distinct note. We hear all the upper partials as tone-colouring.

The lowest partial is called the first or the prime or (most commonly) the *fundamental*. The upper partials may be regular or irregular: if they are regular, they are called *harmonics*; if they are irregular, they are inharmonic, and should strictly be referred to not as harmonics but simply as partials. It is, however, quite correct and common to call harmonics by the more general name of partials.

Pitch depends on frequency: the whole-length vibrations, being the longest, are necessarily the slowest; therefore they yield the

c

lowest partial (i.e. the fundamental). But the part-length vibrations, being shorter, are necessarily more rapid; therefore they yield the upper partials, in ascending order.

What we ordinarily hear in music is a *note* at the pitch of the fundamental but *coloured* by an assortment of upper partials. The sound-vibrations are a combination of those yielding the fundamental and those yielding the upper partials. It is this combination which is called a compound tone. (Harmonics also act like landmarks in helping us to recognize the pitch.)

In a choppy sea we may notice small waves superimposed on large waves, and smaller wavelets superimposed on small waves. These are not 'sound-waves', and as already mentioned, sound-vibrations do not have the physical shape of waves at all; but the comparison may give us a mental picture of how smaller movements may combine with bigger movements to give compound movement.

The Natural Harmonic Series

The vibrations of most musical instruments are substantially regular. When this is the case, the ascending order of partials works out as follows.

The whole-length vibrates at the frequency we hear as the distinct note in question.

The half-length simultaneously vibrates at twice the frequency, giving the octave above.

The third-length simultaneously vibrates at three times the frequency, giving the twelfth (octave plus fifth) above.

The quarter-length simultaneously vibrates at four times the frequency, giving the double-octave (octave plus octave) above.

The same proportions continue (in so far as energy is going into the harmonics) up the arithmetical progression $1 : 2 : 3 : 4 \ldots$

This is called the *Natural Harmonic Series*. Each individual tone in the series is a pure tone. But any combination of these individual tones is a compound tone.

The use of the term harmonic in this connection must be carefully distinguished from other uses directly or indirectly derived from it, as for example when violinists and others describe as harmonics any notes especially produced by inhibiting the fundamental, etc., by methods to be mentioned in due course. In the present connection, it may be helpful to point out that the term harmonic did not arise historically out of any connection with harmony in the musical sense. It arose from a previous method of calculating the pitch of harmonics not by doubling frequencies (as above) but by sub-dividing string-lengths in the proportions $1, \frac{1}{2}, \frac{1}{3}, \frac{1}{4}$, etc.: which is what mathematicians call a harmonic progression.

In addition to the regular partials of the Natural Harmonic Series, there can be inharmonic compounds of which the partials, though regular in themselves, are in irregular relationship with one another. An excellent example of such an inharmonic series of partials is to be found in the beautiful but eerie tone of a fine bell, with its strange humming and throbbing which does not seem quite to belong to the familiar sounds of music, though it is wonderful music in its own special kind.

All in all, the importance of upper partials to the art of music can hardly be exaggerated. It is true that ordinarily we only hear one partial at a time as the note in question. But we perceive the pitch from the series rather than only from the fundamental. We do not ordinarily hear the remaining partials as separate notes in their own right. We do hear them as *tone-colouring*.

Upper partials: the source of tone-colouring

By various kinds of mechanical or electrical apparatus, curves can be recorded which plot the behaviour of sound-vibrations. Specimens of such curves are given in Figs. 1–16.

The reader must not be misled by the fact that these curves show wave-like outlines. They do not depict the shape of the sound-vibrations; they depict the extent and relationship of the displacements occurring in the sound-vibrations. These displacements occur longitudinally: they are in fact in-and-out displacements. In order to record them two-dimensionally on paper, they are translated into lateral curves: they are shown under the convention of up-and-down displacements. Once this convention is understood, the curves give an extraordinarily graphic representation of what is actually happening. Graphic is the operative word. They are a species of graph.

Fig. 17 is not a species of graph, but also corresponds visually to actual sound-vibrations. It shows the pattern produced on the sound-tracks of films by the sound-vibrations in question.

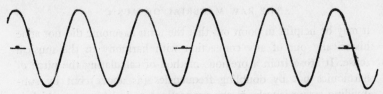

Fig. 1. Sine curve, indicative of the pure tone of a tuning fork

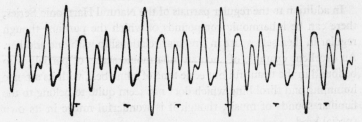

Fig. 2. Integrated curve: just chord on four tuning forks

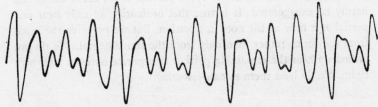

Fig. 3. Tempered chord on four tuning forks

Fig. 4. Beat tone produced between two tuning forks

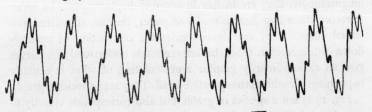

Fig. 5. Preliminary high jangle of tuning fork

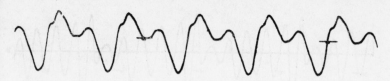

Fig. 6. Flute (nearly pure tone)

Fig. 7. Clarinet (mainly odd harmonics)

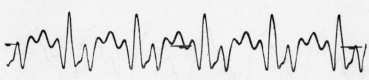

Fig. 8. Oboe

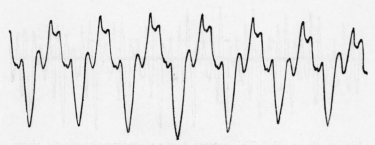

Fig. 9. Saxophone

(Figs. 1–9 from Miller: *Sound Waves* (The Macmillan Co, New York))

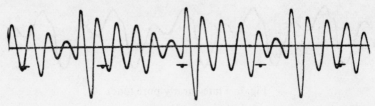

Fig. 10. French horn

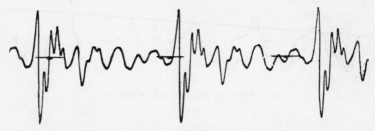

Fig. 11. Trombone

Fig. 12. Violin

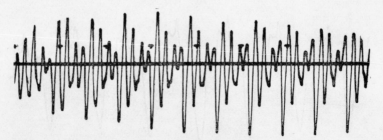

Fig. 13. Piano (*N.B.* This pattern does not repeat quite exactly, showing that the vibrations are not quite periodic, hence that the partials
are not quite harmonic)

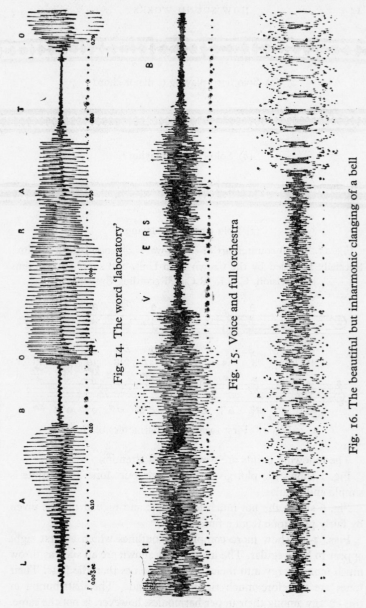

Fig. 14. The word 'laboratory'

Fig. 15. Voice and full orchestra

Fig. 16. The beautiful but inharmonic clanging of a bell

(Figs. 10–16 from Miller: *Sound Waves* (The Macmillan Co, New York))

(a) Solo harp playing C major chord

(b) Solo clarinet playing C

(c) Solo trombone playing C

Fig. 17. Visual counterpart of sound-waves on sound-track of film Specially recorded by the Crown Film Unit, and supplied by Films Division, C.O.I. (R.C.A. Recording System)

Fig. 18. First twenty-one harmonics of C

The following points are worth special attention.

Fig. 1 shows the plot given by a single pure tone: the outline is simple and regular.

Fig. 6 shows the not much less simple and regular outline given by fairly pure tone from a flute.

Figs. 7–12 show more complicated outlines which at first sight appear to be irregular. The instruments shown are all such as throw much more energy into their upper harmonics than the flute. Their tones are therefore much richer compounds. The distribution of this energy among their upper harmonics, however, is not the same. Therefore their plots look different. This represents visually the acoustic fact that their tone-colourings sound different.

On analysis, what appear to be irregular outlines can be shown each to be the product of numerous smaller outlines. These smaller outlines are regular in themselves. They are superimposed to produce a combined outline of the kind which mathematicians call an integrated curve. This represents visually the acoustic fact that the partials of a compound tone may themselves be pure tones. They ordinarily are with most musical instruments.

With these compound tones, the biggest curves represent the slowest but longest vibrations: i.e. the fundamental. The smaller indentations represent the faster but shorter vibrations: i.e. the upper partials.

In Figs. 6–12 the smaller indentations fit an exact number of times into their big curves, so that the pattern recurs at regular intervals. This shows that the vibrations are periodic. In such cases, all the partials are harmonic, following the ascending intervals of the Natural Harmonic Series.

With bowed and blown instruments, the way in which the supply of energy is maintained causes the vibrations to remain periodic, so that the upper partials are all true harmonics. Fig. 13 represents a piano: an instrument on which the supply of energy is not maintained, but intermittently renewed. There is nothing to cause the vibrations to remain periodic; and though they would do so of their own accord if the string were infinitely flexible, this cannot be the case in practice. As a consequence, the upper partials are slightly inharmonic. This is represented in Fig. 13 by the fact that the smaller indentations do not fit an exact number of times into their big curve, so that the pattern recurs a little differently each time. The difference is not great; the pattern is still substantially regular. There is not enough irregularity for the ordinary listener to notice.

A comparison of Fig. 17(b) with Fig. 17(c) shows visually that two different instruments may distribute energy differently among the partials of the same Natural Harmonic Series: in this case the series arising from the fundamental C. Fig. 18 shows in musical notation the pitches of this Natural Harmonic Series as nearly as our normal notation can show them. Many of the higher harmonics do not stand exactly at the note-pitches used by our customary scale-tunings. The seventh, thirteenth and fourteenth come out flatter; the eleventh comes out sharper, and would almost as well be notated as sharp.

We are now in a position to answer the fascinating question why different musical instruments sound different in their tone-colouring. The answer is not complete; but it is a good start.

The flute (Fig. 6) is particularly weak in upper harmonics; very little energy goes into colouring the tone, which therefore sounds almost literally transparent.

The clarinet (Fig. 7) has acoustic peculiarities which starve alternate (even-numbered) harmonics of energy; it is substantially deprived of half the normal series; the tone therefore sounds almost literally hollow, though not transparent.

The oboe (Fig. 8) pours plenty of energy into a rich supply of upper harmonics, many of them rather high; it has not the peculiarities which substantially deprive the clarinet of the even-numbered harmonics; the tone is richly colourful, but with a nasal edge to it which is extraordinarily poignant.

The saxophone (Fig. 9) pours much more of its energy into the lower harmonics; it has a sweeter, fatter tone, but less character.

The French horn (Fig. 10) has a long range of upper harmonics well supplied with energy; its tone is warm and poetic, but can be given a sharp cutting edge.

The trombone (Fig. 11) and still more its very close relative the trumpet (not shown), have the richest possible complement of upper harmonics, and therefore the most brilliantly coloured tone.

The violin (Fig. 12) has an ample but not an extreme complement of upper harmonics, of which the energy is given a distribution so felicitous that of all tones in music this is one of the least liable to surfeit the ear.

The piano (Fig. 13) has basically a somewhat neutral tone of which the lowest few harmonics receive most of the energy; but when allowed to gather resonance by the lifting of the dampers, it can build up a very colourful assortment of upper harmonics.

We shall have many other factors to take into account when we come to consider these and other instruments individually: factors including not only the harmonic content of the tone but the technical means of varying it and articulating it. The above statements have deliberately been put in the most elementary form in order to bring out the present point, which is that every difference of tone-colouring, no matter how it is effected and no matter how it is articulated, is a difference of harmonic content.

There have long been electronic instruments designed to produce individual pure tones at will, either separately or in combination, and in any required distribution of energy. The first I heard was made by the John Compton Organ Company, who are manufacturers, among other things, of electronic organs. To hear pure tones added to one another up the Natural Harmonic Series in this deliberate way was an unforgettable experience. Upper harmonics which in ordinary musical experience are heard mainly as tone-colouring could be heard on this apparatus as a chord comprised of distinct notes, up to the point at which perhaps ten or a dozen had been brought in, from the lowest upwards. Those harmonics which are not attuned to our normal scale did not sound out of tune. They sounded (as indeed they are) in tune on some hauntingly elemental system of their own. The chord itself in its higher reaches becomes full of small intervals which in our ordinary system of music are discords. But in their own literally natural tuning, they sound neither concordant nor discordant, but simply satisfying; neither familiar nor unfamiliar, but simply archetypal. They sound as we might imagine the music of the spheres.

Something of this elemental experience, so revealing of music's archetypal raw material, can be had without the need for special apparatus. Household electric mains in Great Britain supply a current alternating at 50 c.p.s.; this will produce corresponding vibrations in some ordinary apparatus, such as 'reflector' type electric heaters. We may hear quite loudly a long series of natural harmonics. The fundamental in the region of G is extremely clear, with the second harmonic an octave above, and the third harmonic a fifth above the octave. (The sound may cease with rising temperature.)

Under favourable conditions, and with a certain amount of practice, I have been able to pick out as distinct notes harmonics up to the sixteenth: G'; G; d; g; b; d'; f'; g'; a'; b'; c"; d"; e"; f"; f" sharp; g". This needs a deliberate act of discrimination in listening; the moment this deliberate discrimination relaxes, your listening reverts to its ordinary condition, and you hear the upper harmonics not as distinct notes forming a chord, but as tone-colouring attaching to the fundamental. Even then, however, the fifth of the chord and to a lesser extent the major third of the chord may still ring out clearly enough to force themselves on your attention.

Readers who have or come across an electric heater with this pleasant habit of humming to itself (and a great many of them do) may find the experiment worth making. I have also listened to the same result at a very impressive volume from a big transformer supplying the electric railway not far from my previous house. I have been known to go and listen to it for a few minutes before retiring to bed, for the sake of its strangely tranquillizing effect of serenity and completeness.

Another demonstration which I heard on the Compton apparatus consisted in bringing in harmonics at different strengths. When chiefly the first and second harmonics were brought in, the tone was most recognizably flute-like. When a strong series of odd-numbered harmonics only was brought in, the tone was most recognizably clarinet-like. It was a convincing demonstration of the basic fact that tone-colourings vary with the varying relative strengths in which individual pure tones of the Natural Harmonic Series are present.

Fig. 18 shows how much closer, and therefore how much more mutually discordant the higher harmonics are than the lower harmonics. Serene as the overall effect of the Natural Harmonic Series is, and deeply satisfying to our own inner natures, it is an undeniable psychological as well as acoustic fact that a roughness sounds in our ears and minds as a result of this jangling closeness, which gets closer still as the series ascends into microtonic intervals (i.e. smaller than our smallest normal musical interval, the semi-tone). We perceive this roughness subliminally rather than consciously; but we perceive it. The stronger the lower harmonics, the smoother the effect, and the broader the tone. The stronger the higher harmonics, the rougher the effect, and the brighter the tone. The more evenly distributed the harmonics (and the more exactly harmonic) the sweeter the tone. It is in ways such as these, basically, that musical instruments sound different from one another.

Tone-colouring *is* harmonic content; harmonic content *is* tone-colouring.

How does sound-vibration reach the ear?

Roughly, as pressure waves conveyed to the intervening air. But there are complications.

One is *reflection*. Those vibrations which travel straight to the ear arrive soonest. Those which strike the ground, or the walls, floor and ceiling are partly absorbed, but partly reflected, and may thus reach the ear by a slightly longer route, arriving a fraction later.

In a sufficiently resonant room, sound may be reflected back and forth more than a hundred times before sinking to inaudibility. And in a sufficiently large room, it may be some seconds before the last reflection reaches the ear. During that time, therefore, we may continue to hear the sound after its source has ceased: this is called *reverberation*.

Now curved surfaces focus sound as curved mirrors focus light, causing echoes of disconcerting force, such as those experienced in the Albert Hall. But even when more evenly distributed, reverberation has powerful effects.

High sounds tend to lose more energy by absorption than low sounds. A resonant room is therefore kinder to high harmonics than an absorptive room. High harmonics, as we have already hinted, make for brilliance; therefore resonance makes for brilliance.

Again, sound in an enclosed space first builds up energy faster than it is absorbed, so that we hear an increasing loudness. Soon, this build-up is balanced by absorption, so that we hear a constant loudness. Finally, when the source has ceased, the built-up energy is dwindlingly absorbed, so that we hear a decreasing loudness ending in silence.

In a resonant room, the absorption will overtake the build-up more tardily; a greater loudness will be built up; its decrease will likewise be tardier.

Whereas in an absorptive room, the absorption will overtake the build-up more speedily; a lesser loudness will be built up; and its decrease will likewise be speedier.

There is thus a balance of advantages. For if the room is too resonant, the reverberation time, during which we necessarily hear the old sound overlapping the new, will be so long, and the reverberation itself so loud, as to reduce the music to confusion. But if the room is too absorptive, the build-up will be so slow and restricted that players and audience alike will feel burdened by a sense of unavailing effort; reverberation will be so brief as to leave every small blemish painfully revealed; and the undue toll of high harmonics will rob the music of its proper brilliance.

We have, in estimating reverberation, to allow for the audience wearing clothes, which, like all thick, soft fabrics, are very absorptive, especially of high harmonics. This is best countered by surfaces of painted plaster or polished wood, which reflect sound well and impartially. The seats, however, should be upholstered, so as to approach more nearly the absorptiveness of the audience which is to sit in them: in this way, the disconcerting difference between rehearsing in an empty hall and performing in a full one can be reduced to a minimum.

On the basis of experience, the best average reverberation time is about one second in a small hall to two seconds in a large hall; but choral and orchestral music can always do with a little more reverberation than chamber music. To some extent, this adjustment results automatically from the fact that louder sounds take longer to sink to inaudibility.

The loudness of the source of sound should itself bear some reasonable relation to the hall. Even Menuhin's violin cannot really build up sound enough for the Albert Hall; a large choral society in a small and resonant hall can build up all too much.

Apart from absorption, sound decreases in loudness in proportion to its *distance*: not so much because it loses energy; but because the same energy is spread over an ever larger area. Luckily, sound travels with the same speed at all degrees of loudness used in music (very loud noises travel faster). Still more luckily, sound travels with the same speed at all pitches: if it did not, we should presumably hear the harmonics of a compound tone one after the other, instead of simultaneously; and every chord would reach us as successive notes: in fact, as an arpeggio. Incidentally, the ear is more sensitive to faint high sounds than to faint low sounds; which perhaps explains why Menuhin's violin, from the remote gallery of the Albert Hall, sounds not only faint, but thin, disembodied of its low harmonics.

When obstacles (such as the pillars of a cathedral or of an old-fashioned concert hall) intervene between the source and the ear, some of the sound is scattered.

For *light*-vibrations are so small that they are all affected nearly equally by any sizable obstacle: though dust floating in the air is small enough to scatter the shorter, blue vibrations, while permitting the longer, red vibrations to pass, thus causing sunsets. But *sound*-vibrations are comparatively long, and quite a sizable obstacle may scatter the shorter, high-pitched vibrations, while permitting the longer, low-pitched vibrations to pass, thus reducing brilliance: which is the disappointing audible equivalent of sunsets. It is therefore best not to sit behind a pillar when listening to music.

The *speed* of sound being only about twelve miles a minute, is slow enough to raise a practical problem where a very large body of performers is concerned: sound from the most distant performer will reach the ear perceptibly later than sound from the nearest performer; and the result is inevitably a slight raggedness and confusion.

Sound travels faster through warm air than through cold air. The chief practical effect of this is on wind instruments, which rise in pitch as the air inside them grows warmer and vibrates more rapidly. Wind players always warm their instruments with their breath before a concert: even so, if the room gets very hot, the wind goes on rising in pitch; the rest of the orchestra, whose instruments are less susceptible to change of temperature, will do its best to follow: with awkward results if it includes a pianist, who cannot do so.

In the open air, if there is a cold layer near the ground, and a warm layer higher up, the more lofty sound-vibrations will travel faster than the less lofty ones. This causes what is called *refraction*: the faster vibrations are bent down towards the slower vibrations as a marching column wheels when the outside rank marches faster than the inside rank. The effect is not unlike that of a speaking-tube: the sound travels for far greater distances, because it is no longer diffusing energy by spreading upwards, but is concentrated on one level. (In the speaking-tube it is further concentrated in one direction; even a megaphone has something of this effect. An ear-trumpet is the obverse of this principle; it collects sound from a comparatively wide area, and causes it to converge towards the ear.)

A wind stronger at a height than near the ground may similarly cause refraction: if it is blowing with the sound, the refraction is downwards, and the sound travels far; if it is blowing against the sound, the refraction is upwards, and the sound is rapidly diffused, and can scarcely carry any distance at all.

Finally, sound-vibrations can reach the ear (though again with some loss of high harmonics, and therefore of brilliance) through the floor, instead of through the air: but they do not ordinarily do so in strength.

What happens when sound-vibration reaches the ear?

The vibrations impinge upon the ear-drum, which passes them on over a part of the ear called the basilar membrane. This is a structure containing very large numbers of very small but independent fibres, connected by nerves to the brain. The membrane is apparently not under tension, but is capable in some way of picking up and distinguishing vibrations.

Now consider a piano with its dampers raised by putting the loud pedal down. Suppose an ordinary tone sounding nearby. The moment its vibrations reach the piano, any strings of approximately the same pitch as its first or fundamental harmonic will spring into strong sympathetic vibration; any strings of approximately the same pitch as its upper harmonics will spring into similar, if fainter, sympathetic vibration: until the piano is ringing with eerie sounds, though not a note of its keyboard has been touched. What has happened is that energy from the original note has passed through the air and into those strings (but only those strings) whose own free vibration periods are approximately the same as the sounding partials, and which are therefore predisposed thus to respond.

And that is roughly what happens to the fibres of the basilar membrane when the vibrations of a nearby sound reach them. But whereas the piano has strings only for each note of our chromatic scale, the basilar membrane has groups of fibres and a nerve system to carry their messages to the brain at very minute intervals of pitch: hence its amazing sensitivity and selectivity.

With very little mental effort we can hear the simultaneous notes of a chord, not only collectively, but individually (especially if the music happens to be spun contrapuntally, i.e. out of more than one melodic thread at once); which is a little like seeing adjacent colours and patterns in a picture at one glance, not only as wholes, but also as parts.

With greater mental effort we can hear the main harmonics even of a single ordinary tone, not only collectively, but individually (though this does not happen at all in ordinary listening). To perform a corresponding feat of analysis in the case of light, we need a spectroscope. And in the case of sound, indeed, many more separate harmonics can be individually detected with the aid of special selective resonators (the acoustical equivalent of a spectroscope).

1. Renaissance Lyra da Braccio

2. Rebec, Lutes

3. Medieval Lyra da Braccio

4. Portative Organ   5. Gittern

6. Lute, Tambourine, Cymbals

7. Rebec, Bagpipes, Harp

8. Shawms and Trumpets, Dulcimer

9. Singers and Instrumentalists: *including* (1) *Trumpet*,
(2) *Cymbals*, (3) *Portative Organ*, (4) *Lute*, (5) *Tambourine*,
(6) *Psalteries*, (7) *Harp*, (8) *Shawms*

10. Psaltery, Trumpet Marine, Lute, Trumpet, Shawm

11. Trumpets, Portative Organ, Harp, Lyra da Braccio

12. Choir and Instrumentalists

13. Violins, Violoncello, Harpsichord

14. Recorder

15. Viola da Gamba, two-manual Harpsichord

16. Lutes, Viola, Spinet

17. Guittara Battente, Lute, Trumpet, Violin, Tenor Violin and bow

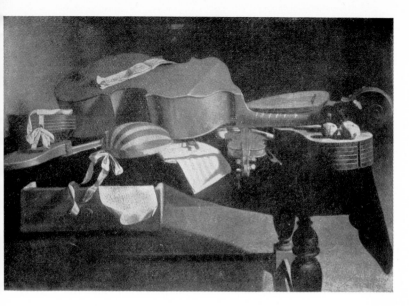

18. Violone, Lutes, Guitars, Cittern

19. Lutes, Guittara Battente, Violin and bow, Viola and bow

20. Viola d'Amore and bow, Lute, Oboe, Trumpet, Harpsichord

21. Guitar, Dulcimer or Psaltery, Flute, Violin and bow

A *resonator* (but not very selective) can be improvised by putting the loud pedal of a piano down, thus raising all the dampers. Play a note of middle pitch softly: once your hearing faculty has the knack you should hear, not only the first or fundamental harmonic (i.e. the note you have played) but also (more faintly) the second (at the octave); the third (at the octave and a fifth); perhaps the fourth (at the double-octave: but this is hard to distinguish from the second); certainly the fifth (at the double-octave and a major third); and probably the sixth (at the double-octave and a fifth) and the seventh (at the double-octave and a minor seventh).

Next let the dampers fall, thus putting your improvised resonator out of action.[1] Play the same note again, and hold it. Though with rather greater difficulty, you should still be able to distinguish the same upper harmonics: thus demonstrating that they are really there in a single ordinary tone, albeit not ordinarily heard individually, but only collectively, through their effect on tone quality.

And finally, you can improvise a *selective* resonator, let us say at the pitch of the third harmonic, an octave and a fifth above. Press down the key belonging to this higher note, but so gently that though its own damper is lifted, its string is not touched by the hammer, and thus remains silent. Hold on to this key, so that its damper remains lifted from the string. Play sharply in the ordinary way the original note an octave and a fifth below the key thus silently depressed: the undamped higher string will now absorb energy from the lower, and vibrate quite energetically in sympathy: thus enabling you to pick out that particular harmonic quite readily from the general mass of sound. To confirm this, let go the *lower* key, thus releasing its damper and silencing its string; but still hold on to the upper key, thus keeping its damper raised. You will now hear the *upper* string going on sounding quite vigorously on its own, though it has never once during this experiment been struck by its own hammer. Or press down the lower and strike the upper key, etc.

If you have two pianos, the same experiments can, of course, also be tried with the identical note struck on one piano and heard

---

[1] Not quite out of action, though, because the topmost notes of a piano are not built with dampers, which, whether rightly or wrongly, are thought unnecessary and undesirable at that pitch. Thus these experiments are not quite conclusive unless the top strings are damped for the occasion with soft rags or a strip of felt.

D

unstruck on the other piano: with even more convincing effect. Think of the struck string as the source of sound, and the unstruck string as the corresponding groups of fibres in the basilar membrane of your own ear; and you will form a fair working notion of the mechanism by which we hear.

How the ear may add further sounds

Astonishingly sensitive and selective as the ear is, it is not a perfect receiving instrument. One of its imperfections has remarkable practical consequences.

There are features somewhere in the hearing system which cause it to be slightly non-linear in its response to incoming vibrations. An incoming sine-wave, therefore, is not picked up quite as a pure sound; the sine-wave is, at least under certain circumstances, slightly distorted, and the sound is heard, even though it did not objectively originate, as a compound sound. The greater the amplitude of the incoming vibrations, the greater the distortion, and the stronger the subjectively heard harmonic content.

One explanation, long accepted, was that the mechanically moving parts of the ear resist inward pressure a little more sluggishly than they relax outwards again: i.e., that they display an asymmetrical drag. But it now seems[1] that this asymmetrical drag in the mechanical parts may not occur, and that the non-linearity must be postulated, if at all, in the cochlea with its basilar membrane, or in the nerve connections, or (as now seems quite probable) in the brain:[2] in short, we do not yet know for certain where, and doubts have even been expressed[3] of the existence of subjective harmonics. But this seems unreasonable, since the evidence for them as facts of perception is both strong and various.

It has further been suggested that beats (i.e. more or less rapid

[1] Georg von Bekesy, *Experiments in Hearing*, New York, 1960, pp. 335ff.

[2] Emile Leipp, *Le Violin: Histoire, esthétique, facture et acoustique*, Paris, 1965, p. 87; Eng. transl. by Hildegarde W. Parry, as *The Violin*, Toronto, 1969, p. 93.

[3] The situation has now really become very unclear, but there is no doubt of there being complex harmonic events in need of explanation. The severest doubts are those now felt on summation tones. The difficulty of separating objective from subjective is greater than had been thought. See John Backus, *The Acoustical Foundations of Music*, New York, 1969, pp. 105–108.

fluctuations of amplitude due to mutual interference among the incoming wave-forms) when their beating itself occurs at a frequency within the audible range, may be heard objectively as a tone; and this explanation appears to accord well with some of the observed facts.[1] But it would be premature to suggest that the causes are properly understood. The results, however, have been much studied, and there seems to be no doubt that something is happening in our hearing which affects our musical experience in ways not directly occurring in the source of sound.

Whatever the causation, when two pure tones of more than a certain loudness are heard, other tones not originating in the source of sound are heard as well. On the assumption that these are subjectively experienced tones, and are the product of the objectively incoming tones in combination, they are known as combination tones.

One combination tone described by Helmholtz as having been heard by him (but now called in question by some) has a frequency equal to the sum of the two generating frequencies: whence it is called the summation tone. It is certainly quite weak: which is just as well; for it is often, as we shall presently see, dissonant even with its own generating tones.

Another combination tone has a frequency equal to the difference between the two generating frequencies: whence it is called the difference tone. It is often loud enough to be distinctly audible as a note separate in pitch; and its effect may be very appreciable even when one of its generating tones is itself a combination tone. Happily it is likely to be consonant with its own generating tones, though not necessarily with the remainder of the harmonic pattern. But in any event, it appears to bring one benefit which may outweigh any possible disadvantages:

Any two consecutive harmonics of a harmonic series generate a difference tone at the pitch of the first or fundamental harmonic of that particular series.

Now music would be greatly different if our hearing faculty did not unhesitatingly accept the pitch of the fundamental as the note of each compound tone. Yet the *objectively* measured intensity of

---

[1] R. Plomp, cited by John Backus, *The Acoustical Foundations of Music*, New York, 1969, p. 108 (an up-to-date and lucid account of the elements, well described for lay readers).

that fundamental may be as little as 0·1 per cent (violin g). Thus it may be partly the accumulation of difference tones generated *subjectively* in the ear that makes the fundamental loud enough to dominate the series; partly our *perception* may recognize the series and attribute its fundamental to it.

This explanation is supported by an even more remarkable fact. Suppose there fall on the ear four or five consecutive *upper* harmonics, of equal or approximately equal intensity. The pitch which we hear is *still* the pitch of the missing first or fundamental harmonic of the series. The ear has actually created subjectively, as a difference tone, a first or fundamental harmonic which does not objectively exist.

When a selection of consecutive upper harmonics (say 10 to 30) is sounded electronically with no lower members of the series, the fundamental, though objectively silent, rings out in the ear, subjectively, with quite uncanny clearness.

This strange phenomenon may best be made clear by one or two examples. A telephone diaphragm (in order to avoid the acute distortion which would result if it possessed any one free vibration period within the fundamental range of human speech) is usually so designed as to be incapable of transmitting the first or fundamental harmonics of human speech at all. It transmits, therefore, only the upper harmonics: objectively, an unintelligible cackle; but subjectively, an adequate reproduction, because our ears reconstitute the missing first or fundamental harmonics from their upper harmonics, very possibly as difference tones.

Again, the formidable expense of a rank of organ pipes vast enough to sound directly the lowest humanly audible notes is often avoided by juxtaposing two ranks of much smaller pipes a fifth apart, which generate the required low notes between them, in our ears, as difference tones. Indeed, where the vast 32-foot (or even 64-foot) pipes are actually built, the ear probably cannot hear their first or fundamental harmonics directly; there is also some doubt whether it can do so even with the lowest notes of the piano. It probably merely hears a strong selection of their upper harmonics, from which it reconstitutes the first or fundamental harmonics as difference tones.

As a matter of fact, asymmetrical drag can occur, quite apart from our hearing, in the structures of musical instruments. This means that *some* sounds of the nature which we have just been discussing *are* actually present objectively. Objective combination tones are often necessarily present when the generators are intense, so that the inertia of the sounding body and the transmitting air ceases to be negligible. (The ear then merely adds to their loudness subjectively.)

Experiment with resonators confirms this conclusion; but it also confirms that in many other instances such sounds *have* only a subjective existence, *in the ear itself*.

The harmonics created by the ear itself must add greatly to the colourfulness and brilliance of what we hear. True, they must also add to its confusion, and even to its dissonance; but this very fact is not without its value, as we shall see.

How do consonance and dissonance differ?

Partly, by force of habit: what is less familiar seems more dissonant. But basically, from a physical cause.

Consider two tones of different pitch sounding together. As the more rapid vibrations of the higher overtake the slower vibrations of the lower, the two alternately coincide and conflict. When they coincide, they reinforce each other; when they conflict, they weaken each other. The result is an alternate intensification and diminution of loudness: this is the phenomenon known as beating.

The lower and closer the two tones, the slower the beats. Play the two bottom notes of the piano loudly together, and you will hear them beating fairly slowly. Play two high notes, and you will not hear them beating; for the beats are now too rapid to distinguish.

When there are not more than about six beats per second, the effect is not unpleasing. Organ builders sometimes introduce them deliberately, by tuning two ranks of pipes just off the unison. But as the beats become faster, their effect grows unpleasantly restless. When they are fast enough to merge indistinguishably, the unpleasantness still persists, till they are very fast indeed, when they cease to make any appreciable effect at all. For moderately high notes, perhaps about thirty beats per second is the most unpleasant.

It is this physical unpleasantness due to beats which is the basic cause of dissonance; the smoothness due to a comparative absence of unpleasant beating is the basic cause of consonance.

Let the two tones be *pure* tones, in the treble stave. Then the dissonance becomes harshest when they are about a semi-tone apart, and vanishes when they are about a minor third apart. Just short of the octave, the dissonance, though less violent, reappears: since the two tones themselves are now much too far apart to beat appreciably, it is probably their difference tone which beats with the lower of them. At the octave, dissonance vanishes; just beyond, it reappears as the difference tone again begins to beat. Yet further on, it once more vanishes.

But suppose the two tones are not pure but *compound* tones, as in ordinary music. We now have to reckon with beats not only between fundamentals (first harmonics), and between one of them and their difference tone, but also between any two upper harmonics, not to mention any further combination tones. For example:

c against c sharp (minor second, or semi-tone): the harshest intelligible dissonance. First harmonics beat with maximum harshness. All upper harmonics beat.

c against d (major second, or tone): slightly less harsh. First harmonics beat, but slightly less harshly. All upper harmonics beat.

c against f sharp (augmented fourth, or tritone): highly disquieting, not quite dissonance and not quite consonance. The third harmonic of c (which is g') beats with the second harmonic of f sharp (which is f' sharp). There is also beating between the fourth harmonic of c (which is c") and the third harmonic of f sharp (which is c" sharp). Also between the fifth harmonic of c (which is e") and the fourth harmonic of f sharp (which is f" sharp).

c against e flat (minor third): faintly disquieting, but accepted as a consonance. The summation tone is d' flat, beating with the second harmonic of c (which is c') and the second harmonic of e flat (which is e' flat). There is also beating between the fourth harmonic of c (which is c") and the third harmonic of e flat (which is b' flat).

c against e (major third): scarcely disquieting at all, and readily accepted as a consonance. The summation tone is d', again beating with the two second harmonics (c' and e'), but less harshly. There is also beating between the fourth harmonic of c (which is c") and the third harmonic of e (which is b'). Also between the sixth harmonic of c (which is g") and the fifth harmonic of e (which is g" sharp).

c against f (fourth): decidedly a consonance. The summation tone is e' flat, beating, but not very fiercely, with the second harmonic of f (which is f'). There is also beating between the third harmonic of c (which is g') and the second harmonic of f (which is f'). Also between the sixth harmonic of c (which is g″) and the fifth harmonic of f (which is a″).

c against g (*fifth*): *still more emphatically a consonance*. The summation tone is e′, which coincides with the fifth harmonic of c, and does not beat with any harmonic of c or g. There is, however, beating between the fourth harmonic of c (which is c″) and the third harmonic of g (which is d″). Also between this latter and the fifth harmonic of c (which is e″).

c against c′ (*octave*): *a nearly perfect consonance*. No beating among the first six harmonics; negligibly high beating between the seventh harmonic of c (which is b″) flat and the fourth harmonic of c′ (which is c‴).

c against c (*unison*): *the virtual consonance*. No beating anywhere between the two harmonic series. Any beating between the seventh and eighth harmonics within each single series (b″ flat and c‴) is too high and rapid to produce the least sense of dissonance.

The analysis above is not all complete: but it is sufficient to illustrate the principle. Beating between very high harmonics, even if they happen to be strong, is likely to be too rapid to have much effect; so that in practice the dissonance of an interval is determined by the amount of beating among the few lowest harmonics and combination tones.

Here is a list of primary (diatonic) intervals, within the octave, with the ratios of their vibration frequencies. Note, in passing, that it is the smoothest consonances which tend to the simplest ratios. (See Appendix IV for a further discussion of the nature of musical intervals.)

Interval	*Ratio*	*Musically*
Unison	1 : 1	Perfect concord
Minor second (diatonic semi-tone)	16 : 15	Discord (very harsh)
Major second (as major tone)	9 : 8	Discord (harsh)
(as minor tone)	10 : 9	
Minor third	6 : 5	Imperfect concord
Major third	5 : 4	Imperfect concord
Fourth	4 : 3	Perfect concord or mild discord according to context

Interval	Ratio	Musically
Fifth	3 : 2	Perfect concord
Minor sixth	8 : 5	Imperfect concord
Major sixth	5 : 3	Imperfect concord
Minor seventh	16 : 9	Discord (not harsh)
Major seventh	15 : 8	Discord (fairly harsh)
Octave	2 : 1	Perfect concord

Intervals which are augmented or diminished by a chromatic semi-tone (secondary or chromatic intervals: save that the augmented fourth and the diminished fifth are normally treated as primary or diatonic intervals) have rather less simple ratios.[1] For example:

Interval	Ratio	Musically
Minor second (chromatic semi-tone)	135 : 128	Discord (very harsh)
Augmented second	75 : 64	Discord (mild)
Diminished third	256 : 225	Discord (harsh)
Augmented fourth	45 : 32	Discord (mild)
Diminished fifth	64 : 45	Discord (mild)
Augmented fifth	25 : 16	Discord (mild)
Diminished seventh	2048 : 1215	Discord (mild)

Intervals larger than an octave may be treated in the theory of harmony as replicas of the intervals one or more octaves smaller: e.g. the tenth (octave and a third) as if it were a third. This is convenient, rather than accurate: their beating, though similar, is not quite the same; nor do they sound the same. Again, a third low in pitch beats more roughly, and sounds less sweetly, than a third high in pitch; hence the warning in harmony text-books against too many thirds in the bass register. But, of course, the similarity between any two thirds, or even between a third and a tenth, outweighs their differences, and in the grammar of music they are rightly classed together.

---

[1] Those given are the orthodox calculations. But the late Dr McClure (a tragic loss) pointed out to me that, for example, the augmented second, the augmented fourth (tritone) and the augmented sixth can be tuned respectively and satisfactorily to 7 : 6, 7 : 5 and 7 : 4, or very nearly so. The actual ratios need not be taken too seriously; they vary with the temperament employed (see Appendix IV). The point to grasp is that simpler ratios favour less beating and therefore less dissonance. None of these augmented intervals is very discordant, however tuned, nor very sharply defined. They make an uneasy and restless effect, rather than a harsh one. They are, tonally, somewhat distressingly ambiguous.

Chords consonant and dissonant

Combinations of two notes are known as intervals: combinations of more than two notes, as chords. It would require computer help to calculate the beat-relations of consonance and dissonance among harmonics and combination tones even of a simple chord of three notes. But the principle remains the same.

It is worth noting that *minor* triads have among their combination tones more notes foreign to the harmony than do *major* triads: which is partly why music in the minor tends to be darker than music in the major.

Another reason is that any minor third beats harshly against the major third already present, in greater or less strength, as the fifth harmonic of the same fundamental. Strike C loudly on the piano, and listen for a time to the harmonic e′ natural ringing out very audibly on its own account. Now play the e′ flat softly, i.e. at about the same dynamic level as the harmonic e′ natural. You will get a delicious but eerie blend of major and minor on this same triad of C; and never again will you wonder why there is something faintly uneasy and ambivalent about all minor tonality.

A chord including a minor *second* (such as e and f) is likely to be quite harsh. A group of notes including two conjunct seconds (such as c, d, e) is probably too harsh to be intelligible *as part of a chord-progression* at all. Yet the same notes spaced out as c, d′, e″ are not unduly harsh (the d′ is then, grammatically, a mere tonic ninth with resolution to the eighth, c′).

All this is understandable enough so soon as it is grasped that dissonance depends on beats; that beats depend on the nearness of harmonics; and that the nearness of harmonics varies with various spacings and inversions of the chord in question.

One final curiosity. We have already seen that some instruments have much more prominent upper harmonics than others. Hence the same chord may sound much more dissonant on some instruments than on others, as every good orchestrator knows.

CHAPTER 2

HOW THE RAW MATERIAL
BECOMES MUSIC

Music as a link with inner experience

Music is not an idle luxury. In common with the other arts, music is
one of the means by which we keep in touch with our inner life.

Our inner life includes our feelings and our intuitions, and it is
these parts of our experience which music is peculiarly apt at expressing. Great music has the merit of presenting us with feelings
and intuitions which we all have to some extent in common, but
inarticulately. The value of the music largely lies in making us aware
of our own inner experience, but articulately, so that we can somehow see the point of it as we cannot so clearly see it without some
such assistance from a creative artist of genius.

Not only can music express our own inner experience for us more
articulately than we could for ourselves, it can also enlarge our experience by sharing with us the experiences of its creative artists,
both the composers and the performers. Creative people tend to lead
difficult and restless lives, but are compensated by being driven to
greater depths of inner experience than average people. They tend
to suffer more, but for that very reason they may see more, and it is
the average people who stand to gain by the vision bought at this
unavoidable cost in suffering.

No artist can altogether avoid his destiny of living out on behalf
of the more ordinary people the extremes of inner experience, and
of concentrating them into the articulate forms of which music gives
examples. But the greatness of the art depends not only on talent,
but also on character. Artists are extraordinarily different from one
another; but an outstanding case may illustrate my point.

The case I have in mind is Beethoven. His genius has never been
exceeded. His character was indomitable to a heroic degree. His outer
life was a succession of disasters relieved only by his fame and

triumphs as an artist; for as a man he was distressingly incompetent in the ordinary business of living. In commercial matters he was so confused that his actual conduct towards publishers and others would have to be called dishonest if it were not so obviously due to the desperation of a neurotic compulsion. He found personal relationships almost an impossibility, and went on increasingly as he began, an irredeemably lonely man. His private tragedy, which was his deafness, exacerbated but did not originate his loneliness, and his own account of how he won through to victory over the despair of it is one of the most moving of human documents.

That victory resounds in his music. Out of all his manifold distress and suffering he forged music which conveys more of the inner meaning of life than any lesser artist would have done. No music tells us more plainly that life with all its pain is the most glorious of mysteries. It tells us this not by leaving out the pain, but by reconciling it with the glory. By accepting the pain, Beethoven was able to experience the glory as few men are privileged to do.

In our deepest intuitions, we not only know that we are mortals who will have to meet with pain as well as delight, and who must one day die; we know that this is the paradox we have voluntarily to accept if we want to be thoroughly in life, and not merely skulking evasively around the edges of it. We know it somewhere; but our knowledge may be so buried in our unconscious that it is of very little use to us until we are brought into closer touch with it. Genuine religion and genuine art can bring us into closer touch with our deepest intuitions. Hence the poignancy of great music.

In music such as Beethoven's, the pain and the delight are not only conveyed in abundant measure; they are brought into such intimate relation to one another that we cannot help feeling that somehow they belong together. This feeling, which we have no need to put into words, and cannot adequately put into words, is more valuable to us than gold and diamonds. We feel in our hearts that this really is what life is like, only that we could never have put it so clearly as the music is doing. We feel that if only we can take our own lives with some of Beethoven's triumph over adversity, we shall share in his delight and strength also. And when I say feel, I do not mean think. I am speaking of experiences which hardly come to the surface in rational terms at all. 'The heart has its reasons', wrote Pascal, 'of which reason knows nothing.'

That such inner experiences are of inestimable importance to us is confirmed by such tangible facts as the continued box-office draw of a Beethoven night, by the crowds of unpretentious music-lovers at Promenade concerts, by the vast popularity of Bach and the packed houses for Wagner: by all the evidence on every hand that ordinary people, and not only sophisticated connoisseurs, need and appreciate music in their everyday existence. Even the ubiquitous radio and TV add their testimony to the same effect. The music going on around us is not all of it very good and still less very great music; but it is music. It takes all sorts to make a world.

The necessity for dissonance as well as consonance

In order to convey pain as well as delight, and to reconcile them with one another and us to them, music needs dissonance as well as consonance. We have seen in the previous chapter how physical a reality discord and concord rest on. This reality is the raw material from which a composer makes up his patterns, together with other realities of melody and harmony, rhythm and timbre. He does so by blending such material into images of which the substance depends on the outer realities of acoustics, but the meaning depends on a correspondence between these outer realities and the inner realities of our common human experience.

Pain and delight are mental experiences, but we associate them largely with physical experiences. The faint, subliminal discomfort as discord beats in our ears, and the relief when concord follows, call up corresponding associations. In countless ways such as these, musical images become symbols for feelings and intuitions so elusive that we could not put them into words, yet so precise that words would be a very inadequate vehicle for them even if we could. It was Mendelssohn who said that the reason why we cannot define the emotions expressed by music is not that they are too vague to be put into words, but that they are too precise.

We could not share musical or any other experiences if it were not that we inherit certain predispositions in common. These predispositions take shape in us as archetypal images. Such images focus age-old experiences of our species, and can be seen in numerous mythologies, religions and traditions of art, not to mention the ordinary man's dreams and fantasies. Our innate familiarity with these images is the common element to which works of art can appeal. I shall always remember my first Wagner as a child. The vivid images on the stage, and the still more vivid imagery woven by the voices and the orchestra, did not fall on my unformed mind as something wonderfully new and unfamiliar, but as something wonderfully familiar to me in some hidden part of myself. What was familiar was not Wagner's actual *Valkyrie*, but the timeless archetypes on which Wagner like other artists was intuitively drawing.

Music as ordered emotion

In drawing on our common background of archetypal imagery, the composer, aided by the performer in so far as he can share in the composer's experience, touches on springs of emotion in us which we hardly knew were there. But music does not only release our emotion. It releases it in a highly organized and ordered form. Discord and concord are not thrown at us in meaningless confusion, but in a meaningful succession of harsh and smooth ingredients.

Very simple sounds, of which the extreme case is pure tones, are smooth enough; but they are so smooth and so simple in their harmonic content as to be positively uninteresting. Very complicated sounds, of which extreme discordance is one example, may be too harsh for us because they are too complicated to be intelligible to us. We can accept any amount of harshness provided that we can detect a meaning in it; if we cannot, it is no better for us than incoherent noise. We do not reject noise, as such; but we do reject what we do not perceive as coherent.

What our minds reject as unintelligible dissonance does not only depend on the degree and persistence of the dissonance; it also depends on what our minds are capable of understanding. Some people have far more aptitude for understanding musical development than others, and some are much better trained at it and practised in it. Even to the most gifted mind, moreover, an unfamiliar innovation may at first seem more or less incomprehensible. With growing familiarity, the connections and recapitulations which make sense of it begin to stand out, until it comes to seem extraordinary that they could ever have been found difficult. In the long run, they may well get to seem too simple to be any longer capable of expressing our deeper emotions. This does not relegate the great music composed in past idioms to the dustbin, since what is once profoundly felt remains profoundly moving; but it does make those idioms useless for the new generation of composers. They must then be replaced by some subtler modification, compression or reaction which, since its artistic precursor is by now all too familiar, will soon be accepted as comprehensible in its turn. There is thus a perennial tendency towards refinement and elaboration, until a more radical reaction sets in, and forgotten simplicities are rediscovered with all the zest of novelty. The limits of what seems comprehensible vary enormously at different times and places. Change may be slow; or, as now, by leaps.

Lacking discord, we should lack the sense of strain and tension which makes the subsequent relaxation into concord welcome. Lacking concord, we should lack the prospect of resolution which makes discord intelligible. Discord and concord are a pair of natural opposites, and their due relationship to one another is a means of symbolizing the opposites inherent in life itself, including pain and delight. Contrasts such as this are of the essence of life, and they are of the essence of works of art, which use them to show symbolically how the dark side and the light side can be reconciled into a totality we can hope to accept.

Acoustically, the varying degrees of beating which we experience as varying degrees of dissonance and consonance are absolute realities. Emotionally, they are relative realities. In music of which the general texture is very concordant, the mildest discord may sound as harsh as the harshest discord in generally discordant music. In music which is unremittingly discordant, the milder discords will assume the function of concords. But there is a certain danger that the degree of contrast available will prove insufficient if dissonance is too persistently maintained.

What applies to the contrasts of harmony applies, not by direct sensation but through immediate memory, to melody also. In most Eastern music of all periods, in antiquity everywhere, and in the bulk of genuine folk music, melody is used without harmonic suggestion or implication. This leaves it free to range through an unrestricted variety of intervals, including microtonic intervals too small to combine as harmony in any system so far envisaged, if ever to be envisaged. In our main Western tradition, our choice of intervals (with rare exceptions of a hybrid kind) is restricted to those which can be combined as harmony; and melody itself is largely conditioned by the implied harmony at the back of it.

Restrictions are themselves an important aspect of the raw material of art, and part of an artist's skill consists in conceiving restrictions as potentialities. He sees the inexhaustible artistic possibilities in the very limits of the style in which he is at work, so that in practice he is not hampered but helped by them. Besides the contrasts of harmony and melody to which I have briefly referred, there are, even within the limits of a single musical style, other possibilities of contrast in rhythm, speed, dynamics, articulation, texture, orchestration and so forth which are likewise in practice inexhaustible. No composer who is able to make contact with the underlying archetypes is ever going to lack for raw material in which to shape his vision and to give it the personal stamp of his own individuality.

The raw material of new music still the same

But what about a composer who rejects, in whole or part, the raw material of music as hitherto understood in our Western tradition?

That is happening today, and it must be taken seriously. Nothing which is happening can affect the physical properties of sound, which are properties of our objective universe, and not amenable to human interference. In that sense, no alteration has been or can be made in the raw material of music.

But composers can alter, and have greatly altered, the selection they make from the raw material available.

Further, new methods can be developed, and have been greatly developed, for drawing upon the raw material available. The chief of these developments, though not the only ones, are by electrical methods of amplifying, of manipulating and of initiating sounds.

The results are startling. There has been a prodigious expansion in the range and variety of sounds we are able to combine in practice. But there has not been anything new in principle. There are new exploitations of sound, but there are no new kinds of sound.

There is new music, but no basically new kinds of music. For music is and can only be the coherent and purposeful organization of sounds.

The organization of sounds into music is and can only be an organization of meaningful contrasts. Harsh and gentle; rough and smooth; fast and slow; high and low; abrupt and gradual; complex and simple; opaque and transparent; dense and sparse; long and short; varied and monotonous; loud and soft: what other contrasts but such as these can go into music ?

The basic experiences which we human beings undergo, from the cradle to the grave, are none other than the age-old experiences of our species, repeated down the generations until patterns of behaviour and response have become ingrained in us which we do not have to learn as individuals, but only to relearn and to renew.

This we do in countless unique variations upon the common themes. But nothing comes to us as basically unfamiliar. When Plato said that all learning is a recognition of what we know already, he meant our intuitive recognition of those archetypal patterns which he regarded as laid up in heaven, but which we may prefer to regard as laid down in the unconscious.

Archetypal patterns are evoked in archetypal images; and neither art nor any other communication nor life itself would be possible if we could not recognize archetypal images as familiar friends, acquaintances and enemies. Animals do it by what we call instinct. We do it by animal instinct and by much else besides which comes through our partial growth into human consciousness.

Love and hate; hope and fear; courage and despair; youth and age; sickness and health; birth and death: there is no one of us but is touched by some variant of these. And whether more consciously or less consciously, there is no art but holds a mirror to them. We see through a glass, darkly; or at times more openly and luminously. But we see.

HOW MUSICAL
INSTRUMENTS WORK

PART TWO

HOW MUSICAL
INSTRUMENTS WORK

CHAPTER 3

INSTRUMENTAL ORDERS

The four orders of musical instrument

Three of them are old and well-tried; one is new but already well established. They are:

I. STRINGS (Gk. *enchordon*, Lat. *tensile*): vibrations from stretched string.

II. WIND (Gk. *pneumatikon*, Lat. *inflatile*): vibrations from an enclosed column of air.

III. PERCUSSION (Gk. *krousticon*, Lat. *pulsatile*): vibrations from a stretched membrane or resonant solid.

IV. ELECTROPHONES (Electronic Instruments): vibrations from a loudspeaker moved by a fluctuating electric current.

These distinctions are not so fundamental as they might appear. An organ pipe can be designed to give much the same harmonics as a violin string: what undeceives us is the lack of the violin bow's bite and expressive nuance. And on the other hand, no two notes are quite alike even on the same instrument in the same player's hands.

Certain parts of a musical instrument are thought to possess free vibration periods of their own, capable of reinforcing powerfully any corresponding harmonics, with a substantial effect on the quality of the tone. Such supposed resonant areas are known as *formants*. The theory of formants is at present (1970) in a very uncertain condition; the following is merely a statement of possible principles.

The hollow, air-filled wooden violin body may have formants whose exact disposition makes the difference between a good violin and a bad one. The tube of a wind instrument may possess formants as decisive for its tone-colour as more obvious factors. The sounding-board of a piano is made of material which ensures the widest possible response, so as to reduce favouritism to a minimum: but favouritism can never be quite eliminated. So, too, a loudspeaker.

Suppose a note sounded: such of its harmonics as tally with the instrument's formants will be selectively reinforced. But suppose another note sounded, having another series of harmonics: the same formants will reinforce harmonics of the same *pitch* as before; but these will not have the same *position* in the second harmonic series as they did in the first. Therefore the second note cannot have quite the same tone quality as the first if the formant theory is correct. In the light of the most recent experiments, this is by no means certain; since, however, the difference between a good violin and a bad one, or a good flute and a bad one, is clearly objective, we are bound to postulate *some* difference in their resonating qualities.

Further, the different strings of a violin are of different gauges and material, besides being stopped by the fingers to different lengths for different notes: low notes and high notes are produced in different ways on most wind instruments; and so on. The player himself may be more or less skilled in coaxing the most favourable assortment of high harmonics; and moreover, since, given the skill, he can on most instruments somewhat vary them at will, his choice of tone-colours will be to some extent individual to himself.

With such points in mind, it is easy to see that no classification of musical instruments can or should be very hard and fast: the grouping into strings, wind, percussion and electrophones is a matter more of convenience and custom than of scientific exactness. Nevertheless, it is convenient and for most practical purposes it is the best description.

How string instruments work

Shake one end of a piece of rope, and watch the impulses undulate to the other end, though the rope as a whole does not move forward. This is a case of *transverse* vibrations (such as occur in a vibrating string), slow enough to see though too slow to hear.

Twang a length of wire fencing: the shorter, the tighter and the less massive the wire, the more rapid the vibrations (now rapid enough to hear, and see indistinctly), and therefore the higher the sound. If the fence posts are of elastic material (e.g. wood) the sound will furthermore be louder, because more amplified by sympathetic resonance, than if they are of inelastic material (e.g. concrete).

In a piano, the higher the note, the shorter the string. In a violin, all four strings must be of the same length, for ease of playing: but too slack a string will sound feeble while too thick a string will be hard to get sounding at all, as well as deficient in high harmonics; hence the bottom string is now always and middle strings are ordinarily weighted by gimping (winding a very fine metal wire round a fairly fine gut or metal core). Gimped low strings are, indeed, usual even (to increase flexibility and avoid inconvenient length) on keyboard instruments. Nylon is now an alternative material, and so is steel, for top strings.

If a string vibrated only as a whole, we might hear only its first or fundamental harmonic (i.e. pure tone): but it also vibrates simultaneously in its quotient parts – in half-lengths, producing the second harmonic an octave above; in third-lengths, producing the third harmonic a twelfth above; and so up the Natural Harmonic Series, the net result of these many superimposed vibrations being, as we saw, a compound tone, at the pitch of its first or fundamental harmonic, but of a quality depending on the relative strength of its upper harmonics.

The string ends, being fixed, are *nodes* (points of least vibration); the centre is normally an *antinode* or loop (point of most vibration). But by placing your little finger lightly on this central antinode, you can make a node of it, thus inhibiting the full-length vibration: which silences the first or fundamental harmonic, and leaves the second harmonic an octave above to be heard as the main note in its place ('natural harmonic'). Similarly, by placing your little finger lightly one-third of the distance along the string, you inhibit both first and second harmonics, hearing in their stead the third harmonic a twelfth above ('natural harmonic'); and this can also be done with any shorter string length held firmly curtailed with the first finger ('artificial harmonic'). But the tone colour ('flageolet tone' so called) obtained in these ways is too peculiar, in the case of string instruments, to be valuable except for certain deliberate effects. (The 'trumpet marine' – Plate 10 – used it normally, however.)

The string ends partly reflect the vibrations back along the string, but partly convey them to the resonating body (corresponding to the wooden fence posts) which, having a much larger surface than the string itself, transmits them to the air in far ampler strength, and enriched in quality (? by the influence of its formants). Such a partnership is called a coupled acoustic system. Strictly, it includes the room and your ear as well: but these latter factors need be considered no further than they have already been.

How wind instruments work

Watch a freight train pass the first slight impact of its shunting-engine from truck to truck along its length, the individual trucks rebounding backwards and forwards, though the train as a whole is still virtually stationary. This is a form of *longitudinal* vibration, such as occurs in a vibrating enclosed column of air, and, incidentally, such as conveys sound, from whatever source, through the surrounding air to your ear. (American freight trains, unlike English, are tightly coupled, and do not seem to show this interesting phenomenon.)

There are two main ways of exciting the vibrations of an enclosed column of air: and in both of them, the exciting tone, instead of (like string exciting tone) imposing its own vibrations substantially on the resonating body, submits substantially to the natural frequencies (free vibrating periods) of the resonating air column.

Watch a flag on a windy day. As the wind strikes the flag-rope, it forms eddies on alternate sides (just as you can often see moving water forming eddies round a fixed post). You can trace these air eddies visibly by the undulations which they impart to the flag as they pass down it; slowly, with a large flag in a moderate wind, more rapidly with a smaller flag in a stronger wind.

It is air eddies of this nature which give rise to *edge tone*, such as excites all wind instruments of the flue class. (Flue is an organ-builders' term for a passage-way directing air across an edge: similar passages are incorporated in all flutes, either by a built-in mouthpiece, as in the recorder, or by pursing the lips to do duty for a mouthpiece, as in the transverse flute.) The edge is not flexible like the flag, but fixed like the river post, and relatively sharp. As air is blown across it, eddies are formed on alternate sides of it: the faster the air current, the more rapid the eddies, and the higher the edge tone (subject to certain qualifications).

Since the air current loses speed as it goes, the eddies can be slowed, and the edge tone lowered, by withdrawing the edge. But if it is much withdrawn or the air-speed *increased* by blowing harder (overblowing), a new factor enters: each eddy breaks into two; and the edge tone jumps to the octave above. More over-blown, each eddy breaks into three; and the edge tone jumps to the twelfth above. And so up the Natural Harmonic Series, though not very far up with this method of tone-production.

Now purse your lips, and make them vibrate by blowing through them. Each time your breath blows your lips a certain distance apart, the elastic tension of their pursed muscles brings them together, thus passing a regular succession of impulses to the outer air.

It is impulses of this nature which occur with *reed tone*, such as excites all wind instruments other than those of the flue class. The reed may be a single 'cane' reed lying on a nearly flat surface, as in the clarinet; or a pair of 'cane' reeds minutely curved from one another, as in the oboe; or simply your lips, as in the trumpet. But the principle in all these cases is the same.

By manipulating with your lip muscles the elastic tension of the reed in question, reed tone, like edge tone, can be jumped to the octave, the twelfth and numerous higher harmonics of the harmonic series. Reed tone is sometimes, as in the harmonium, heard with no resonator: but most wind instruments, like all feasible string instruments, are coupled acoustic systems; and here it is the enclosed air column which is the resonating partner.

Like the string, the enclosed air column vibrates as a whole and in its quotient lengths simultaneously: hence the free vibration periods which (unlike the resonating body of a string instrument) it more or less imposes on its exciting tone (whether edge or reed tone) are once more those of the Natural Harmonic Series.

An air column takes its pitch, in the first instance, from its length, vibrating in wavelengths which are four times the distance from node to antinode.

Hence in a cylindrical *open* pipe (open, and therefore least constricted, at both ends, each of which is thus necessarily an antinode), the longest complete vibration possible must show at least antinode (one end), node (middle), antinode (other end): which gives a wavelength *twice* the length of the pipe itself, to produce its first or fundamental harmonic. The next longest must show antinode, node, antinode, node, antinode: which gives a wavelength half the longest, to produce the second harmonic an octave above. The next must show antinode, node, antinode, node, antinode, node, antinode:

which gives a wavelength one-third of the longest, to produce the third harmonic a twelfth above. And so right up the harmonic series: the result being once more, of course, a compound tone, at the pitch of its first or fundamental harmonic, but of a quality depending on the relative strength of its upper harmonics.

In a *conical* open (at both ends) or closed (at one end) pipe, the wavelengths resemble those in a cylindrical *open* pipe.

But in a cylindrical *closed* pipe (closed, and therefore most constricted, at one end, which is thus necessarily a node, but open, and therefore least constricted, at the other end, which is thus necessarily an antinode), the longest complete vibration will show node (one end), antinode (the other end), with neither node nor antinode between. This gives a wavelength *four times* the length of the pipe itself, to produce its first or fundamental harmonic *an octave lower than an open pipe of the same length*. But that is not all.

The next longest complete vibration cannot show antinode, node, antinode (which would give a wavelength half the longest, to produce the second harmonic an octave above): for though the open end *must* be, the closed end *cannot* be an antinode. Hence the second harmonic is necessarily missing. The next longest can only be that showing node, antinode, node, antinode: which gives a wavelength one-third of the longest, to produce the third harmonic a twelfth above. And so it is right up the harmonic series, only the odd numbers of which can be present, while the even numbers are necessarily missing (except in so far as they are introduced by the exciting tone itself, and reinforced by the formants of the actual tube; or, yet again, formed in the listener's ear as difference tones). That is what gives the clarinet (the nearest orchestral approximation to a closed cylinder) its characteristically smooth and indeed (in the low notes where the exciting reed tone and the formants of the tube can do least to supply the deficiency) cadaverous quality of tone.[1]

Strictly, the antinode necessarily associated with an open end occurs a fraction beyond the opening, since the constrained air cannot immediately become equalized in pressure with the outer air. The difference (known as end correction) is, in general, greater for

[1] Since the second, fourth, etc. harmonics are missing in a stopped cylindrical pipe, its third harmonic is properly called its second partial; its fifth harmonic its third partial, and so on: a source of confusion of which it is as well to be aware.

high partials than for low. Thus each higher partial, if separately excited, is naturally a little more out of tune. But if vibration is mechanically maintained, so that only harmonic partials are possible, then these are more and more out of tune with the natural partials, and therefore more and more attenuated. The more attenuated the partials, the less colourful the tone.

Reed tone, being itself a richer source of high harmonics, will be less affected than edge tone by end correction. End correction, too, is greatest at a narrow or partially obstructed opening: least at a wide and unobstructed opening. It is for this reason, and not for merely decorative purposes, that wind instruments of different timbre end in such a variety of bulbs, bells and flares.

Wind instruments normally and extensively rely for their higher notes on the same device of inhibiting lower harmonics in favour of the next highest which we noted as a special and occasional recourse in string instruments. In many cases, this is facilitated by opening a 'speaker' hole to reinforce an antinode (the obverse of reinforcing a node in the vibrating string, but equally effective, since nodes and antinodes are interdependent); in other cases, the exciting tone is alone manipulated (e.g. forced up by increased pressure of the breath), the air column following suit from its own predisposition to fall into quotient parts (and thus to jump from one harmonic to the next, as the exciting tone is forced up). The ease with which it does so is again conditioned by the bell, and by the general design of the tube and mouthpiece.

Certain new techniques are in course of being developed for wind instruments which greatly expand their resources. Currently (1969) these developments have been mainly concentrated in the woodwind: i.e. flue and reed instruments. It is probable that they can be further extended for lip instruments, though it is uncertain how far. It has long been known how to get chords on the horn (by humming, blowing and combination tones); and some 'flageolet' tones on the flute.

The effect of these new techniques is to force the air column to vibrate in other modes than those hitherto employed. This is done by manipulating the exciting tone in special manners. On those flue instruments (e.g. the flute) having no fixed, built-in air-channel (fipple) for directing the breath across the playing edge, the lips can be opened more widely or more narrowly than the ordinary technique requires for the note in question, and turned to different angles, giving a different direction to the air-stream across the embouchure. On those flue instruments (e.g. the recorder) having a built-in fipple, these methods are excluded, but the others remain, all the more so because there are few or no keys to limit trick finger-ings in which only part of a hole is covered or uncovered, gradually or suddenly. On reed instruments (e.g. oboes, clarinets and bassoons) of which the reed is taken directly into the mouth, the pressure of the lip or lips on the reed can be more or less strong than the ordinary technique requires for the note in question. On all these classes of instrument, the speed and volume of the breath can be greater or less great than the ordinary technique requires for the note in question, as fingered; and by choosing alternative fingerings, the range of these unusual possibilities is very much increased.

By these and other methods, singly or in combination, it is possible to produce the same notes from a great variety of different fingerings (beyond the orthodox variety) and with a great variety of different *colourings*. This results from different degrees of energy sent into different partials, heard as variable tone-colouring for the notes produced by such unorthodox methods.

It is also possible to send so much energy into upper partials that these are heard not as tone-colouring, but as several notes at once: i.e. *chords*. These chords, rather startlingly produced from instru-ments whose normal and familiar use is exclusively melodic, can include four (occasionally more) notes different in pitch but more or less *similar* in volume, colouring and character; or, when some of the sounds arise from acoustic beating, very markedly *different* in volume, colouring and character from one another. Finally, it is possible to produce *microtonic* intervals (e.g. one-third tones, quarter-tones, eighth-tones) both melodically, and chordally; and also glissando effects.

The interest created by these recent developments of wind technique is currently greatest in the *avant-garde*. None of the new effects forms part of the original intention of the instruments con-cerned, or is a planned consequence of its design. All are by-products ingeniously discovered, and enthusiastically exploited, by a genera-tion of composers and performers (jointly) who are above all anxious to get away from traditional idioms, including traditional sounds.

The new wind techniques are special but in no other way abnormal techniques, producing special but in no other way abnormal effects.

They are no doubt being overvalued for the moment by their talented discoverers, pardonably enough; but we should not be too unappreciative of them, either. Like all special effects, they must find their value in proportion to the good uses composers make of them. In themselves, they are neither better nor worse than, for example, harmonics on the violin. The new harmonics on wind instruments are perfectly legitimate extensions of the innate acoustic potentialities of the instruments concerned, and will no doubt settle to their proper place in the natural course of events.

How percussive resonators work

If a stretched membrane, or a solid bar or plate, or a hollow bell, bowl or tube is struck, it may vibrate, like a string or an air column, both as a whole and in parts. But the upper partials will be neither very stable nor very regular, unlike all the harmonic series with which we have hitherto been dealing. If there is a reasonably stable first or fundamental harmonic, we hear a mainly definite pitch, as with the kettledrum. If not, we hear no definite pitch, as with the bass drum.

How electronic instruments work

If an electric current, oscillating with a regular periodic frequency within the range of human hearing, is fed to a loudspeaker, a pure tone results. If other such currents, with frequencies equal to those of a Natural Harmonic Series, are superimposed, an ordinary compound musical tone may be built up, with a quality corresponding to the relative strength of its constituent harmonics. This is an *additive* method (adding sine-waves) of producing musically interesting and varied tones by electronic apparatus. If an electric current is initiated with compound frequencies, a compound tone results. If this compound is rich in all harmonics, all in phase but regularly decreasing (by harmonical progression as $1, \frac{1}{2}, \frac{1}{3}, \frac{1}{4} \ldots$) in amplitude up the series, it may take the form called sawtooth waves; if only odd harmonics, the form called square waves; and from either form (or intermediate forms) harmonics can be subtracted as desired by filtering them out. This is a *subtractive* method of producing musically interesting and varied tones by electronic apparatus.

If an electric current is initiated with the desired frequencies already present, this is a *direct* method, as used, for example, in the Compton electronic organ (for which see Chapter 14 below). But the direct method is not commonly used in electronic instruments: i.e. instruments *producing* sounds electrically with no acoustic source of origin. We must be careful to distinguish these from instruments *reproducing* sounds electrically of which the origin is an acoustic source: for example, a live performance.

For ordinary purposes, such electrical reproduction is direct and (so far as possible) unaltered except by amplification to the original (or any desired) level of volume. For purposes of electronically modified reproduction, for example in concrete music (*musique concrète*), and commonly nowadays in dance music, the harmonic content can be selectively filtered or selectively reinforced; octave doubling can be added on either side (or both sides) of the fundamental; the attack (i.e. the build up of the sound) or the decay (i.e. the decline of the sound) or both (these together comprise the envelope) can be altered; echo and reverberation can be introduced; fluctuation of pitch or of intensity or of both can be caused, to provide vibrato, and certain still more refined modifications can be contrived, for example by a ring modulator, which has two inputs, but one output giving the combined product after mutual modulation by the input signals one upon the other.

Sounds of acoustic, electronic or combined origin can be manipulated in these and other ways for a great variety of purposes and idioms. Electronic sounds can be used to simulate, with varying degrees of closeness, traditional instruments: easily, in the matter of harmonic content (and therefore of tone quality); with more difficulty in the matter of envelope and articulation (and therefore of recognizable overall character). But this simulation has scarcely more to offer artistically than the simulation of orchestral instruments by a pipe organ. Ironically enough, the one such simulation which really does have special value and advantages is the simulation of a pipe organ by an electronic organ.

By far the most interesting and creative use of electronic sounds is for novel effects not obtainable on traditional instruments. The scope for novel tone-colourings is not perhaps so wide as might be expected, since the varieties of harmonic content produced by the various traditional instruments are already so extensive. Perhaps the newest of the new sounds is that produced by a 'white noise' generator giving a random series of frequencies, either over the entire audible range, or (by filtering) over selected bands or portions of it. The curious hissing thus produced is most like the sound of steam escaping under pressure, or of a strong wind rustling the innumerable leaves of a forest: as a whole, it is quite indefinite in pitch; in narrow bands of adjacent frequencies, it is more or less definite in pitch, though still of a certain strange ambivalence.

The scope for novel envelopes and articulations is very wide indeed, and so is the scope for otherwise unattainable rapidity, and for uncanny effects of artificial reverberation and electronic intermodulation and multiple superimposition; indeed, there seem only two conclusive limitations to this sort of special effect. One is when money runs out with which to pay for any more of the very expensive equipment required. The other is when the outer thresholds of hearing are reached, either for extremes of pitch or of intensity (perceptible or endurable), or for the greatest rapidity or complication which the brain can distinguish intelligibly.

There is no foreseeable probability of electronic sounds superseding traditional instruments, which give the performer the advantage of very direct and intimate contact with the sounds produced. Fallible as this contact inevitably is, and imperfect as traditional instruments at their best remain, there is a highly expressive value in this fallibility and this imperfection. An impersonal perfection would no longer represent anything in human nature; for it is human to be fallible and imperfect, and our variability and our unpredictability are what go to make up our character. In so far as electronic appliances respond to and convey the composer's will, they too may serve human purposes; but the mere fact that they are, on the whole, more reliable and predictable, does not in itself make them any better. Imperfections in the medium, and limitations on its potentialities, are themselves part of the artist's material.

We might say that traditional instruments, on the whole, are under the very immediate control of the performer, but are inherently uneven and a shade chancy, wherein lies a good part of their expressiveness. And we might say that electronic sounds can readily be made even and certain, but are less readily brought under the immediate control of a performer for the finer purposes of expression.

But then we should add that there is a growing middle class of instruments in some respects traditional, but in other respects electronic: for example, the electric guitar, in which metal strings, stretched traditionally to pitch, are traditionally plucked; but their vibrations, instead of being conveyed to the traditional hollow resonating body of wood for acoustic amplification, are picked up electro-magnetically for electronic amplification. Here the expression is controlled with traditional directness, but the sounds resulting are very untraditional indeed.

How all this will settle down is obviously still a matter for the future. But so far as this can be foreseen, it does not seem at all likely that any of the traditional orders of musical instrument will be put out of business by the vigorous young electrophonic order. It seems likely that strings (chordophones), wind (aerophones), percussion (ideophones, approximately) and electrophones (including both wholly and partially electronic instruments) will remain our operative instruments of music for a long time to come.

CHAPTER 4

INSTRUMENTAL SPECIES

I: THE THREE SPECIES OF STRING INSTRUMENTS
String instruments played with a bow

The bow is a stick of moderately springy wood, with upwards of a hundred hairs, from the tail of a horse, stretched between its two ends. It is left slack when not in use, but can be tightened to the required tension by a screw knob.

The hair possesses minute roughness, which are made rougher by being rubbed with fine resin. These roughnesses, as they are drawn across the string, pull it minutely to one side, until it grows tense enough to fly back: only to be caught again. By this alternate pull and recoil, it is kept in continuous vibration.

Bowing, as a means of exciting a string to vibration, is favourable to high, accurately harmonic upper partials. But a great deal will depend on the exact technique employed.

For example, the width of hair brought into contact with the strings can be varied both by the angle of the bow and by the degree of pressure. The greater the width of hair in contact with the string, the greater its power to eliminate high harmonics by enforcing an antinode where those harmonics would require a node; and at the same time, the greater the pressure, the louder the tone.

Again, the speed at which the bow is moved can be varied. The faster the bow is drawn, the louder the tone, but the greater the risk that the hair will fail to bite properly, thus throwing more energy into the upper than into the lower harmonics, and detracting from fullness of tone.

Next the point of attack can be varied. The nearer the bow is to the bridge, the louder the tone, and the more brilliant its quality. But too near the bridge, excessive pressure is required before the hair will bite, and squeaks are likely; while too far from the bridge, even slight pressure is too much, and the hair cannot impart sufficient energy to the string. Roughly a seventh to a fifteenth of the way from the bridge gives the normal limits; the average is about a ninth.

In all bowed instruments, the pitch of the strings is first adjusted by regulating their tension: this is done by turning the pegs round which one end passes. The note yielded by a string at its full length is called an open note. Other notes are found by stopping the string with a suitable finger to the length required: these are called stopped notes. The shorter the length, the higher the pitch. Most notes may be played either on a longer length of a higher string, which gives a fuller tone; or on a shorter length of a lower string, which gives a more covered tone.

For special effects, as we have seen, 'harmonics' are available, producing a strange, flute-like quality. A yet further transformation is to clip a mute on to the bridge: this increases its weight, thus penalizing high harmonics, and causing a veiled and distant quality of tone. Further special effects are plucking (*pizzicato*); bowing very near the bridge (*sul ponticello*) or very near the finger-board (*sul tasto*); bowing with the wood of the bowstick (*col legno*), etc.

String instruments played by hand

When a string is plucked with the soft end of a finger, the angle at which it is displaced is not very sharp; the high harmonics are relatively weak; and the tone is full and rounded. When it is thrummed with fingers or thumb, the angle is still less sharp, and the tone still mellower. When it is plucked with a plectrum or with the fingernails, the angle is much sharper, and the tone is sharp and ringing. When it is struck with a soft felted drumstick, the tone is mellow; when it is struck with a hard stick or hammer, the tone is sharp and even jangling, thus revealing the presence of strong and perhaps actually inharmonic high partials.

Further, when a string is plucked, thrummed or struck near its middle, the tone will be relatively round; when near its end, relatively brilliant. As with bowed instruments, the exact point chosen will influence which high harmonics are favoured, and which discouraged. The average distance will again probably be something like a ninth of the way along, where the tone should be bright, yet full and resonant. But the practical limits are much wider; and great differences in tone colour can be gained by varying this factor.

Pitch is varied in much the same way, except that use may also be made in many cases (for example, the harp) of strings differing in length, as well as in tension and in weight.

String instruments played through a keyboard

Adding a keyboard simply means interposing a mechanical action between your fingers and the strings. This limits your control over the quality and volume of tone; but increases your power of playing in full harmony.

Bowing gives direct control throughout the note. Plucking or striking by hand gives direct control, but only at the beginning of the note. Plucking or striking through a keyboard gives more or less indirect control, and that only at the beginning of the note (except the clavichord). The amount of control varies in different keyboard instruments: it is usually considerable, but apt to be greater over volume than over quality.

The point of attack is usually fixed between a seventh and a ninth of the way along the string, which weakens some of the harsher harmonics, and makes for mellowness. Leather plectrums sound mellower than quills; soft felted hammers mellower than hard ones. There is normally at least one string to each note required: and you find your notes by depressing the appropriate keys.

II: THE FIVE SPECIES OF WIND INSTRUMENTS

Flue instruments

These are sounded by an edge tone: whereas all other wind instruments (except for organ pipes of the flue species) are sounded by some variety of reed tone. (See page 44 above.)

The lowest note of a flue instrument is the first or fundamental harmonic of its full length. For higher notes, the player may shorten its effective length by opening a succession of holes; or he may leap to a higher harmonic in the manner described in the last chapter, or both.

Now we have only fingers enough to cover the holes required for a diatonic scale (i.e. such as can be exemplified on the piano by playing the white notes from C to c). For a chromatic scale (i.e. such as can be exemplified on the piano by playing both white and black notes), more complex arrangements are required.

F

When you open a hole, you do not wholly deprive the further part of the tube of its influence. Thus if you now close one or more holes beyond the open hole, you can lower the pitch sufficiently to sound an intermediate or chromatic note. This method is known as cross-fingering or forked fingering.

Alternatively (and this has now become usual in the West) you can drill more holes, and arrange a system of mechanical keys to enable each finger to deal with more than one hole at need. This makes passages involving many chromatic notes, such as have been commonly written during the last centuries, easier to play. Furthermore, the holes can be drilled *exactly* in the sizes and positions which are theoretically perfect, instead of in a compromise such as the unaided fingers can reach and cover. And, on the whole, you can play in tune with less conscious effort of the attention than the older instruments, with one or two, or even no keys, require.

But against these advantages must be set some possible loss (or at the least change) of tone quality: for the keywork is not only surprisingly heavy, but has to be bolted firmly to the tube; and this might (though it has not been established that it does) decrease or change its formants. And in the opinion of some writers, it was all to the good to have to concentrate conscious attention on playing really well in tune, instead of relying overmuch on your mechanism, which anyhow cannot help you to adjust yourself finely to the other instruments with which you are playing.

Keys have come to stay, being a virtual necessity in all very chromatic music: but there are those who think they could with great advantage be somewhat diminished again in complexity and number. *Avant-garde* effects would also be easier.

You have, on flue instruments, extensive direct control over quality and volume, and also over intonation: though not so much as on some other instruments.

Reed instruments

Scientifically, this includes all the remaining species (except for flue pipes on the organ): but conventionally it means instruments using an actual slip of reed (*arundo donax*), sometimes, though inaccurately, called 'cane'; or a similar slip of wood or metal (in harmoniums and reed pipes on the organ); etc.

The tone of such a reed is in any case particularly rich in high harmonics; and the more suddenly and completely the reed, as it beats to and fro, momentarily stops the escaping air stream, the richer its high harmonics.

In modern Western instruments of the orchestra, you take the reed a little way into your mouth, which gives you a good control of quality and volume. When, as in a bagpipe chanter, the reed does not enter the mouth, but is housed in an enclosed passage-way or box, you have little or none.

The methods of finding the desired notes are very similar to those employed in flue instruments.

Lip instruments

Here, the human lips provide a double reed, of exceptional adaptability, owing to the change of shape, size and muscle tension which can be produced at will by a skilled and practised player.

You can usually control loudness within wide limits, and intonation within reasonable limits (though sometimes with difficulty). The quality of the tone is chiefly governed by the design of the instrument and of the mouthpiece used, but also varies with the player. Mutes partly blocking the bell can be inserted in most cases.

Because most lip instruments have a more or less prominent bell or flare, with an important influence on the quality of tone, they cannot satisfactorily be made to give their higher notes by a succession of holes, each shortening the tube when opened, as in flue and reed instruments.

Instead, they make far more use still of the other resource: leaping to a high harmonic in the manner described in the last chapter. Luckily, the very qualities of colourfulness which the bell or flare favours, and which make side holes undesirable, allow you to sound very high harmonics as separate notes. For we must never forget that the selfsame high harmonic can make itself felt in two different ways: either, in the ordinary way, as colourfulness of tone; or, if you have temporarily silenced all lower harmonics, as a separate note.

On some flue and reed instruments, this process can be simply achieved (see page 47) by opening a 'speaker hole'; but this is not desirable on lip instruments. So you rely on what is called over-blowing, which in this case is achieved by adjusting your lips and breath.

That gives you a choice of notes which fall along the natural harmonic series. But there are many large gaps in this series, at its lower end. There is no natural harmonic between the first or fundamental harmonic and the second harmonic, an octave above. The next octave (topped by the fourth harmonic) has one intermediate note (provided by the third harmonic); the third octave (topped by the eighth harmonic) is better provided, having three intermediate notes (fifth, sixth and seventh harmonics); but not till the fourth octave (topped by the sixteenth harmonic) do you get a nearly continuous diatonic scale, with all but one of the chromatic notes still lacking (and that not very well in tune with our normal scale). Higher harmonics yet can be sounded as notes on certain lip instruments by very skilled players, but we need not consider them at this point.

How, then, are all the remaining notes not provided by the Natural Harmonic Series to be found, since *shortening* the tube by holes is ruled out? They are found by the precisely opposite method of *lengthening* the tube. This may be done in different ways.

The most satisfactory is that used in the trombone. This, for the greater part of its length, has a cylindrical tube: it is built in two sections, one of which slides over the other, thus winning the not unnatural admiration of the legendary Shah of Persia who supposed that the trombonists were alternately swallowing and regurgitating substantial lengths of brass tubing. Not only can you lengthen the tube at will; you can do so to any length, within the limits which your arm can reach.

The bottom note is the first or fundamental harmonic of its fullest length.[1] As you shorten it again, you raise the pitch of this first or fundamental harmonic: and also, of course, of its complete Natural Harmonic Series. By juggling about with different lengths, and different members of the Natural Harmonic Series which each different length provides, you can get almost any conceivable note within the instrument's total range: and most of them in more ways than one.

However, a majority of lip instruments are not cylindrical, but conical, for the greater part of their length. That precludes a telescopic slide. The alternative is to insert additional lengths of tubing,

---

[1] In practice, the first or fundamental harmonic cannot be sounded on the trombone when extended to its seventh position. It is merely there in theory. But in all shorter positions it is available in practice too.

either as 'crooks' which can be changed by hand in a few moments, or as permanently attached sections which can be instantly let into or cut off from the operative air column by means of 'valves' or 'pistons'. Here, too, mechanization is not without its cost, but is on the whole necessitated by the many modulations and the chromatic harmonies of much of our existing music.

Both the richness of the upper harmonics as tone-colour and their availability as notes vary enormously with the design of the instrument.

Low harmonics are favoured by a broad, deep and tapering mouthpiece; a short, wide bore; and a slight bell. High harmonics are favoured by a narrow, shallow and angular mouthpiece; a long, narrow bore; and a flaring bell.

Next, mainly cylindrical lip instruments tend to a more brilliant, and mainly conical instruments to a broader quality.

Then there are the endless possibilities of different factors combined. For example: horn and trumpet both have narrow mouthpieces, narrow bores, flaring bells. But the horn's mouthpiece is deep and tapered, the trumpet's is shallow and angular; the horn is conical, the trumpet cylindrical; the horn has a yet more flaring bell than the trumpet. In the upshot, both are very colourful, and capable of very high harmonic notes: but the horn is mellow and the trumpet silvery.

Throat instruments

That is, the voice.

The vocal cords are shaped rather like the lips, and likewise function as a double reed. Under moderate air pressure from the lungs they vibrate, with a pitch governed by their length, tension and weight. These factors are largely determined by sex and age: but within their natural limits they can be controlled very accurately, given the skill. Volume can be controlled by varying the air pressure (not that the singer does any of these things self-consciously in the ordinary way, of course).

The vocal cords are coupled to a system of enclosed air cavities comprising the throat, the mouth and the nasal passages. These are credited with two marked formants: one low in pitch, contributing sonority; the other high in pitch, contributing the ring so valued by operatic connoisseurs. By changing the positions of the jaw, the tongue and the lips, the practised singer has a notable control of tone quality, though he must not modify it too far if he does not want to falsify his vowels, which are similarly controlled.

Keyboard wind instruments

An organ may combine many different qualities of tone, from pipes of different designs, excited some by edge tone and some by reed tone. A harmonium has no pipes: it has powerful reeds which vibrate at their own natural frequency, uncoupled to any resonating system.

There is little or no direct control of quality or volume: but an elaborate organ may offer very extensive indirect control by mechanical means.

III: THE FOUR SPECIES OF PERCUSSIVE RESONATORS

Membrane resonators

A stretched membrane will not of itself vibrate with sufficient regularity to yield a definite note. But if it is stretched across a more or less hemispherical shell, or if two membranes are stretched across two ends of a more or less cylindrical shell, etc., then a quite definite note may result from the resonance of the air within. And within reasonable limits, this note may be tuned by adjusting the tension of the membrane.

Our Western drum technique is of two main kinds, each using drumsticks with heads which may be uncovered wood, or covered with more or less soft material: the harder the head, the sharper the quality of tone. You can strike distinct rhythmic blows, which can be very elaborate, if you have the skill. Or you can merge the blows into a continuous roll, using the elasticity of the membrane to keep the sticks rebounding with great rapidity. In either case, you can vary the loudness by varying the strength or pressure of the blows: and to some extent the quality, by striking at different distances from the rim. Further (e.g. finger) techniques appear in the *avant-garde*.

In Eastern music, drum technique includes traditional methods, in which the separate fingers and the palm of the hand are all employed to produce tone qualities and rhythmical patterns of the most extraordinary subtlety, greatly surpassing our own use of drums until recent years.

Solid resonators

Solid objects of metal, wood or other more or less resonant materials will vibrate confusedly (as a rule) when struck or rattled. If you strike them with a hard material, their higher partials will be more prominently excited, and you will hear a more jangling or metallic quality of sound, than if you strike them with a softer material, which tends to damp their higher partials and bring their lower partials into prominence. But only where one single partial very greatly predominates, as in the wooden bars of the xylophone, or the U-shaped metal bar of the tuning fork, will you hear a more or less definite note: though this note may then be of unusual distinctness and purity.

Hollow resonators

Objects of similar materials, but more or less hollowed out, can be similarly set into vibration. But since they contain air, they form a loosely coupled system, in which the bowl is the senior partner and the air the junior partner. Their acoustical behaviour is notably complex: hence the strangely mixed, elusive sounds produced by such instruments as bells.

Keyboard resonators

Adding a keyboard to a series of resonators tuned to definite notes enables you to play chords, and makes rapid or complicated passages easier.

IV: THE FOUR SPECIES OF ELECTROPHONES

Melodic electrophones

An early method was to find the note by controlling, through some sort of variable condenser, the oscillations of a pair of thermionic valves.

A *single* valve may oscillate at too high a frequency to be heard as sound. Then a *pair* of valves can be made to give what is called a heterodyne frequency, equal to the difference between their several frequencies. This can be brought to any desired point within the audible range of vibration frequency. It can be amplified to any desired volume, and fed to a loudspeaker: either by itself, as a pure tone; or combined with other similarly oscillating currents, to form an ordinary compound musical tone, whose quality can be controlled by varying the combination.

Oscillations within the audible frequency can be generated by many other electronic methods. One which proved very useful for melodic electrophones (and others) is by means of the alternate ionizations and de-ionizations of a gas-tube relaxation oscillator using a neon-filled lamp with two capacitor plates, the output being a sawtooth wave of high harmonic content. The required pitches may be provided, or partly provided, by frequency dividers from one or more master frequencies; and it is essential, for a living quality of sound, to provide a pitch or volume fluctuation, or both, of the order of from five to eight c.p.s., i.e. a vibrato or a tremolo or both combined. Some built-in control of the envelope (attack and decay) is also a musical necessity.

Harmonic electrophones

To design a harmonic electrophone capable of playing not merely in melody but in harmony is very largely a matter of multiplying oscillators or other electronic sources of audible frequencies, together with the auxiliary circuits required. When the electrophone is strictly electronic (as opposed to photo-electric, electromagnetic or electrostatic), the commonest sources were vacuum-tube oscillators and are now transistors. These may be provided for each note separately; or twelve master oscillators may be provided, one for each semitone, with frequency dividers, or synchronized subordinate oscillators, for octave intervals at all pitches required.

There are a great many different possibilities open to designers, and there is really no end to the varieties of circuit capable of the primary task of setting up frequencies within and throughout the range of audible vibrations. Auxiliary circuits to control tone-colouring, envelope, volume and other elements of expression are of inexhaustible variety and ingenuity. Merely to provide the keys for different notes of the keyboard with appropriate switching is no simple matter; it is not enough to provide for an open and a closed position, since this gives a preternatural suddenness of attack and decay; some sort of cunningly delayed action must be incorporated. Further cleverness of design is needed to give ready control over the electronic organ's equivalent to what would be different registers on the pipe organ, including means of coupling them and pre-setting them. In these and other matters, new ideas and improved methods are being put forward all the time.

Photo-electric tone-generators provide frequencies of any desired wave-form by passing light through suitably designed interceptors, revolving at constant speeds. The light produces matching responses from photo-electric cells, on the same principle as is used by the sound track (variable area or variable density) of cinema films.

Electromagnetic tone-generators may yield sine-wave frequencies which can be combined for more complex wave-forms, as for example in the older Hammond Electric Organ to be described below, where, however, the frequencies are not strictly harmonic, being derived from generators tuned in equal temperament. This is, however, a system of exceptional constancy and reliability.

Electrostatic tone-generators resemble the photo-electric method in providing frequencies of any desired wave-form, but set up in physical matter (for example as in the Compton Electric Organ to be described below), by engravings on one of a pair of capacitor plates, the other of which scans it by revolving close to it at constant speed.

Acoustic electrophones

There is an interesting and rapidly growing category of instruments in which the main frequency and its initial harmonic content are provided by traditional acoustic methods, but the vibrations are not acoustically amplified by the traditional resonating bodies of the instruments concerned. Instead, the vibrations are picked up electro-magnetically or electrostatically, and amplified electronically with or without secondary modifications of the harmonic content, the envelope or other factors in the emerging sound.

This method can be applied to instruments having or capable of having metallic strings, such as the piano, the violin or the guitar. In such cases, the instrument may be retained in its traditional form, and remain capable of being sounded in its traditional ways; or it may be deprived of its resonating body (sound-board, or hollow body), and become incapable of being sounded in its traditional ways. On the first alternative, acoustic resonance may blend audibly with electronic emission; on the second alternative any acoustic emission from the primary source (the exciting tone) becomes negligible, and the entire audible effect depends on electronic amplification, modified or unmodified.

The method can also be applied to wind instruments using a vibrating reed as primary source (exciting tone); examples are one kind of electric organ (the earlier electric Wurlitzer organ), and the electric clarinet. The earlier Wurlitzer applies the principle electrostatically by using a vibrating reed as one plate of a capacitor, and a pick-up (or a choice of pick-ups) as the other plate. The reeds are enclosed so as not to be directly heard; their main frequency and its initial harmonic content are heard only by electronical amplification and emission.

So rapidly are the applications of this and similar principles expanding that it is unrealistic to regard such instruments merely as variants upon their traditional originals. Their effect may, at the extreme, be almost or quite unrecognizably different. Since they nevertheless retain an exciting tone which continues to operate in an acoustic and not in an electrical mode, the name for them which is suggested here is acoustic electrophones.

Synthesizing electrophones

An *electronic music synthesizer* is a very extensive and costly complex of appliances indeed. It can be given instructions, in one example (the R.C.A. synthesizer at Columbia University) by perforations punched in a continuous roll of paper (very much like a computer instructed by punched cards – and indeed, in this particular respect not unlike an old fashioned player-piano!). In response to these instructions, it can supply electrical oscillations within the audible frequencies, and of the desired wave-forms, with a vast range of auxiliary characteristics. Tone-colourings, envelopes, volumes are all selectable.

Alternatively, a composer can instruct a *computer* to work out numerical equivalents for every parameter of the sounds he desires (pitch, timbre, volume, envelope, etc.). The numbers are passed through a digital-to-analogue converter whose output is corresponding electrical impulses. So fantastically high is the speed and total of numbers required for a faithful acoustic equivalent that not even a computer can so far keep up with the required calculations at the actual speed of music, except on a relatively crude and unambitious level. Speed and efficiency are greatly increased by storing blocks of previously computed material in the computer's memory, to be drawn upon ready-made. At the time of writing (1970), performance-speed computing is rapidly advancing as a practicable proposition.

The products in both these cases, therefore, are translated into signals usually stored on magnetic tapes, single or multiple. These signals can be reproduced and further modified by any of the many available devices of electronic music, including acceleration, retardation, reverberation, modification by ring modulator, amplitude modulation, frequency modulation, direct splicing, electronic superimpositions and combinations from any tape tracks to any other tape tracks. The end-result is one tape of up to four individual tracks, each track being feedable into its own loudspeaker, perhaps one at each corner of the room or hall.

That is the performance. There has been a composer, and he has been working long and hard to conceive the sounds wanted and to ask the synthesizer for them by giving the necessary instructions. There have been electronic engineers, usually needed to help the composer. But in any traditional and human sense, there has been no performer.

The traditional performance of music has been, and remains, a creative partnership of two kinds of artist depending one upon the other: the composer and the performer. It has, of course, always been possible to combine these artists in one and the same person. This happens whenever a composer performs his own music; and, by the way, it does not necessarily follow that he is the best one to do so. A performer who is not the composer can often interpret his music not only with much greater technical competence and fluency, but with fresh insight into its potentialities which its composer himself did not have.

Another variant is where a performer starts to improvise, and becomes his own composer for the time being. All these combinations of the two main roles in music were practised in past centuries, improvisation being perhaps the most ancient of any.

Improvisation was still of radical importance in the Baroque period, where it took care of most accompaniment and much ornamental figuration; it did not die out even in the nineteenth and early twentieth centuries, when composers went furthest in notating what they wanted and expecting to get it from performers; it is back in strength by our time, particularly in jazz and in the music of the *avant-garde*.

Another and more humble precedent for dispensing with one member of the creative partnership is the old-fashioned player-piano, which itself had numerous precedents in barrel organs and musical boxes and other applications of mechanical ingenuity to musical performance. To set up the pins in a barrel or to raise the notches in a cylinder takes craft and calculation rather than musician-ship, and was not normally done by the composers whose music was thus set up for performance. Thus the principle of performance without performers is an ancient one, and need not cause us any surprise or disapproval.

But no two live performers will perform the same piece of music (whether their own or anybody else's) in quite the same way. Each will bring out rather different aspects of its potentialities: the one, perhaps, taking a rather slower tempo and bringing out the utmost of the possible tenderness and nuance; the other going for a rather faster tempo, with less time for nuance, but bringing out the utmost of the possible brilliance. Even the same performer will not perform the same music twice quite in the same way. All these personal modifications, provided that they remain within the latent potenti-alities and inherent implications of the music, and are not merely arbitrary impositions upon it, are legitimate, valuable and creative. It is the element of human individuality which is creative. The variability is part of the value.

One of the disadvantages of recorded music (among its obvious advantages) is the freezing of the performance to one interpretation, identical every time the recording is played through. A similar disadvantage attaches to music produced tapewise on an electronic synthesizer, just as it attaches to concrete music and any other form of electronic music which takes its final physical shape as a tape or other recording, playable as often as one wants, but only playable as that identical interpretation. The performer is dispensed with; the performance is built in, and it is therefore the same performance except in so far as the man running the tape recorder chooses to manipulate the controls. And that no more nearly approaches genuinely fresh performance than manipulating the 'expression levers' did on the old player-piano.

It is possible to go a further stage and dispense with the composer. This can be done by instructing a computer to pick out numerals either at complete random, or by a random probability arising from the previous numerals. Further instructions may provide a set of restrictions corresponding, for example, to the rules of traditional counterpoint, or to the rules of serial composition (twelve-note or any other – including, very readily, those wholesale inversions and retrogradations which are so crucial to the serial idioms), or whatever else the programmer's choice may be; the computer will then reject any numeral not falling within these restrictions, and come up with another try. The numerals are converted to frequencies, amplitudes, etc., by a digital-to-analogue converter which supplies electrical impulses corresponding to the coded numerals. These impulses are transferred to magnetic tape, and the performance, which has required neither composer nor performer, consists in playing the tape.

This is still, of course, the result of human ingenuity, and therefore cannot be wholly devoid of personality. That, the tape in effect tells us, is the kind of person who feels it is worth while to set this remote and largely random cycle of occurrences into operation. So what? So it takes all sorts to make a world, including those who just like playing with gadgets; but also, perhaps, those who will go the limit in evading conscious responsibility as artists.

There are plenty of ways of producing aural or visual patterns mechanically. We may find some of these patterns beautiful and even meaningful; but that is because we project associations on to them, as the patient projects images when asked to describe what he can see in a choice of ten Rorschach ink-blots. The images may tell us something about the patient's psyche, though not about the blots. We can see and we can hear images where none were planned; but that comes from our inherent and indeed archetypal capacity for coming up with images. Our images themselves, however we put them there, are always meaningful, although we may often have little or no conscious knowledge of what our own images symbolize.

The arts rest very largely on unconscious symbolism. But conscious craftsmanship and conscious expression are ingredients just as significant; and though the proportions may differ very greatly, there is probably no art where there is no fruitful interplay both of unconscious and of conscious factors. Art is communication primarily in the sense of communication between unconsciousness and consciousness; and secondarily in the sense of communication (on both unconscious and conscious levels) between personalities. That is to say, between people (and possibly in some unknown degree between animals who carry out courtship dances or communicate however unconsciously by bird-songs, and the like).

Broadly speaking, then: no persons, no art. A machine is no person, not having a psyche; and this difference is unbridgeable and ineradicable. There can be no music of machines.

PART THREE

MUSICAL INSTRUMENTS
DESCRIBED

22. J. S. Bach's C major Trio Sonata at the Carmel Festival, California, with the author playing the gamba

23. Audience Involvement: Richard Hervig's *Antiphons* in performance by the Center for New Music at the University of Iowa, with William Hibbard, conductor and musical director

24. The First and Second Violins

25. The Violas

26. The Violoncellos and the Double Basses

27. The Flutes and the Piccolo

28. The Oboes

29. The Clarinets

30. The Full Orchestra

31. The Bassoons

32. The Horns

33. The Trumpets

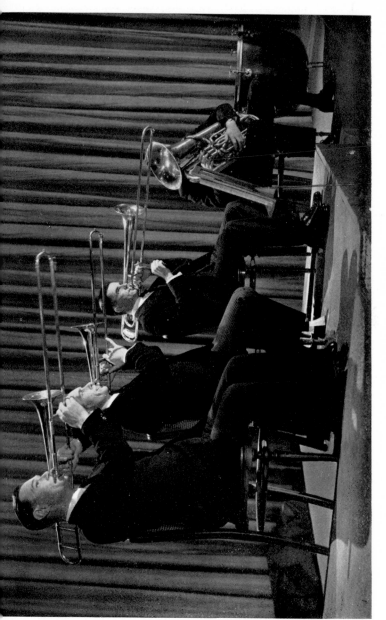

34. The Trombones and the Tuba

35. The Kettledrums

36. The Harp

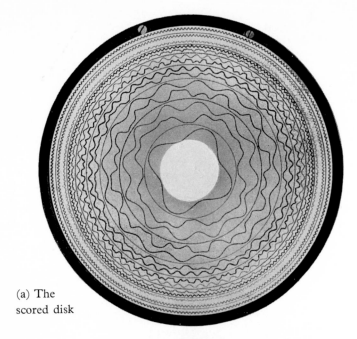

(a) The
scored disk

37. Operative principle of the Compton Organ

(b) The
scanning
disk

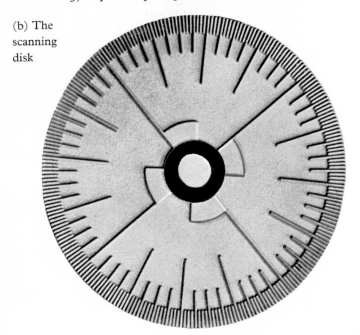

BOWED STRINGS

The Family of Violins

A good many musicians, perhaps a majority, consider the violins[1] the reigning family of the musical aristocracy. They are the foundation of the symphonic orchestra: the other constituents may vary within considerable limits, but it is rare in symphonic music to employ an orchestra in which the usual complement of violins of all sizes is not present. A wind band without violins is a noble music: but it does not hold such a ruling position in our musical traditions.

This ruling position only dates from the seventeenth century. The violin family emerged during the sixteenth century, becoming well established by about 1550; but like its near relative the rebec (see below) the violin was then regarded as chiefly suitable for dance, tavern and theatre music. About 1600, Monteverdi was making excellent use of it; and thereafter the violin family was not long in achieving its present leadership (while the humble rebec became a rural rarity and, in some localities such as the Balkans, a persistent folk-instrument).

The leadership of the violins is not the result of their tone quality alone; for while this is, properly handled, extraordinarily beautiful, it is not, in its own kind, more beautiful than are many other instruments in their different kinds.

The principle involved here is of general application and great importance. As we saw in Chapter 2, music, being an expressive and not merely a decorative art, requires sounds of many contrasting kinds: harsh as well as mellow, brilliant as well as tender, cool as well as colourful, bitter as well as sweet. Some instruments have, of course, a wider and more varied range than others: but no one instrument can excel or even compete in all directions; and there is

---

[1] Plates 13, 16–22, 24–26, 30.

1. The body (or sound-box)
2. The neck
3. The head
4. The scroll
5. The peg-box
6. The peg-box cheek
7. The tuning peg
8. The nut
9. The fingerboard
10. The bridge
11. The tailpiece
12. The saddle
13. The end-pin (or tail-pin)
14. The belly
15. The back
16. The ribs (or sides)
17. The upper bouts
18. The middle (or centre) bouts
19. The lower bouts
20. The button (or neck plate)
21. The neck bracket
22. The corners
23. The edge
24. The groove
25. The purfling
26. The neck block
27. The end-pin block
28. The corner block
29. The linings
30. The bass-bar
31. The sound-post
32. The F-hole
33. The F-hole notch
34. The waist
35. The scroll eye
36. The tailpiece loop

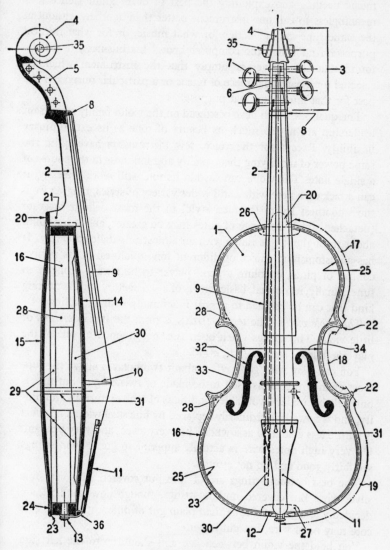

Fig. 19. The violin

music needing and exploiting the best of every kind. Hence it is meaningless to call one instrument better than another, without at the same time asking: better for what music, or for what musical purpose? And where the composer knows his business, it will be found that the answer is simply that the instrument which he selected for a particular piece of music or a particular purpose is the best for that music and that purpose.

The qualities which have bestowed on the violin family its present leadership are not so much its beauty of tone as its extraordinary flexibility. Except for the voice, few instruments have quite the same power of modifying their quality and loudness in the course of a single note. The violin can sustain its tone still more tirelessly; it can attack each note with a still wider variety of styles, ranging from the smoothest legato (bonded style) to the most delicate staccato (detached style). Its range of notes may be greater, and it can jump about throughout this range with an almost unparalleled agility. It has an astonishing choice of different tone qualities: it has perfect control of pitch, enabling a good player to be always properly in tune. Finally, its normal, basic tone is of a satisfactory and fascinating kind that can be listened to almost indefinitely without palling.

The treble violin. The term VIOLIN is from the Italian *violino*, or little viola. The strings when open (i.e. not stopped by one of the player's fingers) sound: *g*; *d'*; *a'*; *e"*.

You can play with good effect about two octaves above the topmost open string. This used to be made of twisted gut: but that is only reliable under favourable conditions of temperature and humidity, and is nowadays ordinarily replaced by fine steel wire. The effect is a little less colourful as a whole, but very sweet and very brilliant. On very high notes wire is actually superior to gut. Nylon strings are fairly good and do not stretch.

The best bottom strings are of thin gut covered with very fine silver wire. But covered middle strings, though now standard, are decidedly less good for tone than plain gut of different gauges. The core may be of wire, but gut is better.

You hold the violin between jaw and shoulder: to the left side (unless you are left-handed). You can place your chin to left or right of the tailpiece: the former position is now universal, though both have been in equal fashion. The neck rests between your left thumb and forefinger: lightly, so that your hand can slide up and down smoothly to reach the different fingering positions. The usual Baroque manner of supporting the violin did not, as is commonly stated, interfere with the player's facility in making shifts of position (up to the seventh on all strings in Geminiani). Your right hand holds the bow (more or less at the end, though the Baroque and older grips were variable).

The fittings of the violin have been considerably altered since the greatest period of violin-making, in the seventeenth to eighteenth centuries. The modern bass-bar (supporting the belly beneath the bridge at the opposite end to the sound-post) is heavier, to sustain the added tension of the slightly tighter and longer strings now used, the neck having been lengthened by about half an inch, and the standard pitch raised to about a semitone higher than what appears to have been that most prevalent among the varying pitches of the early eighteenth century. The modern bridge has also been raised and more highly arched, the angle of the neck being thrown back to correspond.

The purpose behind this train of changes was to increase the volume of the sound. This has been to some extent achieved, at a certain cost in colourfulness and transparency. The violins of the modern orchestra are more powerful as well as more numerous than those of a typical seventeenth- or eighteenth-century orchestra. This has genuine value for nineteenth- and twentieth-century music, particularly the great romantic composers such as Wagner and Mahler. For Baroque music such as Bach or Purcell it is a disadvantage, since it thickens the texture and makes the counterpoint less clear, as well as obscuring the sounds of such typical Baroque instruments as the harpsichord, the recorder, the lute or the gamba. It has become a difficult problem to balance the harpsichord in a modern orchestra, even a small string orchestra such as is now generally and rightly used for Bach and other Baroque composers. The string tone, even if not actually too loud, is apt to be too massive to let the harpsichord through with its own natural ease and brilliance. In part, however, this is a problem of playing-style, and not only of the modern fittings of the violin family.

Some violins of the classical period culminating in Stradivarius respond better than others to the increased tension and heavier bass-bar: in many cases there is no doubt that the result is magnificent, in others harmful to the verge of disaster. More discrimination is very desirable. The raising of the arch of the bridge should also be given some reconsideration. It makes it easier to apply great pressure and speed of bow with less risk of inadvertently sounding the adjacent strings; but it makes it harder to play three-part chords (and still more so four-part chords) without undue harshness and violence. Schering's theory, followed by Schweitzer, that chords in Bach's unaccompanied violin solos were played by relaxing the hair tension of the bow while playing is totally erroneous, and no longer accepted by any up-to-date authority; such chords were partly treated as close arpeggios, but also require a moderately low arching of the bridge. It is undesirable for general purposes to use too flat a bridge, which allows insufficient clearance for loud, free playing; but a somewhat less highly arched average than the present might be found advantageous, at least in Baroque music.

The viola. The Germans call the VIOLA *Bratsche*, for reasons to be seen at the end of this chapter, when the history of bowed string instruments is briefly touched on. The French call it *alto*, quite correctly; for it is the true alto violin. We sometimes call it the tenor, because normally it plays the tenor part in modern music, the alto part being played by the second violin. But this is misleading, and undesirable, since the true tenor violin is a different instrument, to be described below.

The viola is tuned a fifth below the violin: *c*; *g* (commonly wire-covered gut); *d'*; *a'* (still sometimes uncovered gut).

A body length of at least 16¼ inches is desirable; but many shorter instruments of good tone exist, as well as larger ones up to a maximum of nearly 19 inches. The size of the resonating cavity cannot be the only determinant of the harmonic response, or every instrument of the same dimensions would give the same tone, which is contrary to experience. There is some tendency to cavernous low notes and nasal high ones. But a skilful composer will often turn this anomaly to good effect, while a good player can draw from his instrument a peculiar richness of tone.

Even on a small viola, however, the highest notes cannot be reached with quite the same agility as on the violin, so that the viola's upper range is for most practical purposes a little less. But a good player can overcome this obstacle too in astonishing degree.

The tenor violin. Until perhaps the later seventeenth century, the true TENOR VIOLIN is thought to have been in use, filling that awkward gap between viola and violoncello which no ingenuity on the part of composers can quite bridge. For if you bring your violas low or your violoncellos high, they are neglecting their own proper functions, and giving, moreover, an out-of-the-ordinary quality of tone best reserved for deliberate effects. In fact, there have been several modern attempts to reinvent the tenor violin, in apparent ignorance of its once flourishing existence. Arnold Dolmetsch, however, revived it successfully. It is easily learnt by violoncellists, and its return to general use would be an interesting and perhaps valuable development. Yet it was always a rarity since Monteverdi's days, no doubt because five-part writing declined and even four parts became less usual than three. Even the viola was in some disrepute during the eighteenth century, sometimes given uninteresting parts, sometimes doubling the bass-part an octave up, sometimes left out entirely. But the viola came back into its own with the string quartets of Haydn and Mozart, especially the later ones. The tenor violin did not.

The tenor violin at first lay a fifth below the viola, but settled down one tone higher: that is, an octave below the violin, or *G*; *d* (covered); *a*; *e'* (uncovered).

The tone is satisfactory even in the extreme registers, for the instrument is played violoncello-wise, and can thus be made to the size ideal for its proper pitch. But if it is tuned to violoncello pitch for children to learn on, it naturally sounds wretchedly feeble and unhappy.

The violoncello. The Italian word VIOLONCELLO means little *violone* (as if we should say, little double bass). The violoncello has always stood a fifth below the tenor violin: that is, at first, *B*, *flat*; *F*; *c*; *g*; but later, *C*; *G* (covered); *d*; *a* (previously always uncovered).

As on the violin, you can play about two octaves above the topmost open string: but it is an exceptional accomplishment to coax a really good tone so high, and classical chamber music does not demand so extreme a compass.

Until the mid-nineteenth century the violoncello, like the tenor violin, was played resting between the knees. In the mid-eighteenth century it was still sometimes (as it had been normally) bowed like a viol. Now there is a peg to support the instrument, and the bowing is modelled on that of the violin. The bowing was changed in the mid-eighteenth century; the peg only became established in the mid-nineteenth.

As a solo instrument, the violoncello has not quite got the versatility which makes the violin so pre-eminent in this direction. The violin seems able to adapt itself to almost any mood or idiom; the violoncello is a little more apt to impose its own mood and idiom on the music. Its fundamental character is strong and noble. In music which draws suitably on this character, it is a very fine soloist indeed; elsewhere, it may not have quite enough lightness. It is magnificent in the orchestra, whether as soloist in a concerto or in its regular bass or tenor capacity. Possibly the most splendid of all its functions, however, is as the bass of the string quartet. A good 'cellist in this role makes sounds of a beauty and expressiveness which could not possibly be surpassed.

The double bass. The true double bass violin was quite common in Handel's day: there is an eight-footer in the Victoria and Albert Museum stated to have been used in contemporary performances of his music. But playing it was 'a labour fit for a horse',[1] and it was possibly kept for noisy occasions where a suspicion of coarseness might be overlooked.

True double bass violins of a more ordinary size and musical refinement undoubtedly existed, but the question remains an obscure one for lack of sufficient evidence. Both the double bass violin and the double bass viol might be known by the Italian name of *violone*: so might an ordinary bass viol or an ordinary 'cello. Whatever the historical explanation, the double bass as we know it not only today but in the numerous specimens surviving from the past is not in any strict sense a true double bass violin; it is an instrument with some features of the violin family, but others of the viol family. It is a violin in having a relatively thick and heavy construction, with a considerable weight of wood, and strings which are somewhat thick and tightly stretched; it is a violin in having no frets to give the tone a sharper edge. It is a viol in having generally a flat back and cut-away, sloping shoulders, both very great conveniences in an instrument so large to handle (a body length of 44 inches is usual, and such an instrument stands over 6 feet in height); it is a viol in being ordinarily tuned not in fifths (standard throughout the higher members of the violin family) but in fourths, again a matter of great convenience in reducing the amount of shifting needed for its long stretch (due to the great sounding length of the strings); it is still

[1] Johann Mattheson, *Das Neu-Eröffnete Orchestre* (1713), p. 286.

occasionally (and was once ordinarily) a viol in being bowed under-hand as opposed to the overhand bowing of the violoncello since the mid-eighteenth century.

But what is really important is that, on account of its relatively thick wood and tight strings, the DOUBLE BASS (*Contrabasso*; some-times misleadingly, 'bass viol' or just 'bass') sounds not like a viol but like a violin. Its more powerful tone, when really well produced, differs in colouring from that of the double bass viol, but can be made nearly as sharp and quite as pure. It is wonderfully beautiful in skilful hands.

The commonest present tuning is E_i; A; D; G. Most big orches-tras now include at least a few double basses with downward exten-sion to C_i by bringing in an extra length on the E_i string. The technique is violoncello-like, and scarcely less agile: only less so because long strings need time to change from one vibration speed to another, thus precluding the rapidest succession of different notes. The upper range is somewhat shorter. In chamber music, decidedly small 'chamber basses' are sometimes used with excellent results.

In the orchestra, the double basses often double the most impor-tant notes of the violoncellos an octave lower; but during the later nineteenth century it became increasingly usual to give them an independent line of their own. Plucked notes (*pizzicato*) are par-ticularly effective, and may be used to pick out the bass line of the harmony with admirable clarity.

The double bass has always rested on a peg, like the modern violoncello; the player stands or rests against a stool. Bowing, originally viol-wise, is now almost universally violoncello-wise.

Outlying members of the violin family. The violino piccolo (little violin) was usually tuned a fourth or a minor third above the violin: it was used by J. S. Bach, but was becoming obsolete in Mozart's day. The tone is sweet and pure at its proper pitch, but wretched if tuned to violin pitch for children to learn on.

The *kit* or *pochette* was still tinier, being carried by dancing-masters in their pockets. It stands about an octave above the violin, with a small but clear tone; and it is either a diminutive violin or a diminutive rebec (see below).

The *viola d'amore*[1] is played violin-wise, but is variably tuned with

[1] Plate 20.

six to seven strings of gut, covered or uncovered. *Beneath* the finger-board lie (but not invariably) wire strings which sound by sympathetic vibration, giving the tone a peculiarly sweet and silvery quality, rather apt to cloy in time. Bach used the viola d'amore on occasion; but it has comparatively little special literature. (But the same name was also applied to an ordinary violin tuned with wire strings. Both forms date from the last third of the seventeenth century.) The *baryton* was a similar, bass instrument, but short-lived.

The *quinton* has existed as a five-stringed violin: *g*; *d′*; *a′*; *d″*; *g″*, and the name should not be used for the late five-stringed treble viols. There is some slight evidence for a contralto or true *second violin*, a little larger than the normal violin, and tuned a tone lower: another instrument to have been abortively reinvented in modern times; but not nearly so standard (once) as the tenor violin.

The *viola pomposa* was almost certainly a five-stringed alto violin: probably *c*; *g*; *d′*; *g′*; *c″*. The *viola da spalla* (of the shoulder) is a small violoncello of standard tuning, carried in processions on a shoulder strap. The *viola di fagotto* (of the bassoon) is a variant with wire-covered strings and an allegedly bassoon-like tone. The *violoncello piccolo* (little violoncello) is a slightly small, five-stringed violoncello: *C*; *g*; *d*; *a*; *e′*. (This is probably the same as the *violoncello alto* of Boccherini; and pretty certainly J. S. Bach's violoncello 'a cing acordes' in his sixth Suite for Violoncello.)

Violin bowing. All sizes of violin have similar bows of different weight. You hold the bow from above: and you play accented notes so far as possible at the end nearest your hand, where maximum weight and maximum muscle power combine; unaccented notes at the other end. This is a technique well suited to the music of the violins, in which more or less regular accents have often prevailed.

The modern violin bow-stick (perfected by Tourte towards the end of the eighteenth century) is incurved, lying nearest to the hair in the middle. The curve is logarithmic, of which the effect is that the tension does not either increase or decrease however hard you press. This favours a smooth, sustained, massive style, suited to the general character of nineteenth- and twentieth-century music.

The stick of the earlier type of bow, besides being commonly an inch or two shorter and upwards of an ounce lighter, is out-curved, standing furthest from the hair in the middle. Hence the more you press, the tighter the tension grows. This favours a sharp, articulated and pure style, suited to the general character of sixteenth-, seventeenth- or early eighteenth-century music. Its firmness helps with chords. For dance and orchestral use, many early bows were short. For solos and chamber music, they tended to be long, and were sometimes extremely long.

The Family of Viols

Historians used to believe that the viols[1] were the primitive ancestors of the violins. This was an unwarranted aspersion: they are cousins, and flourished side by side for some two centuries after the rise of the younger, violin branch. The last celebrated bass-violist prior to modern times, Karl Friedrich Abel, died, aged 62, in 1787.

The viols have a good deal in common with the violins. Like all satisfactory bowed instruments, they have a superb command of nuance: they are extremely expressive in capable hands. Their tone is also beautiful, but of a different quality; the technique required (e.g. for some bass viol solos) may be of high virtuosity.

It is just as difficult to draw the finest tone from a good viol as it is from a good violin: no instrument should ever be judged except when played by a player of the first rank. But when the true tone of a good viol is heard, it proves, first, quieter than the violin tone; and second, edgier.

These qualities are well suited to the most typical music written for the viols. This is usually of a contrapuntal character: in other words, several strands of melody are heard at once. And to hear them clearly, you need a tone which does not either over-assert itself, or blend too smoothly with its neighbours. The sound of a full 'consort of viols' is rich and homogeneous; but it is not so homogeneous that the separate threads fail to stand out distinctly. You can always follow them with ease, even when the part-writing is very complex. That is what I mean by calling viol tone more edgy: it has edge enough to stand out individually. For its own contrapuntal music, this is an essential virtue.

The viol and the violin use exactly the same principle of a stretched string gaining vibrations from the friction of the bow, and passing these vibrations through the bridge to the belly, the back, the air

[1] Plates 15, 18.

1. A viol
2. The belly of the viol
3. The back
4. The neck
5. The fingerboard
6. The nut of the fingerboard
7. The frets
8. The pegs
9. The bridge
10. The tailpiece
11. The sound-post
12. The bow
13. The hairs of the bow
14. The nut of the bow
15. The peg-box
16. The figure-head
17. The hook-bar
18. The ribs
19. The upper bouts
20. The middle bouts
21. The lower bouts
22. The bass-bar
23. The upper cross-bar
24. The lower cross-bar
25. The cross-strip
26. The corner fillet
27. The upper block
28. The lower block
29. The linings
30. The linen reinforcement strip
31. The sound-hole
32. The neck bracket
33. The length of body
34. The purfling
35. The shoulders

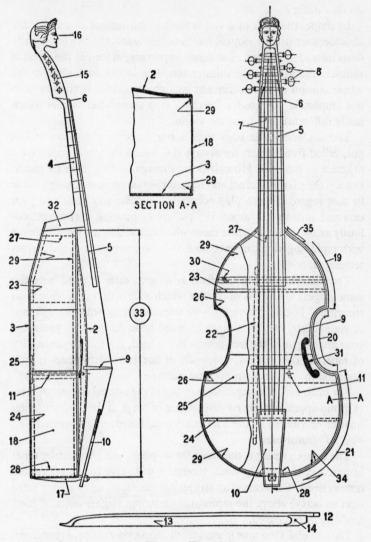

SECTION A-A

Fig. 20. The viol

within, and from the body outwards to the open air. In what, then, do they differ?

In shape, the back of a viol is usually flat instead of arched; the shoulders are usually sloping instead of rounded; the ribs are usually deep instead of shallow. Far more important, in weight the wood is thinner; the strings are thinner too, but longer and slacker; the whole tension of the instrument is slighter, so that it vibrates with less amplitude but greater freedom. It is these latter factors which really differentiate it from the violin.

The tendency to an edgy tone is reinforced by the pieces of fine gut, called frets, which are always tied round the viol's fingerboard at semitone intervals. Historians have imagined that these are meant to keep the player in tune; and indeed they do serve as a rough guide in that regard. But to play accurately in tune you must use your ears and adjust your fingers (by pulling or pushing) just as meticulously as the violinist: while those who assume that the frets interfere with rapid fingering can have no first-hand knowledge of the correct technique.

The real function of the frets is to give each stopped note the same ringing sharpness of quality which only open notes possess on the violin. For on the violin, you stop the string with the soft end of your finger, and get a more rounded tone: on the viol, you press your finger against the fret, which, being hard, gives a sharper quality of tone. In this respect, too, each of the two instruments is well designed to fulfil its own peculiar purpose.

The treble viol. The topmost member of the normal consort of viols (a group approximately corresponding in range to the modern string quartet of violins) is the TREBLE VIOL, tuned: *d*; *g* (covered); *c'*; *e'*; *a'*; *d''* (uncovered).

The bottom string is too short for its pitch, and has a tubby tone: in practice, it is hardly used, though it will serve for an occasional note at need. The remaining strings are excellent, up to rather more than an octave above the topmost open string. Higher notes of good quality can be coaxed.

The alto viol. One tone lower stands the ALTO VIOL: *c*; *f* (covered); *a* (or *b*); *d'*; *g'*; *c''* (uncovered).

The alto viol is not always present in the consort, its place being more often supplied by a second tenor viol. The reason is partly that the strings of each member of the viol family are more numerous

than are those of the violin family: partly that treble viol parts lie on
the average lower than first violin parts, and therefore less distant
from the lower members of the family. Even so, where the music is
written in four or more very evenly spaced parts, the alto viol has
its own proper place. The tone is slightly sombre but good throughout, though still a little weak on the lowest string.

The tenor viol. A fourth below the alto stands the TENOR VIOL:
G; c (covered); f; a; d'; g' (uncovered). Tone excellent throughout,
the bottom string being scarcely weak at all.

The bass viol. A fourth below the tenor stands the BASS VIOL
(commonly called the *viola da gamba*, or gamba for short; though
strictly that name, which means 'viol of the leg', applies to all viols
alike): (A,); D; G (covered); c (often covered); e; a; d' (uncovered).

The low seventh string, when present, is not always satisfactory
except for its lowest, open note. But the six-stringed instrument is
superb throughout (its bottom D was tuned down to violoncello C
at need).

A good bass viol can be played quite easily, and with a unique
beauty of tone, one and a half (with adequate skill two) octaves
above its topmost open string: that is to say, in a register where the
violoncello needs a deal of coaxing to draw a not wholly reposeful
quality of tone. That is simply due to the lighter, less tense construction of the viol.

For this reason, though the violoncello is a most noble instrument, the leading solo member of that family is the treble violin.
With the viols, matters are the other way about: the leading solo
instrument of the viol family is the bass viol, whose magnificent
resources have been exploited (though not very extensively) by
composers down to and including J. S. Bach.

It is unfortunate, from our modern point of view, that in the
greatest age of the gamba its leading exponents were performer-
composers most of whose inspiration was spent in improvising
virtuoso music never set down on paper. From the mid-sixteenth
to the mid-seventeenth century we know of a number of such
improvising masters of the gamba, among whom the Englishman
Christopher Simpson was pre-eminent. He left enough written-out
examples in his text-book, *The Division Violist* (1659), to reveal his
poetry as well as his brilliance, but there is no wide repertoire of this
kind surviving. In the early eighteenth century, the French school

of Marais and Forqueray contributed works of typically French elegance and tenderness, and there are a number of German works for gamba in addition to the three justly famous sonatas (and several obligatos) by J. S. Bach. But to a certain extent the solo gamba is an instrument more limited in its literature than in its capabilities.

The gamba may eventually attract the interest of modern composers, since its qualities are quite outstanding. It has a certain snarling clarity in the bass register, a certain nutty warmth in the middle register, a certain ringing edginess in the upper register, all very different from 'cello sonorities, and all uncommonly attractive in their own right. Its only marked disadvantage is that it cannot be made to sound so loud, at least in the massive fashion of which the 'cello is capable. It is surprising, however, how assertive a sound the gamba can be persuaded to produce if the handling of it is sufficiently strong and skilful. In really expert hands its tone can be not only expressive and beautiful beyond the ordinary, but much louder than is commonly supposed.

Besides its solo capabilities, the gamba makes an excellent string bass for continuo accompaniment, with a characteristic colouring and transparency of its own which in many circumstances gives a better effect for accompanying voices or chamber instruments even than the 'cello; especially as the gamba adds up better with the harpsichord in chamber music than the 'cello does. In any capacity, the gamba should be played with its frets and its underhand bowing as the true bass viol it is, not fretless and overhand as an inferior kind of bastard 'cello.

The violone. An octave below the bass viol stands the double bass viol, normally referred to by its Italian name of VIOLONE: $D\prime$; G' (covered); C; E; A; d (uncovered).

The violone has a tone of quite remarkable silkiness, purity and ease of speech throughout its compass, softer, but perhaps more free, than our present double bass. A good violone doubling a bass viol or a violoncello at the octave below is a wonderful musical effect.

Outlying members of the viol family. We need only mention here the *pardessus*, a fourth above the treble viol, with a sweet, glittering tone of its own. The *division viol* is a small solo gamba; the *lyra viol* a yet smaller version, variably tuned to suit certain full chords.

Viol bowing. All sizes of viol have similar bows of different weights. Like the earlier violin bow, but unlike its modern successor, the viol bow curves outwards from the hair, and grows tauter the more you press on it.

You hold the viol bow from below: and you preferably play accented notes at the end furthest from your hand. But in this method of bowing, there is very little to choose between one end and the other. If anything, you can thrust more vigorously at the point (far end); if anything, the weight of your hand and arm tells more at the heel (near end); hence there is no strong predisposition to regular accents at either end, as there is at the heel in violin bowing.

And this is a technique as well suited to the most typical viol music as violin technique is to violin music. For the former, being ordinarily very contrapuntal and very free in rhythm, calls for many subtle accents irregularly distributed; while the latter, being less often very contrapuntal or very free in rhythm, calls more commonly for sharp accents regularly recurring. As usual, technique is the faithful servant of expression.

The Family of Lyras[1]

This is distinct both from the classical lyre (a plucked instrument), and from the lyra viol mentioned above.

The late medieval *lyra da braccio* (lyre of the arm) is played violin-wise with a nearly flat bridge and a long soft bow: its five strings sound more or less at once, the top having the melody and the remainder a drone harmony in fifths and octaves much like the drones of a bagpipe.

During the Renaissance, the bridge grew more arched, the strings became seven (tuned unevenly), and genuine chords were employed, as well as drone harmony. The two lowest strings were to the side of the fingerboard, and not meant to be stopped. The five strings over the fingerboard and meant to be stopped might be tuned: g; g'; d'; a'; d''. The tone is smooth but ringing.

The *lyra da gamba* (of the leg), a tenor lyra with up to sixteen strings, had a great vogue, especially for accompaniment, and mainly in Italy, during the later sixteenth century and the seventeenth century. It too is played with long sweeping strokes.

The bowed Welsh *Crwth* may have some connection with the Lyra family, with which it has both drones and flat bridge in common.

[1] Plates 1, 3, 11.

H

The Family of Rebecs[1]

This can be traced under a diversity of names and in various sizes through the Middle Ages. By the Renaissance it had declined socially, to become mainly a dance and tavern instrument. It was then a complete family with several members, of which, however, only the smallest was at all prominent.

Shaped often like a narrow pear sliced down the stalk, the rebec has usually three strings, but is otherwise tuned and played violin-wise. There is normally no sound-post. The tone is a surprise: loud and pungent, with a wonderfully fiery colouring. A violinist can learn its technique with no great difficulty.

An outline genealogy for bowed strings

The early history of most instruments is obscure and controversial. But picture a wealth of medieval stringed instruments, with fluctu-ating forms, shifting names, and almost interchangeably bowed or plucked. Many may be of Eastern origin; and Eastern influence, especially through Moorish Spain, may have continued. But pres-ently three great bowed families emerge with tolerable distinctness.

One is the lyras, not unlike violins in shape and handling, and possessed of an important feature common to both viols and violins: the sound-post supporting the bridge and joining belly to back.

Another is the viols, always fretted, always held upright, and never under the chin violin-wise. Their shape and name vary; but instru-ments having these visible characteristics in pictures and sculptures can be traced far back into the Middle Ages.

A third is the rebecs, not bellied like viols and violins, but flat-tabled like lutes; properly lacking, also like lutes, the sound-post; but held, played and even tuned much like violins, and, likewise, unfretted.

Lack of sound-post and lack of belly-arch are related factors. For where the sound-post supports the belly a node must be caused: the belly is held stationary. The remainder of the belly is arched to leave it free to vibrate on another plane: 'sound-holes' so called being cut lengthwise to help it to do so. This combination of rigid sound-post and arched belly has proved the best for tone produced continu-ously with a bow. Lyra, viol and violin share it in common.

[1] Plates 2, 7.

Contrast with this the flat-tabled, sound-postless rebec. Here, there being nothing to impose a node, the table can vibrate freely as a whole, with a maximum towards the centre. It is the back which arches, so steeply (in the standard pattern) as to join the table with no side-ribs in between at all. Such a vaulted back contributes much more substantially to the tone than the flat or slightly arched back of viols, lyras and violins. And it is this combination of flat, free table with steeply arched, vaulted back that proves best for tone produced intermittently by plucking. The lute is its acme, as we shall see.

The fourth great family, that of the violins, did not emerge until the sixteenth century, when it seems to have borrowed its shape, its sound-post and its mode of handling chiefly from the lyra; its tuning and perhaps its bowing chiefly from the rebec; and nothing essential at all from its nearest collateral, the viol. Yet these cousins, viol and violin, though they are distinct, and the one is in no sense the ancestor of the other, are near blood-relatives. Their very names bear witness to that.

The member of the violin family which got the standard name was the alto member, called then, as now, viola; which is simply Italian for viol. To distinguish the two families, the violins were loosely referred to as *viole da braccio*, or viols of the arm, despite the fact that the larger members, when they appeared, were played downwards, being too big to hold violin-wise. To this day, as we noted, a German name for viola is *Bratsche*. And the viols, being all played downwards, were quite accurately referred to as *viole da gamba*, or viols of the leg.

The viols are now again in use for the sake of their own excellent body of solo and chamber music, especially in early seventeenth-century England, and late seventeenth- and early eighteenth-century France and Germany. Their virtues being distinct from those of the violins, both families are needed, as complementary rather than competing instruments.

CHAPTER 6

PLUCKED STRINGS

The Family of Lutes

The LUTE[1] is the best of all the sliced-pear instruments, whose acoustic properties we considered when dealing with the rebec. But the lute has a much wider flat table, and a correspondingly larger vaulted back, made of jointed strips or ribs, and of remarkable resonance. The pear, so to speak, is a much bigger and finer pear. There may be an ornamental 'rose' cut in the centre of the table. The ribs are astonishingly thin, and the table, of pine like most such sounding-board resonators, is not much thicker. The resonance is so free that you can feel the instrument picking up vibrations even from a speaking voice near by; for the same reason (lightness of construction) the maximum amplitude is not great. There are plenty of ringing upper harmonics to give a fascinating tone-colouring, but not much massive energy in the lower harmonics to give volume.

As a consequence, lute tone is not very loud, but (when well produced) peculiarly colourful and expressive. When badly played, however, the instrument sounds dry and prickly. It is a difficult instrument; chiefly because the technique has to be so very accurate for good tone-production; but there is also a certain problem in keeping a lute really well in tune. All stringed instruments are in some degree troublesome to keep in tune: but thick, tense strings stand best. Thus the piano gives little trouble; the violin, not much trouble; the viol, a little more; the lute, with its many thin strings, more still. But a good lutenist will contrive to keep his intonation very good indeed.

Like the viol, the lute has frets of fine gut tied round the fingerboard at semitone intervals. These help in catching full chords rapidly and surely: but as on the viol, their real function is to give a sharp and ringing quality on stopped notes. You cannot wholly trust

[1] Plates 2, 6, 9, 10, 16–20.

90

to the frets to keep you properly in tune. For unless you use your fingers nearly as accurately as a violinist does, you may be but indifferently well in tune; and your tone, too, will sound lifeless, lacking its proper ring and beauty.

While the fingers of your left hand are busy finding their exact position, precisely on the hinder side of the appropriate frets, your right hand is plucking the strings, not clumsily with the ball of the finger, but delicately with the extreme tip of each finger (except the little finger, which rests on the table, to support and steady the hand), and the extreme edge of the thumb. Occasionally, for certain full chords, you sweep fingers and thumb across the strings in opposite directions simultaneously.

The strings of the classical lute (except for the topmost string) are not single, but tuned in unison pairs or sometimes (lowest three) octave pairs (*courses*). You must pluck each string of the pair (both with one fingertip) very evenly and truly to produce a proper tone: and you may be plucking as many as four pairs at once (including the thumb). There were generally six courses on a sixteenth-century lute, lying over the broad fingerboard, and stopped with the left hand as required. But from the latter part of the sixteenth century there may be further courses, often lying outside the fingerboard, and played open: that is to stay, unstopped. These, the diapasons, add a wonderfully deep and resonant bass to the instrument; besides which, they vibrate sympathetically even when not played.

There are many sizes and varieties of lute, from the smallest *treble lute* with no diapason strings, to the *theorbo* with its separate peg-box mounting diapasons of greater length than the higher, stoppable strings: a length appropriate to their lower pitch, so as to give them the best possible tone. A still larger lute, with the second peg-box up to twice as far from the lower end-piece as the first peg-box, giving basses of quite exceptional depth and resonance, might be known as *chitarrone*. *Arch-lute* describes any large lute.

The tunings of the lute are too diverse to be listed here. A standard sixteenth-century tuning would be G, c, f, a, d', g'. The left-hand technique of the lute and of the viol is very similar.

There is no bridge on the lute, to raise the strings near their lower end, as there is on bowed instruments, where you could not bow the strings separately at all if they were not raised to different levels by the arch of the bridge. As in most plucked instruments of the lute and guitar families, the strings are simply fixed, at their bottom end, to an end-piece glued to the table.

There is another common difference between bowed and plucked instruments. Violins, viols and the like, whatever the rest of their outline, must needs be given waisted sides, so as to leave space for the bow to tilt sufficiently to reach the top and bottom string without first coming into collision with the sides of the instrument. Of bowed instruments, only the rebec does not need these incurved waists, because it is so narrow anyhow. But plucked instruments have no need of waisted sides, though they may have them. This fact makes possible the noble simplicity of the lute's outline.

The MANDORA family is another branch of the lute family: its best-known relative is its treble, the *mandoline*. But of that the strings are normally plucked with a hard plectrum instead of with the finger-tips, and as the strings themselves are mainly wire, instead of gut or wire-covered gut, the tone is less colourful and the technique less subtle and expressive. Both in form and technique this is nearer to the medieval lute (often plucked with a plectrum and somewhat small in the body) than it is to the highly developed lute of the sixteenth and seventeenth centuries.

The Spanish VIHUELA is a versatile instrument, with a shape closely resembling a guitar. Plucked with the fingers (*vihuela de mano*), it is musically a lute; plucked with a plectrum (*vihuela de pendola*), it is not far off a mandoline. There is also a bowed vihuela, which is structurally the same but technically a different instrument: in short, a viol.

The Family of Guitars[1]

The GUITAR has slightly waisted sides, though, being plucked, it does not need them. But stringed instruments in the Middle Ages had a way of fluctuating between the two modes of tone-production: as the vihuela (a very close relative of the guitar) always did. The waisted shape is as old as Babylon and had originally to do with the feminine symbolism of string instruments.

The guitar back is commonly flat, like a viol. There are gut frets (in modern times, fixed metal frets, which are perhaps less good, since they cannot be adjusted at will to temper the intonation of a

[1] Plates 17–19, 21.

slightly false string – and most strings go a little false before their life is up). The table is always flat; it may have an ornamental 'rose'.

The Renaissance guitar is double-strung, with five courses. It is easier than the lute, and though less beautiful and expressive, not excessively so. Lute music sounds very well on it.

Early in the eighteenth century, the *double-strung guitar* gave way to the *single-strung guitar*, with six single strings, and a tone which, though good of its kind, is no longer comparable to that of the lute. This is the modern instrument, which in Spain exists as a complete family of four sizes: *guitarillo* (with five strings); *requinte*; *tenore*; and *guitarra* (bass guitar: the one normally most familiar). Segovia has gained as well-earned a glory for the guitar today as Dowland once did for the lute.

The guitar has two basic techniques: plucking proper, as in the lute: or thrumming. Glissandos are delicate unless, as is now very common, the guitar is greatly amplified electronically. This makes really a different instrument of it, but a very effective one.

The *ukelele* is a diminutive four-stringed guitar of little resonance. The *Hawaiian guitar* has metal strings and great resonance. It is played unfretted, flat on the knee, with finger-pieces called 'thimbles'.

The Family of Citterns

The CITTERN[1] or CITHREN has rounded sides, like the lute (though more nearly circular); but a flat back, like the guitar. It is not to be confused with the gittern,[2] which is a late-medieval relative of the guitar. (The so-called English guitar is, however, a form of cittern.)

The cittern exists in many sizes, possessing from four to twelve pairs of strings. That is to say, it is double-strung, like the lute and the early guitar. But its strings are properly of wire, like those of the mandoline. It is played either with the fingers or sometimes with a plectrum; but in neither case is it particularly expressive, unless unusually well played. It was an extraordinarily popular lowbrow instrument in Elizabethan days.

The *pandora* or *bandora* is best classed as a branch of the cittern family, large enough to act as a cheaper substitute for the theorbo in accompaniment. It is not to be confused with the mandora, which,

---

[1] Plate 18.   [2] Plate 5.

as we saw, is the name of that branch of the lute family whose smallest and most familiar member is the mandoline.

The *orpharion* and (distantly) the *poliphant* are further cittern variants, of which the first-named is interesting for one characteristic feature: the end-piece to which the strings are fastened at their lower end is glued slantwise, so as to give a greater sounding-length to the lower than to the higher strings; the fixed inlaid frets are proportionately slanted to correspond. It was a cheap substitute for the lute, and similarly tuned.

The *banjo* may conceivably derive its name from the bandora. Instead of a hollow wooden body, it has a shallow metal hoop with a membrane stretched across the top. It has, in one form, four pairs of metal strings, played with a plectrum, when it has a hard but brilliant note (the mandoline-banjo). Normally it has five to nine single gut strings, played with the fingers.

The Family of Harps

Unlike the instruments so far described, the HARP[1] has no fingerboard. You do not ordinarily stop the strings to get different notes: you pluck another string. There are more or less numerous strings of different lengths, mounted on an approximately triangular frame, one side of which is a hollow wooden box, acting as a resonator after the same fashion as a violin body.

The *Irish harp* or *clarseach* has up to forty-five wire strings, and a brilliantly ringing tone; the so-called *Celtic harp* has up to fifty gut strings, and a softer but more expressive tone. Each is tuned diatonically: that is, in a selected mode and key, without extraneous (chromatic) semitones.

The *chromatic harp* has strings for each semitone. An early form was Monteverdi's *double harp* with two rows of strings, one for diatonic notes, another set parallel for chromatic notes; it was thought to be a late sixteenth-century Irish development, but this is uncertain. The *hooked harp* is diatonically tuned, but has a set of pivoted hooks, each of which, when turned sideways, can be made to press on one string, and thereby to raise its pitch by a semitone. The *single-action pedal harp* has foot-pedals for operating these hooks with the foot, in the actual course of a piece; and finally, the modern *double-*

[1] Plates 7, 9, 11, 30, 36.

action pedal harp, perfected early in the nineteenth century by Erard, has pedals for raising the lowest pitch of any or all strings by either one semitone or two. This is the normal orchestral instrument of today, fully adapted to the needs of our freely modulating music, and of a clear and telling though not especially brilliant or expressive tone. It is, however, extraordinarily beautiful in the orchestra when well composed for, and has the useful virtue of being decidedly loud.

The *Aeolian harp* is not actually a plucked instrument at all. Its strings of fixed pitches are exposed to a current of air, which sets them in motion as the wind sets telegraph wires in motion (by air eddies on alternate sides). As the strength of the breeze varies, different members of the harmonic series of each string are heard, the result being that unearthly harmony descibed by Thomas Hardy in *The Trumpet-Major*. It was, I suppose, an aeolian harp which gave rise to that most fascinating of all musical fairy legends: the harp that plays itself.

The PSALTERY[1] and the DULCIMER are close relations of the harp. Structurally, they both consist of strings of varying length, stretched on a triangular or rectangular frame, over a sound-board. You pluck the psaltery with your fingers or a plectrum: the tone is extremely bright and resonant, indeed a confusing jangle unless you deftly damp the strings by hand between the notes. The present representative of the psaltery is the *zither*, with five metal melody strings over a metal-fretted finger-board, and a number of open (unstopped) accompanying strings of gut (covered or uncovered), whose softer tone sets off the metallic brilliance of the melody.

You play the dulcimer with a pair of hammers or drumsticks held one in each hand. The modern form heard in Eastern Europe includes chromatic semitones. The tone is colourful; rapid tremolo effects are telling and exciting; but confusion likewise results unless the strings are deftly damped by hand. The current name is *cembalon* in a great variety of spellings. The virtuosity with which this simple instrument is played in many folk-orchestras is unforgettable once heard.

[1] Plates 9, 10, 21.

CHAPTER 7

KEYBOARD STRINGS

The Clavichord Family

Beethoven said: 'Among all keyed instruments the clavichord was that on which one could best control tone and expressive interpretation.'[1] In his day the CLAVICHORD was going out. But it was a favourite instrument of J. S. Bach, and is particularly well-suited to many of his immortal Forty-eight Preludes and Fugues.

The clavichord did not come into prominence before the sixteenth century, though the principle is much older, and the instrument itself may date before the fourteenth century. This principle is what is called tangent action.

The tangent is a brass wedge set upright at the far end of a pivoted wooden lever. When you depress the near end (the visible key), the tangent is raised smartly into contact with the string (or often course of strings: for a unison pair is usual, the material being covered or uncovered brass).

The string is divided into unequal lengths, of which the shorter is kept voiceless by interwoven strips of felt. The longer, however, is caused by the impact to vibrate, giving a note predetermined by the weight, length and tension of the string in question.

But not wholly predetermined. For though the tension has been set within very fine limits by adjusting the tuning-pins in the ordinary way, within still finer limits the player can control the tension directly, by pressing more or less firmly on the key.

This gives him something of a violinist's direct finger control over that expressive, faintly but regularly fluctuating variation of intonation which is called vibrato. But when he releases the key the sound is instantaneously damped.

Now in apparent theory, since every increase in pressure must needs raise the pitch, it ought to be impossible to vary the expression

[1] Cited in Grove's *Dictionary of Music and Musicians* (1927 ed.), i, 662.

without playing out of tune. This has misled some historians (perhaps prejudiced already by hearing a bad clavichordist) into deducing that the clavichord is inherently defective. But it is the theory which is defective, not the instrument.

By striking more sharply, you can heighten the *velocity* of the tangent, thus increasing the loudness, without appreciably altering the pitch. If, however, you are clumsy, you may then exaggerate the *pressure*, thus playing out of tune. This is especially liable to happen to pianists casually essaying the clavichord. For the touch of these instruments is radically different: and it is impossible for the pianist

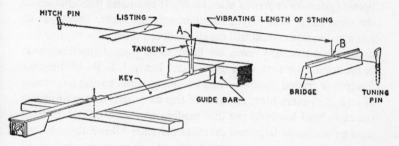

Fig. 21. Clavichord action

to unlearn in a moment the almost unconscious muscular habits acquired by years of drawing the best results from his own instrument. Even if he does not play the clavichord out of tune, he cannot hope to make it speak in its finest tones without proper study.

When well played, the clavichord, though less brilliant than the harpsichord and less massive than the piano, is, as Beethoven noted, more subtly expressive than either. Its loudest tones are very soft, but its softest tones are unbelievably softer still: and your control over this whole dynamic range is, from the nature of the action, more intimate than any other keyboard instrument affords. And, indeed, a (relatively) loud chord on the clavichord sounds more explosive than the (absolutely) loudest chord of the mighty piano itself, so that those sudden outbursts, for example, which punctuate the closing passages of J. S. Bach's Chromatic Fantasia acquire, by sheer contrast, a tragic power and horror on the tiny clavichord which no concert grand piano can approach.

Again in fugal music, to make a fugal entry stand out clearly on the piano, you have to play it decidedly more loudly than the accompanying parts. But on the clavichord the tone is of such clarity that the counterpoint is more easily made distinct, while the fugal entries can be given a more expressive nuance by direct finger control, as on no other keyboard instrument. And finally, the sensuous beauty of good clavichord tone is itself very moving. But because of its overall softness, the clavichord is essentially unsuitable for public performances; nor is it satisfactory when electronically amplified. It can be recorded well – if played with the volume low.

Clavichords prior to the early eighteenth century were made with more than one tangent striking each course of strings at different points (*gebunden* or *fretted clavichords*). If two notes thus effected on the same string were played together, only the higher would sound; but a good player could trill rapidly between them. The fretting was so arranged that only notes not likely to be wanted simultaneously in the commoner keys were 'gebunden'. But in J. S. Bach's time the *bundfrei* or *fretless clavichord* had become general, having one course of strings to every note; and it is in this more satisfactory form that the clavichord has been put into modern production. C. P. E. Bach used an unusually large and excellent clavichord (his Silberman was famous) the tone being notably louder. Such an instrument might be especially valuable today.

The Harpsichord Family

At about the same time at which the clavichord emerged, another family of keyboard stringed instruments made its appearance upon the early Renaissance scene. This is the family of which the general name, and also the particular name of its most elaborate member, is HARPSICHORD.[1]

In principle, a harpsichord is a psaltery to which a mechanical action and a keyboard have been attached. In its simplest form, this instrument has one keyboard working a single set of wire strings (covered and uncovered) stretched (but unlike the clavichord, fully stretched) above a sound-board; the pitch of each string being determined by its weight, length and tension, and finely adjusted by tightening it or slackening it where it passes round its tuning-pin.

The string is plucked by a plectrum, made of quill or leather, and carried sideways on an upright jack. The jack is raised by the further

[1] Plates 15, 20, 22.

end of a pivoted lever, when you depress the nearer end, which is the visible key. When you release the key, the jack falls back, bringing a small piece of felt into contact with the string, and thereby instantly damping its vibrations. The plectrum does not pluck the string a second time, when the jack falls back; but is hinged so as to slide past the string as noiselessly as possible, and the slight jangle thus caused is damped at once.

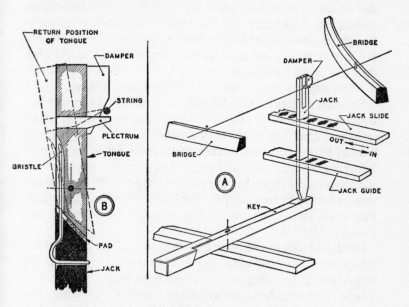

Fig. 22. Harpsichord action

This simple harpsichord with a single set of strings, operated from a single keyboard, was the first to evolve; in England it is known alternatively as the *virginals* or the *spinet*.[1] The *harpsichord* proper is simply a more elaborate version of the same instrument. It has two, three or four complete sets of strings, operated by separate sets of jacks. If two sets of strings, they are likely to be tuned in unison, and a hand stop, knee stop, or pedal may be added for throwing one set out of operation at will. The unisons, when sounded together, have a peculiarly ringing quality of great beauty. Until about 1650 the word virginals was used of this full-sized harpsichord, as well

[1] Plate 16.

as of the smaller version nowadays more usually intended by virginals.

Where there are further sets of strings, one is usually tuned an octave higher (the 4-foot register), and when brought in, adds further brilliance; another, very rare prior to modern times, is tuned an octave below (the 16-foot register), and adds solidity and depth. Their separate pitch is not consciously detected, but merges with that of the unisons (the 8-foot register). But if the unisons are thrown out of operation, and the 4-foot or the 16-foot register is brought in alone, either will be heard at its proper pitch, yielding two further qualities of tone. Another, very eerie tone results when the 4-foot and the 16-foot are combined, without the 8-foot unisons. A 2-foot stop two octaves above the 8-foot is not unknown.

Yet other devices are found in some harpsichords. There may be a separate set of jacks so placed as to pluck one set of strings nearer to its end (lute stop): this gives a rather hard but powerful and brilliant tone. There may be stops which bring felt or leather pads lightly into contact with the strings, thus partially damping them, and resulting in a somewhat muffled tone (harp or buff stops). Where some sets of jacks are equipped with leather plectrums, and others with quills, their warmer and colder tones can be effectively contrasted or blended.

Louds and softs can be contrived in two ways, singly or combined. Added stops (or simply added notes) can be brought in until the full harpsichord is sounding; or withdrawn until only a single set of strings is sounding. And if (as is found on a number of modern instruments) the jacks are set on controllable slides, they can be brought a little closer to their strings, or a little further from them: in the first case, the plectrum plucks more sharply, and gives a louder tone; in the second less sharply, and gives a softer tone. This change can be gradual or sudden: but it is a modern device. In the later eighteenth century there was occasionally a third method, by opening or closing wooden shutters placed over the strings; but this is not at all satisfactory, since, when shut, they muffle not only the loudness, but also the characteristic brilliance of the tone.

It will be seen that the harpsichord, like the organ, employs a good deal of machinery for its effects. The player, by his touch, cannot very substantially alter the volume of the resulting tone. But he can alter it quite sufficiently to make a slight accent, and also to make a slight difference between loud and soft. The effect of accentuation, as on the organ, can be immensely increased by making a cunning silence of articulation *before* the note, which then appears to be much more prominently accented than it can be (if at all) in actual dynamics. Good phrasing is as indispensable as on the organ: there is nothing without it. The silences of articulation and of phrasing must be long and conspicuous enough really to get across to the listener, which means longer than most players may be inclined to realize.

There are three fundamentals of good harpsichord technique, and it is particularly important that players coming from the piano should be aware of them.

(i) The touch is by grasping the keys as firmly as possible, never weakly, and never violently. To hit the keys from above gives the plectra no chance of gripping properly on their strings, and they fly past, making a tinny, dry sound of no lasting quality. Conversely, to press the keys down feebly puts insufficient strength into the pluck, and the sound is thin and miserable. You can tell a good harpsichord touch by the power with which it carries the sound to the back of the hall. If the sound there is difficult or impossible to hear, the touch is as likely to be at fault as the instrument.

(ii) All chords of more than two or three notes need to be rolled or spread, with a powerful, grasping roll which sends the sound ringing out into the hall with redoubled force. Chords absolutely simultaneous do not exist in harpsichord technique, for the same reason that unison strings are never plucked absolutely in simultaneous attack on a well-regulated harpsichord. When the attack is absolutely simultaneous, the sound is harsh and ineffectual, quite the opposite of the harpsichord's characteristic mellow ring. The spreading of most chords will be so slight that they do not sound spread, to the ear, but merely rich. Some chords can be more conspicuously spread, for musical reasons: these can range from moderately swift to quite slow, and perhaps returning several times up and down (as on final chords, or when accompanying recitatives). Whatever the spreading, slight or extreme, swift or slow, one rule is invariable: the first (usually the bass) note takes the beat, and everything else comes afterwards.

(iii) All notes in the same harmony are held down so long as fingers can possibly be found to hold them down, and except where good articulation or good phrasing requires a break. A normal harpsichord has no damper-raising (sustaining or 'loud') pedal; and when the finger is lifted, the damper must fall back and the sound will cease. Only by keeping the fingers down, wherever possible and desirable, can the sound be caused to build up through sympathetic vibration and general resonance. Then the whole harpsichord begins to ring with glowing sonority and sustaining power. Otherwise, it is an instrument dead and dry; and although this, too, can be a valuable effect on rare occasions, it is thoroughly uncharacteristic of the harpsichord's basic technique and idiom. In the arpeggiation, for example, of the first (C major) Prelude of J. S. Bach's 48, not only must the fingers stay down, but they must be put back and kept down again after the arpeggiation has passed them by. Only at each change of harmony are they finally released.

It must be remembered that our modern pedal-mechanism for changing stops was nearly (not quite) unknown on Baroque instruments. Much modern registration is too fussy and complicated for the music, and could not have been done at the time. Showy pieces may gain by it, but profound pieces may lose, and it is often better to be more reticent for simple reasons of good musicianship. Nor were 16-foot stops at all common then, nor are they necessary. They add a lot of pressure on the sound-board; and instruments without them tend to have a better resonance.

The tone of the harpsichord family is, like that of the clavichord, well-adapted to contrapuntal music, each thread of which stands out with ready clarity. Elizabethan keyboard music is often well designed for the little virginals, and is then best on this simple form of harpsichord. On the other hand, the great Toccatas of J. S. Bach, and the like, demand the surge and brilliance of the big harpsichord; while some eighteenth-century harpsichord music imperatively demands the double keyboard of the larger instruments. For accompanying music of the seventeenth and eighteenth centuries, the harpsichord is highly desirable, since it is a much more transparent instrument, with a better power of blending and less tendency to cover other instruments, than the piano.

It will be as well to warn the reader that old harpsichords are rather commonly to be heard which have been very faultily restored, so that their tone is feeble and perhaps uneven. Some new ones are as weak; others, in a misguided endeavour to gain greater absolute loudness, have been given an excessively harsh, metallic tone and unresponsive touch. Neither the feebleness nor the harshness is proper to the instrument. The tone of a good harpsichord, correctly played, should be brilliant, but satisfactorily sustained, full, round, warm and colourful.

The Pianoforte Family

The PIANOFORTE is to the modern age what the lute was to the Renaissance, and the clavichord and harpsichord to the Baroque. It is the common solo and accompanying instrument of the home. For this, being, like them, an instrument of harmony, it is self-sufficient: a whole world of music beneath your single pair of hands.

Besides its domestic popularity, the piano, like the big harpsichord of the Baroque age, has a public function to fulfil. It was no accident that the nineteenth century, with its taste for romantic grandeur and its unprecedented cultivation of the public concert, evolved the modern grand piano. A great literature has been written to exploit this massive but expressive instrument, both as a recital soloist and as the solo partner in concertos for piano and orchestra; the *avant-garde* has found new uses for the instrument.

For public purposes, the full-size *concert grand piano* is used; for domestic purposes, the smaller grand pianos, down to the *baby grand*, are more suitable. Where space and expense are considerations of importance, a good *upright piano* will give admirable results (better than an indifferent or over-small grand); next come smaller upright *cottage pianos*, and so down to the little, obsolete, horizontal *square piano* (it is really an oblong) so popular in the eighteenth century. The oldest surviving pianos were made by Cristofori at the beginning of the eighteenth century: but these are thought to have had forgotten precursors.

The pianoforte (Italian for 'soft-loud') acquired its name from its power of passing through insensible gradations from soft to loud and back again, by touch alone. As one of J. S. Bach's sons (C. P. E. Bach) wrote: 'A good clavichord possesses – with the exception that its tone is weaker – all the beauties of the former (the pianoforte).'

The novelty of the early piano, in short, was not its expressive touch alone, nor its loudness alone, but its combination of the two.

In its essential principle, the piano is a dulcimer to which a

I

mechanical action and a keyboard have been added, just as the
harpsichord is a psaltery with the same additions. But as a matter of
historical development, the first pianos closely resembled harpsichords provided with a hammer action in the place of a plectrum

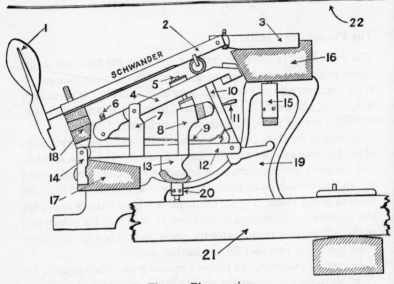

Fig. 23. Piano action

1. Hammer head
2. Grand shank and roller
3. Grand flange and repetition
   screw
4. Repetition lever
5. Repetition lever regulating
   screw
6. Repetition spring regulating
   screw
7. Repetition lever flange
8. Bent block
9. Repetition spring and cord
10. Grand jack

11. Grand jack regulating pin
    and button
12. Grand lever
13. Grand lever block
14. Grand lever flange
15. Set-off button and pin
16. Grand butt rail
17. Grand lever rail
18. Grand rest rail and baize
19. Grand standard
20. Bass capstan screws
21. Key
22. String

action; though two or three unison strings, simultaneously struck by
the same hammer, are normally provided for each note. When you
depress a key, the impetus is transmitted through a more or less
complicated action to the hammer, which flies up to strike its strings
with a velocity proportionate to the impact of your finger; while at

the same time their damper is raised, until the key again is released: when, unless the so-called 'loud' pedal (the damper-raising pedal) has been depressed, the damper is restored and the string falls silent.

A piano action has to be more complicated than a harpsichord action (and much more complicated than a clavichord action) to provide for two essential stages. First, the hammer is not merely to be pushed briskly up to the string, like the tangent of a clavichord; nor is it to be pushed sharply past the string, like the plectrum of a harpsichord; it must fly towards the string at speed. Second, it must be able to rebound instantly, so as not to damp the vibrations of the string by remaining in contact with it any longer than necessary; and it must rebound in such a manner as to be ready for an almost immediate repetition of the stroke.

In the modification known as double escapement (patented by Erard in 1821), the hammer can be given a renewed blow well before the key has returned to its original level: an arrangement greatly facilitating the rapid repetition of the same note.

The tone of the first known pianos, built lightly and strung lightly like large harpsichords, is much less different from harpsichord tone than piano tone has since become. This has been confirmed by acoustical analysis.

The harpsichord and the early piano are both comparatively deficient in low harmonics, but are possessed of a long and ample range of higher harmonics. That is merely the scientific way of saying that their tone has more brilliance than body.

When all the stops of a big harpsichord are brought into action, the effect is not only brilliant, but full as well. The piano has no such added stops to bring in; and the early pianos have a not much more resounding tone. This, however, is not an unqualified defect. The early piano is beautifully translucent throughout its compass. Even massive chords in its bass register, which are apt to be muddy on a modern piano, and are therefore usually avoided by comparatively recent composers, will sound sharp and clear on a grand piano of the time of Beethoven, who not infrequently employs them.

By the same methods of analysis, the tone of the clavichord can be shown to possess a considerably fuller range still of upper harmonics. This range, in fact, extends even higher; but as a whole, the very high harmonics are rather less prominent, while the moderately high harmonics are much more prominent. That, again, merely confirms that the tone of the clavichord, though soft, has exceptional fullness, colour and fascination.

The modern grand piano can be shown to possess a narrower range of harmonics than any of the older keyboard stringed instruments, including the early piano. The very high harmonics are totally absent or inappreciable; so are the moderately high harmonics. But the somewhat low harmonics are fairly rich, and the very low harmonics are very rich indeed. This merely confirms that modern piano tone has, in itself, more body than colour or brilliance.

As we saw (page 15), only a string infinitely thin and flexible could perfectly execute the motions which were theoretically attributed to it in previous chapters. Now, the strings of the clavichord, of the harpsichord, and of the early piano, though departing more or less substantially from infinite thinness and flexibility, are all decidedly thin and flexible by comparison with the strings of a modern piano. Keyboard string instruments, unlike instruments whose tone is artificially sustained, are not given the minute periodic impulses which could cause their upper partials to approximate to an exact harmonic eries: and the less thin and flexible their strings, the less harmonic, as well as the less energetic, their upper partials.

Even the early piano needed rather stouter strings than the harpsichord, to withstand the impact of the hammers. But in the course of the nineteenth century, a desire for ever greater volume overtook musicians and instrument-makers, piano-makers among them. To make pianos louder, their designers specified stouter and stouter strings, able to withstand more and more violent blows of the hammer. To take the vastly increased tension of the stouter strings, an iron frame was gradually evolved to supplant the old wooden one. To achieve a sufficiently mellow tone from this tightly braced mechanism, whose internal tension now amounts in extreme cases to over thirty tons, the hammers, which were at first small and hard, became steadily larger and softer. To increase the volume obtainable from such hammers, the stiffness of the touch was increased, until, in this particular respect, a reaction presently set in. But in other respects, the tendencies of the later nineteenth century continue to this day.

These tendencies all lean one way. For the stouter the string, the less energy it can throw into its upper harmonics; while the larger and softer the hammer, the greater the string-length it makes contact with for the longer time, and the more damping its effect on the upper harmonics. This is why the gain in volume on the modern piano has been paid for by loss in colourfulness and brilliance. These losses are partly remedied, however, by skilful pedalling, which plays an essential part in colouring piano tone.

Of the two pedals with which the modern piano is generally equipped, that to the *left* is known as the Soft Pedal. This operates, nowadays, in one of three ways. It may interpose a strip of felt between hammers and strings, thus still further reducing the harmonic content, and stifling colour and brilliance as well as volume. Or it may bring the hammers nearer the strings, thus reducing the force of their impact; and this, though less drastic, has a similar effect. But there is a third and better method, favoured in the finest modern pianos: the hammers are so shifted as to strike only two out of the three strings provided to each note. The dampers, however, operate as usual, rising from all three strings so soon as the key is depressed. Result: the vibrations of the struck strings excite sympathetic vibrations in the unstruck string.

These sympathetic vibrations of the unstruck string, unlike the direct vibrations of the adjacent struck strings, are not inhibited by any contact with the hammer. They have therefore a more extensive range; and though they are not loud, they are sufficient to colour the resulting tone, and to lend the piano a valuable resource in soft passages.

In Beethoven's day this resource could be carried further by leaving two out of each course of three strings unstruck. That is the meaning of the express instruction *una corda* (one string) attached to many passages in his Piano Sonatas: an instruction which the modern piano has lost the power to execute literally.

The pedal to the *right* is known as the Loud or Sustaining Pedal. This operates by raising the dampers from every string of the piano at once: a device of immense value in every respect. But what here concerns us is that to raise all the dampers immediately permits sympathetic vibrations, not merely in the adjacent unisons, but throughout the instrument. These, added to the still undamped struck vibrations, make themselves felt as a surge of volume, growing rapidly until its maximum is reached, or until the dampers are restored by releasing the pedal. But what is added is not merely volume.

The subtle use of the damper-raising pedal, often momentarily, and never long enough to confuse the harmony unduly, gives the judicious pianist his chief control of colour.

There is a further factor which tends to rich colour in loud passages. We saw that loudness was the bait which led nineteenth-century makers to exchange the hard, unsubstantial but colourful tone of the Beethoven piano for the substantial but rather neutral tone of the modern piano. It may, then, seem a paradox that the piano yields more high harmonics, and is therefore more colourful, when loudly played. But the explanation is a simple one.

For loud playing, the hammer is flung more quickly towards the strings, and rebounds correspondingly quickly. This gives it less time to damp the high harmonics; especially as the felt is itself compressed to more than its usual hardness. The result is artistically favourable; for it is in loud passages that brilliance is most required.

If over-soft felts are fitted (a vice to which some manufacturers are prone), this welcome access of brilliance is forgone; for the deep pile keeps the hammers longer in effective contact with the strings. The result is an over-mellow and unvirile tone. Hardness is in the nature of hammer instruments, and any attempt to breed it out is quite misguided. The best modern pianos are free from this mistake, and make the utmost of their own proper virtues.

These are very numerous. To begin with, the piano excels all other solo instruments (other than the organ) in sheer power: not the supreme musical quality, it is true, but nevertheless exhilarating in its proper place.

Next, piano tone is more sustained than either clavichord or harpsichord or lute tone. This quality comes from the heightened tension and heavy metal frame: as we saw, it was purchased at a cost; but it is of real musical value, and is the chief recommendation of the *modern* piano in the case of music designed, like Beethoven's piano music, for that distinctly different instrument, the late eighteenth- and early nineteenth-century piano. We should perhaps insist on using an early piano for early piano music: but experience suggests that the mechanical and acoustic limits of the early piano were very real. One quite practical course would be to use a mid-nineteenth-century piano, mechanically a very efficient instrument, and much nearer to the early piano in general character and tone than our somewhat exaggerated modern titans.

Another virtue of the piano is the intoxicating crispness with which, when played 'staccato', it can enunciate musical rhythms. This it owes to being, literally, an instrument of percussion, struck with hammers. Yet it can sustain a good and smooth 'legato' as well. And finally, it is capable, when the dampers are raised, of weaving a soft and glamorous web of sound in which little is distinct, and everything melting, warm and romantic.

That is a remarkable assortment of virtues, and precisely such as to commend the piano to nineteenth-century taste, which did so much to develop it. There are, of course, certain limitations inseparable from the instrument. The piano can never compete with a voice, a violin, and many others in producing a really unbroken, 'singing' flow of tone: no keyboard string instrument can. Nor can the piano ever sound so sparklingly brilliant as a harpsichord, or so translucently expressive as a clavichord. But this is merely to say that the piano, like all other instruments, has the inevitable defects of its virtues.

There is no lack of fine pianists at the present time: but the instrument is far from easy, requiring the most delicate finger-control and judgement for a good 'touch'. This consists partly of feeling each key with your finger before depressing it, for the sake of a smooth control and neatness of technique; and partly of beautifully independent finger-movements by which to match each note in loudness, to mould each phrase at will, to join an unbroken 'legato', or to space an exactly regular 'staccato'. At the same time you must be 'pedalling' with skill and insight.

Apart from 'pedalling', you have no more control of the tone from the moment the hammer flies towards the strings. Up to that moment, you can control the velocity of the hammer: and this, as we saw, governs both the loudness and the brightness of the tone. The infinite subtlety with which notes can be joined and separated probably accounts for much of the vast difference between a merely good and a really great pianist.

CHAPTER 8

FLUE INSTRUMENTS

The flutes a species, not a single family

All the instruments to be considered in this chapter are, strictly, to
be described as flutes: a name covering any pipe excited to sound by
an edge tone, the air for which is supplied by breath.

In ordinary modern usage, the word 'flute' has a more restricted
meaning. We mean by it the family of transverse flutes represented
in the symphony orchestra. These receive their name simply from
being held transversely across the face when played. In the eighteenth
century, they were frequently known as the German flute, to contrast
them with another important family of flutes, known as the common
flute. This latter we now generally call by one of its other names:
the recorder; sometimes, the English flute.

So important was the recorder during the early eighteenth and
previous centuries that when we meet the word 'flauto' (flute) or its
equivalent in music of that period, the supposition is that the recorder is intended. When the transverse flute is intended, we meet
the word 'traversa' (transverse) or its equivalent.

The playing position is not the essential point of difference between the transverse flute and the recorder. The transverse flute is an
example of a class of flute in which the air stream is directed to the
edge *by the lips alone*; and this class includes some vertically held
members. The recorder, on the other hand, is an example of a class
of flute in which the air stream is directed to the edge *by a mouthpiece*; and this class (sometimes called fipple flutes or whistles) includes some horizontally held members: while the vertical flute, in
one early form, has the mouthpiece of a recorder but the fingering of
a transverse flute.

The liquid tones of the flute species

As we shall see, the flute species contains several distinct varieties of tone. But in contrast to other species the flutes contribute a peculiarly limpid, pure and innocent colouring to the composer's palette. These qualities have not the universality or the indispensability of string tone; but they are such as no other instruments could imitate or replace.

> *Sabrina fair, listen where thou art sitting*
> *Beneath the glassy, cool translucent wave.*

If there is any tone in music glassy, cool, translucent, it is the tone of the flutes, with their especially pure quality, weak in high harmonics, particularly when low and soft.

The Family of Transverse Flutes

The TRANSVERSE FLUTE[1] (German flute, cross flute, Querflöte, etc.) is an open pipe played by blowing across a sharp-edged hole near its upper end. This end is itself blocked and inoperative; the edge-hole assumes its acoustic functions. But the hole is narrower than the tube; which would cause inaccuracy, unless corrected, in the harmonic series.

The simplest flute is a plain cylinder: intonation is corrected by the player's breath. This needs skill and a good ear; but the result is then very satisfactory and the tone extremely pleasant. This is the *natural flute* and this Renaissance and early Baroque flute is now being made and played again.

About 1680, the flute was modified constructionally, by giving it a conical bore, except for a cylindrical head-joint. Intonation still needs exceptional care; but it is by no means an unmixed disadvantage for the player to have to keep his ear on the alert. The tone is very characteristic, of a cooing quality, but rather brilliant in the upper registers. This is the *conical flute* (the cone is always widest at the blowing end, and narrowest at the further end; unlike most other conical wind instruments). Since its most typical early specimens have six finger-holes and one closed key (for e' flat or d' sharp), its first form is best known as the *one-keyed flute*. It can have a tone of quiet but extraordinary charm, and some excellent work has been done in recovering it for Baroque performances.

[1] Plate 27.

During the eighteenth century, the conical transverse flute enjoyed an astonishing popularity as a solo instrument of both amateurs and professionals. It acquired a number of further keys from about the last quarter of that century onwards to fill in the semitones and its compass was extended downwards to c'.

Halfway through the nineteenth century, Theobald Boehm once more redesigned the flute as a cylindrical pipe with conical headjoint. This (rather than the original cylindrical instrument) is what is called the *cylindrical flute*. He had already reorganized its fingering on the famous system known by his name. This was to calculate the ideal number, positions and sizes of the holes, irrespective of the limitations of the human fingers; then to devise keys to enable the fingers to manage them.

These changes brought more gain than loss. The one-keyed flute is by no means easy to play well; it is quite unsuited even to moderately chromatic passages such as modern music abounds in; but it can be mastered, and has been revived with pleasing results for early flute music. The conical flute is still to be found; but in its modern form, with eight keys and six finger-holes, it has changed considerably since its early days. The cylindrical flute is still more different. With its many large and well-placed holes, almost all controlled by keys, it is louder, more even, and in some ways much easier to play: genuine advantages which commend it to modern players. Though it has inevitably lost something of the older flute quality in the process, it has become a more virile, reliable and generally useful member of the orchestra, less pastoral and charming than before, but thrilling in its own stronger way.

The orchestral flute. The normal compass of the treble FLUTE (concert flute, grande flûte, grosse Flöte), which is the standard concert flute in the modern Western orchestra, is three complete octaves from c' to c'^{v}. (Its basic tonality is d', with a downward extension of one tone.)

The flauto piccolo. The 'little flute' or PICCOLO, as normally used in symphony orchestras, lies an octave above the treble flute. Its compass lacks the downward extension to c'', but is also almost three octaves in expert hands: d'' to c^{v}; though the highest notes are difficult and need skilful management. They are the highest notes of the symphonic orchestra. (The Boehm piccolo is still made with a conical bore to lessen shrillness.)

The *flûte d'amour* lies a minor third lower than the treble flute; its silky and rather intriguing tone is caused by a proportionately narrow bore. The *alto flute* (called in England bass flute) lies a perfect fourth lower than the treble flute; it is in pitch the alto of the family: the flûte d'amour is in pitch a slightly higher alto. There is a tenor register *bass flute* (the Albisophone) in *c* (with *B* extension), but seldom used: while a genuine bass flute made in 1932 by Rudall Carte, with a lovely tone right to its bottom note (*C*), is scarcely yet scored for. Some other tonalities and compasses have been used, especially in military bands or drum and fife bands; the names of all the flutes are confused and fluctuating.

The Family of Recorders

The RECORDER[1] (English flute, common flute, direct flute, echo flute, beak flute, flûte douce, Blockflöte, etc.) does not differ in essential principle from the transverse flute. It is a slightly conical tube, with the narrowest end at the bottom; and a straight whistle edge in place of a round edge-hole. The player's breath is directed towards this edge, not by his narrowed lips, but through a mouthpiece.

This is a considerably easier technique: in fact, the recorder is possibly easiest of all truly satisfactory musical instruments, which accounts for its immense vogue since its revival in recent decades. There is a great place in music for amateurs with no leisure, and perhaps no inclination, to learn a very exacting technique, but with plenty of musical feeling to play expressively in reasonably simple music on a reasonably simple instrument. The recorder is such an instrument. The viol, though much more difficult to play, is another, in virtue of possessing a literature of chamber music profound in spirit but relatively undemanding in technique.

The chief technical problem of the recorder is to control the breath so steadily as to produce an even flow of pure and limpid tone, accurately in tune. Your intonation, indeed, if your skill is adequate, should be of satisfactory exactness: you control it by subtle variations in the flow of breath. You can vary the loudness within narrower limits than the transverse flute, where the intonation can be adapted better. The difference in quality between a good player and an indifferent player is conspicuous enough: the former, crystalline and

[1] Plate 14.

melting; the latter, breathy and awkward. The fingering is unassisted by keys except for the bottom notes of the largest instruments: it is quite rapidly acquired. Chromatic semitones are found by cross-fingering. Of course, as on any other instrument, a virtuoso technique takes a great deal of mastering. But the early stages are both easy and rewarding: an average quartet of amateurs should be able to play a Bach Chorale purely and movingly within a month or two of starting.

We are once more indebted to Arnold Dolmetsch for solving the problem of making first-class modern recorders, and to his son Carl for first revealing their virtuoso potentialities. There are several very fine makers now in the field, a number of good makers, and others who fall short of a satisfactory standard of tone and intonation. Plastic recorders can be of high quality, though they often are not.

The Renaissance recorder, like the Renaissance flute, is simpler in bore and purer in tone. It is being made and played again. A good Baroque recorder is a little edgier and more colourful. Purcell, Bach, Handel and other seventeenth- and eighteenth-century composers, even down to Mozart and Gluck, have scored for the recorder in passages which should preferably not be transferred to the transverse flute: not because that is not beautiful too; but simply because it is not the same. And unlike the piccolo, the smallest recorder (*sopranino*) is capable of reasonably soft tone even in its highest registers: it was scored for by Handel in his operas *Acis and Galatea* and *Rinaldo* under the style of flauto piccolo.

Members of the recorder family. The smallest member of the recorder family, not normally used in consort, is the little sopranino or piccolo recorder mentioned above. The largest great bass recorder descends to *F* or occasionally to *D*, when it requires a length of nearly 8 feet; the normal bass recorder to *c* at lowest. There are eight sizes of recorder described in Praetorius's *Syntagma* of 1615. But for modern consort purposes, the family has four standard sizes.

The *descant recorder* (serving the treble role) has a range from c'' to d'^v (it is called *soprano* in America).

The *treble recorder* (serving the alto role) lies a fifth below, with a range from f' to g''' (it is called *alto* in America).

The treble (i.e. alto) recorder is the normal solo instrument of the family, with an extensive repertoire. Handel intended certain sonatas for it, by the side of others designated for the transverse flute. It is also the instrument most commonly used in the eighteenth-century orchestra; though recorders in *d'* or other keys are also met with.

The *tenor recorder* has a range from *c'* to *d'''*, the top notes being rather difficult to sound.

The *bass recorder* has a satisfactory range of rather less than two octaves, from *f* to about *d''*; sometimes *c* to about *b'*. The tone is gentle when heard alone, but telling in consort with other instruments.

All sizes of recorder, when joined with different instruments or voices, are apt to deceive the ear into misjudging their pitch for an octave lower than its actual sound: a fact for composers to bear in mind. A probable cause is lack of high harmonics.

A near relative of the recorder is the *flageolet*, and a lowly one is the *penny whistle*. (The French *flageolet* with four finger- and two thumb-holes was of seventeenth-century date, as used by Pepys. The *English flageolet* with seven finger-holes and one thumb-hole was an early nineteenth-century instrument with double and triple flageolets as offspring. The *quadrille* was a Boehm system flageolet.)

The *three-holed pipe*, another nearly related cousin of the recorder, is used in that ancient and honourable accompaniment of the folk dance, the PIPE AND TABOR. You play the pipe with your left hand: the tabor (a little two-headed drum) with your right hand. Your little finger and the one next to it hold the end of the pipe between them, leaving only two fingers and the thumb for stopping holes.

The secret lies in using only rather high members of the Natural Harmonic Series. Suppose your pipe has a first or fundamental harmonic *c'*. You ignore that (in fact it is scarcely to be sounded on so narrow a pipe as this, designed specially to make the higher harmonics easy to sound). For to play a diatonic scale up to the next or second harmonic *c''*, you would need not less than six holes: which, of course, means two hands.

Your scale begins with the next or second octave. You can play *c''* by merely 'overblowing' it as the second harmonic of your unused fundamental *c'*: so you need no hole for that. And *g''* you can 'overblow' as the third harmonic: you need no hole for that. You only need holes for the three notes between: *d''*, *e''*, *f''*.

And these three holes are all the instrument requires: for every higher diatonic note which the instrument can reach may be sounded as a third, a fourth or even a fifth harmonic either of the full-length fundamental c', or of one of the shorter-length fundamentals established by opening these holes one, two or three at a time. With skill, this gives you a diatonic compass of one and a half octaves or more, with some chromatic notes, to be got by cross-fingering as well. The tone is clear, pure and very pleasing, with its sharp, accented accompaniment from the tabor to mark the rhythm and keep the dancers alert and accurate.

CHAPTER 9

REED INSTRUMENTS

The high colouring of reed instruments

The strings lead the orchestra: the flutes provide its coolest tones.
But the reeds lend some of its strongest colourings. Being prone to
some very distinctive assortments of prominent high harmonics,
they have always a certain poignant intensity. They are often heard
alone, or nearly so: but when blended with other instruments, they
colour that blend pervasively, a single oboe or clarinet making itself
felt easily through a mass of strings. Such powerful resources need
judgement and restraint: but well used, they are among the most
telling which the orchestra possesses.

The Family of Shawms

Of modern orchestral instruments with double reeds, the basis is the
ancient family of shawms and pommers. Shawm (schalmey, shalmuse,
shalmele, etc.) and pommer (bombard, bombart, etc.) are really alternative names: but there was a tendency to call the smaller members
shawms and the larger members pommers. Being a characteristic
instrument of the waits (a city watch which turned into a municipal
band), the shawm was also, in England, called the wait (wayte, waight,
etc.); hautboy (hoboy, etc.) was another name (whence oboe), derived
from the French *hautbois* or 'high wood' (meaning loud wood), but
fairly indiscriminately used for various sizes of shawm. To save
confusion, I shall follow one well-authenticated usage, and call the
instrument, in all its sizes, the SHAWM. (Plates 9, 10.)

The shawm has a rather wide and stiff double reed, and a conical
bore widest at the bottom: the tip of the reed acts for acoustic
purposes virtually as a closed end. The bell is rather flaring, which
helps the high harmonics and makes for colour and brilliance. So do

117

the large finger-holes. The net result is a tone of astounding pungency, described thus by Mersenne in 1636:[1]

> It is proper for large assemblies, such as Balls (though the Violins are now customary in their place), for Nuptials, for village Festivities, and for other public rejoicings, by reason of the grand noise which they yield, and the grand Harmony which they evoke, for they have the most powerful and the most violent tone of all instruments, excepting the Trumpet.

The shawm, essayed by Dolmetsch, has since been successfully revived, and experience shows the verisimilitude of the above description. When the reed is taken into the mouth, the shawm is moderately expressive as well as magnificently virile. If played with a box covering the reed, the shawm can be made raucous beyond belief. In the West, however, there is normally a small ring or 'pirouette' which leaves the tone almost as raucous while permitting some control of the reed in the mouth.

The shawm family are shown by Praetorius (1620) from the small discant shawm, going up to b''', to the great bass pommer, or bombardone, going down to $F_{,}$. The shawm continues to be an extant folk instrument in Spain (especially Barcelona) and elsewhere.

The Family of Oboes[2]

During the sixteenth and much of the seventeenth century, the terms OBOE (hautbois, etc.) and shawm were interchangeable. When French makers from about 1660 began to decrease the taper and narrow the flare, thus reducing the pungency, the oboe embarked on its independent career as the first treble wood-wind to become standard in the orchestra. But not until the nineteenth century did it begin to acquire its present exceptional equipment of keys and holes (including two or three speaker-holes to assist 'overblowing'). There is no 'pirouette'; finger-holes are relatively small.

By far the most prominent harmonics of an oboe playing middle c' were shown on analysis to be the fourth and fifth; the first or fundamental harmonic showing, objectively, scarcely any intensity at all (though the ear or our perception stresses it). There is also thought to be a group of high harmonics attributed to formants,

[1] *Harmonie Universelle*, ii, 303.   [2] Plates 20, 28, 30.

close together in pitch, and exceeding the intensity of the first or fundamental harmonic by some four times.[1]

The French have since developed a peculiarly silvery yet delicately nasal form of oboe, with a slightly feminine, very expressive technique proper to it; elsewhere, as in Germany, makers and players have remained more faithful to the veiled eighteenth-century instrument. A distinction is possible not only between these two varieties of standard oboe, but a third: the oboes d'amore, with their incurved

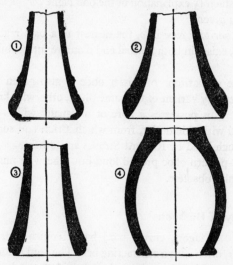

Fig. 24. Oboe bells: old; da caccia; modern; d'amore

bell, narrow bore, and veiled, mysterious timbre. It might be an advantage to the symphonic orchestra if all three could be developed, so far as is physically possible, into complete families, separately available. At present the situation is confused, especially since the French have begun to prefer a rather larger bore and robuster tone again. This, however, is desirable; the French oboe was getting too refined for proper oboe character.

The standard soprano *oboe* in *c'* has always a certain bitter-sweet expressiveness, with a compass from *b* or *b* flat to *a'''*, of which the top few notes are very uncertain. There has been a *tenor oboe* in *f* (called *taille* in Bach's time).

[1] See Miller, *Sound Waves*, p. 54. But Saunders' findings do not confirm (*J. Acous. Soc. Am.*, 18, 2, 1947).

K

The *oboe d'amore* proper is an alto instrument in *a*, but with incurved bell and veiled tone: a great favourite of J. S. Bach; and revived in 1874 by Mahillon of Brussels for performances of Bach's music.

The *oboe da caccia* is an obsolete (often curved) tenor oboe in *f*, scored by J. S. Bach and others. It ended by acquiring the oboe d'amore form, in which shape it may have begotten the following.

The so-called *cor anglais* or *English horn* is a tenor oboe d'amore in *f*. No satisfactory explanation of the odd name *cor anglais* or *inglese* has yet been given.

The true *baritone oboe* in *c*, the nearest to a bass reached by the oboe family, exists in both normal and d'amore forms; but is a rarity in either.

The name of baritone or basset oboe is also given to an early twentieth-century variant of the same pitch, otherwise known as the *heckelphone*. This possesses a bore of unusually wide taper, and a globular bell with side outlet, from which a rich and sonorous tone emerges, much liked by Richard Strauss and others.

A Boehm-pattern oboe proved loud but otherwise unsatisfactory, and is virtually obsolete.

The Family of Bassoons[1]

The BASSOON (fagott, curtal, etc.) has a conical bore of rather narrow taper, often with a contracting bell. The reed is comparatively wide, and resembles that of the shawm and the early oboe much more than that of the modern oboe. 'Overblowing' gives the second, third and even higher harmonics: in very skilful hands a compass of over three and a half octaves can be achieved, throughout the whole of which the technique is remarkably flexible and agile. There has been much the usual history of added keywork, though not quite in the same extreme degree.

Now the bassoon, though very close to the shawm, is not, like the oboe, its descendant, but a collateral instrument, first appearing distinctly in the sixteenth century. Its special feature is the way in which its tube is doubled back on itself, so that it is twice as handy as the awkwardly lengthy, straight bass shawm, which it tended to replace. And when the smaller shawms changed into the oboe family,

[1] Plates 30, 31.

the bassoon remained with them, to become the customary bass to the oboes in the modern orchestra.

This is, theoretically, a compromise. Bassoon tone is considerably smoother and less colourful than modern oboe tone, especially in the lower registers, where the bassoon has a cavernous quality which the oboe cannot match. Indeed, the bassoon lends itself to comedy more readily than most instruments: though grandeur and even tragedy are by far its more important roles. It makes, indeed, a fine solo voice in the orchestra. As the standard bass to the wood-wind group (flutes, oboes and clarinets), it serves extremely well: but not, perhaps, ideally well.

It would be possible to enlarge our modern orchestra with certain new wood-wind members to complete its several families so far as they can be completed. A genuine bass flute has been proved an acoustic possibility: and a bass oboe should be feasible enough. We could include a full family of four sizes of oboe (perhaps further divided into a silvery French branch and a more veiled German branch); and another full family of four sizes of oboe d'amore; and yet another (if not two, as with the oboes) of four sizes of bassoon. The double bassoon sounds different yet again.

The modern tendency is, on the whole, to have fewer different kinds of instrument playing simultaneously. We are less given to thick mixtures of many different instrumental tones at once: we place more reliance on simple, unmixed colour-washes from a single instrumental family at a time. Of course, mixed colourings are just as valuable when used with skill and imagination. But for either purpose the more complete the several orchestral families, the wider the composer's choice of resources. It must be admitted, however, that the orchestra as at present constituted is so superbly resourceful in practice that such an enlargement might well be undesirable if only on financial grounds.

Like the oboe, the bassoon has itself diverged somewhat, into a reedy English and French version (the more traditional), and a mellow German version. Both have their qualities: but I hope the more silky oboes and bassoons will not oust (as they have already very largely done) the reedier types: for the one is no substitute for the other.

The standard bassoon. The standard bassoon of the modern symphony orchestra possesses the astonishing range A, at lowest, or normally B_i flat to e'' flat, f'', or even, in very skilled hands, playing modern instruments, a'' flat: the topmost notes being, however, not so satisfactory as the others and very unreliable.

The *double bassoon* (contrafagotto) stands an octave below the standard bassoon, with the range $B_{,,}$ flat to b flat in skilful hands, or three notes higher as a difficult special effect; f is the limit in usual practice, since the tone above that is rather forced and lifeless. Heckel supplies a model going down to $A_{,,}$; but few orchestral players have instruments going lower than C_i.

Other bassoons. In the Renaissance period, when every conceivable instrument was given as complete a family of members as possible, the bassoon family included a *discant fagott* or treble bassoon, with a range from a or g to c''; *quint-fagott* or doppel-fagott, with a range from F_i to g; and several intermediate sizes of which the most important was the *quart-fagott*, a tone above the quint-fagott and a fourth below the standard bassoon. At various times, there have flourished an *octave bassoon* (soprano bassoon) at the octave above the standard bassoon; an *alto bassoon*, at the sixth above the standard bassoon; a *tenor bassoon* (tenoroon), alternatively at the fourth or the fifth above the standard bassoon; as well as a rare curiosity, the *subkontrafagott* (sub-double-bass bassoon), two octaves below the standard bassoon, with the phenomenal bottom note $B_{,,,}$ flat, though whether that abysmal pitch can be directly audible to the human ear is more than doubtful, for reasons into which we have already entered (pages 25 and 26). All these are obsolete.

The Family of Clarinets[1]

All the reed instruments to which we have so far attended are examples of the conical stopped pipe, played with a double reed. The CLARINET belongs to a new class: it is a cylindrical stopped pipe, played with a single reed.

Of these differences, by far the most important is the shape. The effect on tone quality of changing from a double to a single reed is not crucial, as may perhaps be illustrated by the fact that for a time bassoons with single reeds in place of double reeds were not absolutely unknown. But the effect of changing from a conical to a cylindrical bore is crucial.

[1] Plates 29, 30.

Being a virtually stopped cylinder, the clarinet can, as we saw (page 45), only sound the odd-numbered members of the Natural Harmonic Series. This, of course, affects its fingering, since certain notes which on an oboe might be found by 'overblowing' to an even-numbered harmonic, must be found on the clarinet by opening a special hole. But what is more important, the absence of the even-numbered harmonics affects the tone of the clarinet as well, giving it that finely cadaverous, and almost literally 'hollow' quality by which it is distinguished in its lower register.

True, the even-numbered harmonics are not, even in theory, totally missing from the tone: for the tube is not a pure cylinder either at the mouthpiece or at the bell. Still, they are mostly weak at the best, especially in the lower register. The topmost register of the clarinet has a much brighter quality: supposedly because these high notes are much nearer in pitch to some high formants of the tube itself. These formants are alleged to be weaker than the oboe's, and more widely spaced. But a reed is always a potent stimulant of high harmonics: and the clarinet, for all its strange and haunting quality in its lower regions, is decidedly brilliant in its upper notes.

Analysis shows that the strongest upper harmonics of a clarinet playing middle c' are the ninth and – unexpectedly – the eighth: further proof that we do not wholly understand as yet the influences governing the appearance and the relative strength of the harmonics which lend each individual instrument its characteristic quality of tone. The formant theory, though plausible and perhaps fundamentally correct, has not received sufficient confirmation from actual experimental analyses to be advanced without hesitation.[1]

The clarinet has fairly elaborate keywork working on various systems (including a Boehm clarinet). The instrument itself is a comparative newcomer of rather uncertain origins, apparently late in the seventeenth century. A pair of clarinets became standard in the orchestra from about 1870: Mozart being one of the first composers of genius to exploit the instrument to any great extent.

The standard *soprano clarinet* has the remarkable extreme compass of nearly four octaves, from c sharp to c'^{v}; but most of the top octave

---

[1] See Miller, *Sound Waves*, p. 54. The clearest simple account of the formant theory will be found in Jeans, *Science and Music*, but his conclusions are not all confirmed by other authorities. Saunders' work has been highly critical (*J. Acous. Soc. Am.*, 17, 3; 18, 2; etc.).

is unavoidably strident. B flat or A is the usual key in which it is pitched, since the clarinet in C is considered unsatisfactory in tone. The E flat clarinet, a fourth higher, is very shrill, and needs more discretion in the composer than the lower clarinets. The still higher clarinets in F, G and A flat are not favoured by symphonic writers. There is an *alto clarinet* in F or E flat; a variant miscalled the *basset horn* in F, of narrower bore and more coloured tone; a *bass clarinet*, usually in B flat an octave below the standard clarinet; a double bass *pedal clarinet* an octave lower still; as well as a *clarinetto d'amore* in G, with an incurved bell and a mellow tone. Other sizes and tunings are or have at various times been in use.

The Family of Saxophones

The SAXOPHONE, introduced by Adolphe Sax in the mid-nineteenth century, has the conical bore of an oboe, though wider; the single reed of a clarinet, though more massive; and the material of a brass instrument. It was designed as a complete family of many sizes, the commonest of which are now *sopranino saxophone* (*e'* flat), *soprano saxophone* (*b* flat), *alto saxophone* (*e* flat), *tenor saxophone* (*B* flat), *baritone saxophone* (*E* flat), and *bass saxophone* (*B,* flat). The compass is up to two and a half octaves, two speaker-holes facilitating 'overblowing'.

The wide taper militates against high harmonics, especially as the bell is not very widely flared. The first or fundamental harmonic is unusually strong, while the strongest upper harmonic is the fourth, at the double octave, with moderate intensity in the fifth and sixth harmonics and a dwindling intensity thence upwards to the fifteenth. Jeans postulates certain high formants not unlike the oboe's; but the effect of the saxophone on the ear is decidedly more smooth, and even cloying.[1]

The saxophone has been recommended to symphonists as a useful bridge between wood-wind and brass-wind tone. Whether from prejudice, or whether from a dislike of so comparatively characterless a quality of tone, they mostly reject this advice. (But there is a fine use in Vaughan Williams's Sixth Symphony.)

The *sarrusophone* is a conical brass instrument with wide taper, played with a double reed. It was evolved by the French bandmaster

[1] Miller, *Sound Waves*, p. 54; Jeans, *Science and Music*, pp. 148ff., based on experiments by Herman-Goldap.

Sarrus in 1856; and it bears the same relation to the oboe and bassoon families as the saxophone bears to the clarinet family. It exists as a complete family in eight sizes; but, with the possible exception of the bass and contra-bass members, it does not now appear to have much hold on life. A nearly related contra-bass is at present popular in Italian military bands, under the name *contra-basso ad Ancia*; and in American wind bands.

The Family of Bagpipes

The essential feature of the BAGPIPES is a leather windbag from which air can be squeezed by pressure of the elbow. This serves as a reservoir, and enables a continuous sound to be maintained, without pause for breath. You keep the bag inflated by blowing through a blow-pipe, or by bellows worked by your arm.

To this reservoir there are attached single- or double-reed pipes in varying number and design. There may be only one pipe, known as a chanter, with finger-holes for playing melodies. But the characteristic bagpipe has, in addition, at least one, and usually several further pipes, known as drones. These are tuned to a fixed pitch, at the octaves and fifths of the chanter's tonality.

In the special case of the *Irish uilleann pipes*, there is yet another set of pipes, known as regulators. These have keys manipulated by pressure of the wrists, and they add to the chanter and drones an occasional simple harmony: the tone is very pleasing. The chanter overblows to play a second octave.

The French *musette* has two chanters, one higher in pitch than the other: the tone is sweet and docile. (There is also a bagless musette still surviving: it resembles a treble shawm and is actually called bombarde, which is one of the names for shawm, to this day, in Brittany, where it is always played in company with, and at the octave above, the Biniou or Breton bagpipe with single drone.) At the other extreme come the *Highland pipes*, with their wonderful barbaric power and uncanny intervals, not quite those of any ordinary modern scale. Many other nations have bagpipes of varying designs and quality.

Where there are the characteristic drones, the bagpipes stand outside our Western art of harmony, giving in return a haunting fascination which we should have to travel a long way East, or a long way back into history, to parallel.

CHAPTER 10

LIP INSTRUMENTS

The adaptability of all lip instruments

Lip instruments are the hardest of all to classify. To begin with, their exact dimensions have a crucial effect on their tone quality, so that by gradually changing the shape, you produce an almost continuous gradation of tone quality between one lip instrument and its nearest relative. Yet at the extremes their tone quality is as different as could well be.

Their names, too, are in a state of confusion. What denotes one instrument in England may have a different connotation in some other country; and many distinctions without a difference have been introduced for the sake of eluding extant patents.

Finally, many important qualities of lip instruments are governed, not by their design at all, but by the skill and physical endowments of the player. Your lips are in effect a part of your instrument: and no two players are quite alike in this respect.

The strings owe their endlessly satisfying tone quality to their wealth of evenly distributed upper harmonics; the flutes owe their limpid fascination to a relative sparseness of high harmonics; the reeds owe their poignancy to compact, uneven groups of high harmonics. The lip instruments, in turn, are distinguished by an exceptionally massive array of upper harmonics; and by a remarkable adaptability, due to the peculiar flexibility of the human lips, from their loosest and most ponderous state to their most tense and delicate.

The noble sonority of lip instruments

The brass department includes sombre as well as brilliant qualities. But it is seldom without a certain noble sonority, fit to express dignity, splendour, sinister power, triumphant rejoicing, tragedy and even mystery in turns. For however you use the brass, you can hardly rob it of its grandeur. True, if your music is trivial, the brass will not save it: no orchestration can. But if you have something generous or fateful to say, the brass will help you to say it in a peculiarly telling manner.

Sibelius once called the modern symphony orchestra a perfect instrument but for the lack of a sustaining pedal, which the composer must remedy by skilful scoring. The brass is invaluable here: the most intricate figuration for strings or wood-wind may be floated on a sea of brass tone, comprising nothing but a few simple chords. Again, the brass may carry Wagnerian melodies clean through a maze of surrounding figuration; or it may, like other orchestral groups, be heard alone. But in every role, sonority and nobility are its salient qualities.

Varieties of lip instrument

It is not possible, for inescapable acoustic reasons, to construct complete families of every kind of lip instrument. For if you so design the instrument as to excel in its higher register, where a treble instrument should excel, you automatically endow it with a brilliantly colourful tone. But if you so design it as to excel in its lower register, where a bass instrument should excel, you automatically endow it with a broader and less highly coloured tone. And instruments whose tone is substantially different cannot be regarded as members of the same family.

If you use a narrow air column of more than a certain length, it will flatly decline to vibrate at full length: hence, however skilfully you play, you will be unable to make it sound its fundamental note. But it will vibrate readily enough in half-lengths or less; so that there is no difficulty in sounding the second harmonic (an octave above the fundamental) and upwards.

Indeed, you will be able to sound exceptionally high notes on such an instrument. In compensation for losing the bottom octave, you may be able to climb as high as four (or even, as a very freakish stunt, five)[1] octaves above the (normally impracticable) fundamental. And

[1] Harold Stambaugh, the New York trumpeter and cornet-player, published cadenzas, and instructions for playing them, with this fantastic range, fundamental and all!

the reason why you can, by 'overblowing', sound such exceptionally high harmonics *as notes* is simply that there is an exceptional wealth of high harmonics already present in the tone itself, *as colourfulness*. That is the acoustic consequence of a tube unusually narrow in proportion to its length.

But if you use a short air column of more than a certain width, it will almost as flatly decline to vibrate in many parts; though it will vibrate readily enough in one length (sounding the fundamental), or in a few part-lengths (sounding a few of the higher harmonics as notes). And by the same token, the high harmonics will be less prominent in its quality of tone. That is the acoustic consequence of a tube unusually wide in proportion to its length.

In practice, a good deal depends on the mouthpiece, and still more on the player's skill; but there are always limits to what the cleverest player can extract, with any mouthpiece, from a given design of tube. The majority of lip instruments are only practicable up to three or three and a half octaves above their fundamental, which is some-times good and usable, sometimes poor, difficult or unobtainable. Conversely, to sound exceptionally high harmonics even from a long but narrow tube needs such contraction and tension of the lip muscles that they are sometimes damaged by the strain. Lip instru-ments are therefore (in practice) normally used in the register where they excel, rather than through the total compass (theoretically) available with more or less uncertainty and more or less unevenness of sound.

When an unusually narrow tube is long enough for its fundamental octave to lie within a bass compass, it will inevitably prove too long actually to sound that low octave, at anyrate with satisfactory readi-ness and true bass sonority. And if we think to remedy this limitation by widening the tube, we shall merely discourage its very high harmonics, thus robbing it, not only of its top notes, but also of its uniquely colourful tone.

On the other hand, when even such an unusually narrow tube is long enough to encourage the very high harmonics, it will inevitably prove too long to lie within a treble compass. And if we think to remedy this limitation by shortening the tube, we shall again merely discourage its very high harmonics, and rob it, not only of its top notes, but also of its uniquely colourful tone.

Hence it is that neither a true bass instrument nor a true treble instrument is a physical possibility, in this kind, sometimes roughly known as four-octave instruments: of which the horn and the long, true early trumpet are the outstanding instances. The lowest is strictly a baritone; the highest is strictly an alto. But since with skill their individual range is exceptionally extensive, this limitation is less constricting than it might appear. And what are sometimes roughly known as three-octave instruments, though their individual range is less extensive, are less subject to limitation in forming complete families.

The Family of Cornetts

The early CORNETT (zink, etc.) is nowadays so spelt, or called cornetto, to distinguish it from the modern cornet, an early nineteenth-century invention to be described below.

The cornett is a roughly two-octave instrument of relatively wide bore; with a cup-shaped mouthpiece of small to moderate size; without bell. There is also a variation called the *mute cornett*, of which the mouthpiece is carved out of the tube itself; it has a less emphatic tone.

The lack of a bell is probably responsible for the two-octave basic compass and tone quality of what we should otherwise expect to be a more extended and colourful instrument. But it also permits what is impossible in any modern lip instruments: perfectly satisfactory pitch alteration by side holes, of which there are six in front for the fingers, and one behind for the thumb, except for French instruments, which have no thumb-hole. By opening these, the scale is completed, and the upper compass enlarged into the third octave.

The material is wood, or more rarely, ivory. The shape is either straight, or curved; the latter cannot be drilled out on a lathe, and is therefore nearly always made in two half-bores joined edgewise, and covered with leather to conceal the joint.

During the Renaissance, the family normally included a *cornettino* in *e'* or *d'*; a *cornetto* in *a* or *g*; and a *cornone* or great cornett in *d*, with a key *c*; each with an average compass of about two and a half octaves. There was also a high bass cornett in *G*; but neither this nor the great cornett in d were very popular, and the general practice seems to have been to use a trombone (sackbut) to provide the bass, the tenor, and even very frequently the alto (leaving one or two treble parts to the cornett itself). No very satisfactory bass cornett was, in fact, evolved.

Towards the close of the sixteenth century, a true bass in *C* was allied to the cornett family (without, however, anywhere superseding the use of the trombone). This, from its very wavy outline, is called the *serpent*. Later, a larger serpent was built, a fifth below; and even a monster a fourth lower yet. But these latter were the merest freak instruments. Nor is the standard serpent itself strictly a cornett proper; it has a wider bore and thinner walls, besides lacking the cornett's thumb-hole at the back. It was primarily designed to accompany plain-chant in churches and cathedrals, and there is no actual evidence that it was ever employed for any other purpose until the latter half of the eighteenth century, when it became a popular military-band instrument (particularly in England); but by that time the cornett family proper had fallen into disuse. However, so close a cousin is the serpent of the cornett family proper that they are best treated together, especially since the serpent is the only successful bass instrument of the cornett group.[1]

The serpent is a quite remarkable instrument. To begin with, it readily reaches three octaves above its pedal tone of *C* or *D*. Next, its original six finger-holes (later, several additional holes were operated by keys – still no thumb-hole) are placed, so as to be within reach, in theoretically quite incorrect positions for many notes, which can nevertheless be sounded, given adequate skill, in perfect intonation. Finally, it can, if the player has the skill and the physique to loosen his lips sufficiently, take several notes *lower* than its fundamental proper: down to A_i at least.

The explanation of these last two phenomena is as follows. The notes which a lip instrument will sound most readily and sonorously are, as we know, the natural harmonics of its air column. But in any coupled system, the exciting partner may draw the responding partner to some extent out of its natural pitch. It is by this means that players of wind instruments, especially lip instruments, ordinarily adjust their intonation to a fine exactness.

[1] The 'Lysarden' listed in the Hengrave Hall Inventory of 1603 was, in Galpin's original opinion, a serpent. (F. W. Galpin, *Old English Instruments of Music* (Methuen, 1910, etc., 1932 ed.), p. 195.) But he appears later to have considered it a tenor cornett.

Now it happens that on the serpent, and also, as we shall find, on the horn, the lips can exert this influence, in a downwards direction, to a rather unusual degree. Hence they can not only pull their notes into fine intonation; they can, given the skill, actually sound notes which are not theoretically provided for at all. This is called forcing; and the notes thus sounded are called factitious notes.

The serpent outlived the remaining cornetts; in France, it was still played in rural churches within living memory, while Thomas Hardy knew it in England, at least by repute. 'Old things pass away, 'tis true, but a serpent was a good old note; a deep rich note was the serpent.'[1] The indefatigable Dolmetsch family revived it long ago; and I can vouch for its astonishing compass, and its full, flexible tone, ranging from a gentle cooing to the noisy bellow of an ox.

Cornetts were often used to double voices, with which their rather pure tone fitted them to blend. Mersenne (*Harmonie Universelle*, 1636) likens this tone to 'a ray of sunshine, which appears in the shade or the darkness, when one hears it among the voices in Cathedrals or Chapels'; Holme (*Academy of Armory*, 1688) calls it 'a delicate, pleasant, wind musick, if well played and humered'; Evelyn (*Diary*, 1662) says 'now no more heard the cornet which gave life to the organ'; and North (*Memoirs*, about 1720) adds: 'Nothing comes so near or rather imitates so much an excellent voice as a cornett pipe; but the labour of the lips is too great and it is seldom well sounded.' (The labour for *soft* playing, however, as we learn from Mersenne, and as experience confirms, is exceptionally light.) Bach used the cornett in eleven of his Cantatas.

The cornetti have now been most successfully revived; but we have still to train players with the fabulous virtuosity and sureness of which this difficult but glorious instrument is capable, as many contemporary descriptions make quite plain.

The *key bugles* and keyed *ophicleides* (whose bass member supplanted the serpent in the orchestra, to give place in turn to the bass tuba) were successors and the *Russian bassoon* and the *bass horn* were variants (the ophicleide was still listed by Couesnon, Paris, in 1916). The incredibly pure, clear and silvery sounds that can be produced from a treble cornett, and the comparative ease with which it is sounded, augur well for the future of this once indispensable family.

[1] *Under the Greenwood Tree.*

The Family of Bugles

The BUGLE family has, in general, the following characteristics: roughly three-octave compass; wide conical bore; large or varying mouthpiece; varying bells. Tone inclined to be broad and imposing, especially in the lower register.

The highest bugles are generally known as *flugel horns*, made in various pitches, of which the lowest and most important is in *b* flat. Next come three instruments varying in timbre: the most general names being *tenor horn* (*E* flat: medium bore), *baritone* (*B* flat: medium bore), and *tenor tuba* or *euphonium* (*B* flat: wide bore). These are all in fact of baritone register; but the euphonium has the most solid and most bass-like timbre, and can reach down chromatically to its fundamental with the aid of its fourth valve. Then follow two *bass tubas* or *bombardons* in *F* and *E* flat, and a *contra-bass tuba* or bombardon in *B,* flat. The tubas (euphonium and bombardons) are among the most important brass units in the modern symphony orchestra, where, in addition to other functions, they often provide a weighty bass to the trombone family.[1] Finally, a giant *sub-bass tuba* has been built in (theoretical) *E,* flat, and even vaster *sub-contra-bass tubas* in *C,* and *B,,* flat.

The tubas can legitimately be regarded as ophicleides ('keyed bugles', as we have seen) with valves instead of keys.

It would serve no good purpose here to give further details of these instruments, whose compass varies with the number of valves provided. But *N.B.* the French six-valve C tuba, chromatic compass *C,* to *c″* or higher! – and two further complications.

In 1845, Adolphe Sax, the inventor of the saxophone, patented a complete family of *saxhorns*, of which the lower members but not the upper members now valve their fundamental (pedal) octave in practice. The upper members are virtually flugel horns; the lower members are virtually tubas. Sax had, however, been anticipated by Stölzel of Berlin with a complete family of valved bugles some years before.

Rather later in the nineteenth century, Richard Wagner, wanting to exploit a hornish form of bugle tone in full harmony, introduced his so-called *Wagner tubas*. Of these, the 'tenor' was a roughly three and a half octave instrument using its fundamental octave, and in

[1] Plates 30, 34.

quality resembling the tenor horn. The 'bass', however, did not use its fundamental: it had a compass and timbre somewhat resembling the true horn in F, though a little less rounded in quality. Both tenor and bass Wagner tubas were played with horn mouthpieces. Finally, the contra-bass Wagner tuba, unlike the others, was a true tuba, and played with a tuba mouthpiece.

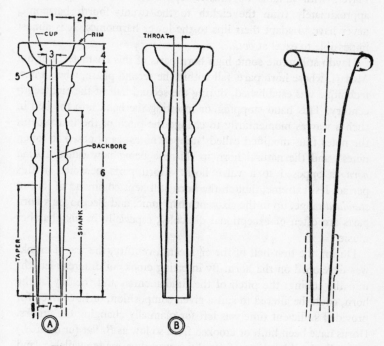

Fig. 25. Trumpet (A, B) and French horn mouthpieces

The Family of Horns

The HORN family has the following general characteristics: compass extending through the fourth octave above the fundamental or even higher (the fundamental, when available, being of varying quality according to the pitch of the horn); narrow conical bore; narrow but more or less tapering mouthpiece; widely flaring bell. Tone superbly colourful, but mellow.

The orchestral horn (no longer strictly French horn) passed

through three main phases. First, the valveless *natural horn* in Bach and Handel's time was played (like the contemporary trumpet) with a special technique for sounding notes up to the twentieth harmonic, or even beyond, in which region the notes of the Natural Harmonic Series lie close enough together to permit of melody: a technique subsequently lost, but recently almost recovered in another form. Players with suitable lip muscles specialized on the top register, approximately from the eighth to the twenty-fourth harmonic, never have to adapt their lips to the lower harmonics. It is almost impossible to excel at *both*.

Haydn still wrote some high horn parts of this character; but not Mozart, whose horn parts fall within the second phase, when a new technique was established, during the second half of the eighteenth century. This hand-stopping, or inserting the hand into the bell in such a way as momentarily to change the pitch of the instrument, the notes thus modified called 'stopped notes' as opposed to 'open notes', and the natural horn in this use being now called a *hand horn* as opposed to a valve horn.[1] Horn parts became, at this period, less extreme, though the horn still kept command of its full *standard* range, up to the sixteenth harmonic, and Beethoven's horn parts are often of exceptional difficulty, especially in his chamber music.

During the first half of the eighteenth century, the use of crooks was developed on the horn. By inserting crooks of different lengths into the tubing, the pitch of the fundamental, and the key of the horn, could be altered to suit a given composition, or in course of it provided sufficient time was left for manually changing the crooks. Horns have been built or crooked from so low as $B_,$ flat (or even $A_,$) upwards. A wide range of tonalities was thus made available, and each was associated with a perceptibly different quality of tone. In each key, with its proper crook, notes not available as harmonics could, both diatonically and chromatically, be produced more or less successfully by stopping with the hand. The quality of the stopped notes differs from the quality of the open notes. This difference, however, can be reduced by skilful playing so that it is not too disturbing when it is not wanted, while it can also be valuably exploited as a special effect when it is wanted.

The third main stage began to develop during the first half of the

[1] Plate 32 (valve horn).

nineteenth century, and became established during the second half. This is the stage of the *valve horn*. Piston or rotary valves of varying designs are arranged to add (or in certain instances to subtract) short lengths of tubing at the touch of a finger or thumb, in course of actual playing. This made the horn a fully chromatic instrument on open notes, though the technique of hand-stopping was still retained as a means of most subtle variation; indeed, it contributes some of the idiomatic elements in the highly colourful character of the horn. Crooks inserted by hand were gradually reduced to those in F, E flat and E; and by the end of the nineteenth century, the horn in F, with about 12 feet of tubing, had become the standard instrument of the orchestra.

At about the same time, however, a higher horn in B flat alto acquired growing popularity, to facilitate horn parts of a high tessitura; and as a further development in the same direction, double horns were built in F and B flat. About 3 feet of tubing can be brought in or taken out, in course of actual playing; and though the F portion and the B flat alto portion thus brought into operation at will have a natural disposition to give different qualities of tone, this difference can be largely and perhaps wholly overcome by the skilled manipulation of a highly accomplished player. The conveniences are so considerable that the double horn is now replacing the F horn as the standard instrument. Nevertheless, many first horn players retain the B flat alto horn, generally with an added valve giving a downwards extension to A.

As with the modern trumpet to be described below, the modern horn tends to grow away from the old, long-tube instrument into a new, short-tube instrument with some loss of nobility to set against the undoubted gain in facility. This loss, it is argued, can be largely and perhaps wholly recovered by fine playing, since the horn is a very flexible instrument for those who know what kind of tone they are aiming at, and just how to coax it out. Nevertheless, the decrease in length must change the acoustic situation. And there are two further changes, of which the consequences also combine with the first. One is an increase in width of bore, disposing the instrument towards a tone more full and sonorous, but less coloured by high harmonics. The other is a more cup-like and less funnel-like mouthpiece, disposing the instrument slightly in the direction of a trumpet's brightness.

L

During the first half of the nineteenth century, the bore of the horn already diverged into two opposing categories: a wide bore especially characteristic of the Germans, and a narrow bore especially characteristic of the French. The wide bore tends to a mellow power; the narrow bore tends to a poetic colourfulness. But the ideal of tone at which the player aims (influenced as he ordinarily is by his own national tradition) may have at least as much effect upon the results produced. Typical French horn playing sounds rather thin to those preferring the German ideal, and typical German horn playing sounds rather coarse to those preferring the French ideal. The Austrians appear to have reached an attractive compromise. But as always, the only true criterion is suiting the tone and the technique to the idiom and the music. We need, perhaps, both extremes of horn quality.

The narrow-bore French horn has now clearly lost the battle to the wide-bore German horn. But the standard of horn playing seems to remain as high as its variety; and there is only one current fashion (favoured especially in France and in Russia) which appears, on musical grounds, to be quite contrary to anything within the natural disposition of the horn. This is the very prominent use of vibrato, which has just the same incongruity, and, I think, distastefulness, as a prominent tremulant on the organ. This does not mean that vibrato could not be used effectively on the horn if that were what the composer deliberately wished into his music. It does mean that vibrato is a very undesirable effect indeed in classical or romantic horn parts composed for the natural dignity and poetical colourfulness of the horn as traditionally understood.

Like the serpent, the horn can 'force' its lower notes downwards to a remarkable extent (as much as a fourth at times). There are no horns basically of higher than alto register, though their extensive upper compass enables them to climb remarkably high in practice. The lower horns would rank as bass instruments but for the fact that their bottom registers lack true bass sonority and power, thus placing them for practical purposes in the baritone class. The middle register is particularly characteristic, and often acts as a most effective orchestral cement, as when a horn holds a long internal 'pedal' around which other instruments weave a shifting web of harmony. This is also an excellent register for horn solos. There are no other instrumental sounds quite so glowing as well-played horns.

The Family of Cornets

The CORNET family has the following general characteristics: very variable compass (up to five octaves as a quite exceptional stunt); rather narrow mainly conical bore; moderate mouthpiece; moderate bell. Tone very flexible and moderately brilliant.

The *cornet* proper of modern usage (cornet-à-pistons, cornopean, etc.) was developed early in the nineteenth century on the basis of the simple French posthorn; it has been used in various tonalities, of which the most important are now *b* flat and *a*. Its bore is partly wider than that of a modern trumpet; and it includes more of a conical taper. These factors make it more easy to play; it has, in clever hands, a quite astonishing agility. Since its tone (especially if it is played with a trumpet mouthpiece) has rather similar qualities, it has been much used as a substitute, in which role it is tonally inferior. In its own right, however, it has more valuable attributes.

Lower cornets have been built, but have never been of serious importance.

The Family of Trombones

The TROMBONE family has the following general characteristics: fundamental usable only in smaller sizes and shorter positions of the slide; very roughly three-octave compass; rather narrow cylindrical bore; mouthpiece moderate; bell moderate. Tone rich and powerful.[1]

There has existed a complete family of soprano, alto, tenor, bass and contra-bass slide trombones. Since the early trombones (*sackbuts*) of the late Renaissance and early Baroque periods often appear in chamber music together with other single instruments of small or moderate power, it is clear that their style of playing, at least under these circumstances, was more delicate and restrained than that most commonly associated with our orchestral trombones today.

In modern use, the soprano trombone is obsolete, and the alto trombone a rarity. The *B* flat tenor trombone is a standard instrument, and its performers now cultivate such ability in its higher registers that they can take most alto trombone parts (often, for example in Beethoven, quite high) in their stride. In order to facilitate the use of these higher registers, a tendency set in to diminish the bore of the tenor trombone, and consequently the fullness of

[1] Plates 30, 34.

tone so valuable to it in its modern functions. But this tendency was fortunately held in check. It might be thought desirable to revive the alto trombone in *e* flat. The *B* flat tenor, however, is thoroughly comfortable up to *b'* flat, or *c"*. It is just viable for about a fourth higher; but so high as this, a trumpet can take over its work with more satisfactory effect.

There is also a standard bass trombone in *F* (or, in England, *G*). The bore is wider, and the mouthpiece and the bell are larger, to favour depth and solidity of tone.

But the arrangement now mainly established in the orchestra is to use a form of double trombone comparable to the double horn. Both in the rather lighter form of the tenor trombone, and in the rather heavier form of the bass trombone, the standard instrument is in B flat with F attachment: i.e., there is *B* flat tubing to which further tubing can be added by a rotary valve, controlled by the left thumb, when the combined lengths give an instrument in *F*. In its heavier form, as a bass trombone, this double instrument can be further extended downwards by a slide which can be pulled out to lower *F* to *E*. But the *F* attachment so lengthens the tubing that the seventh (longest) position of the slide cannot be reached while it is in use. The contra-bass trombone was introduced into the modern orchestra by Wagner; it is a fine instrument in *C,* or *B,* flat, but so seldom written for that players cannot ordinarily afford to cultivate it. The bass of trombone harmony is often, though not quite homogeneously, supplied by bass tuba (bugle) instruments.

The slide trombones have an electric effect in the orchestra when boldly handled. In addition, they can create an atmosphere of majesty, both in full harmony by themselves, and when used to sustain other departments of the orchestra.

There are also *valve trombones*, of which Wagner's bass trumpet has been called one, but wrongly; it has the true trumpet bell.

The Family of Trumpets[1]

The TRUMPET is a close relative of the trombone, both possessing mainly cylindrical tubes of not very different bore. But the most aristocratic members of the trumpet family (namely, the early long trumpets) stand out both from the trombones and from the more plebeian members of their own family (namely, the modern short

[1] Plates 8–10, 33.

trumpets). Indeed, were it not for the fact that these two branches of the trumpet family merge at their boundaries, their difference being only one degree, it would be necessary to treat them here as separate families, so considerable is that difference at the two extremes. Finally, the modern short trumpet is now even tending to lose its mainly cylindrical shape, in favour of a largely tapered one, thus approximating to its upstart and formidably agile rival, the cornet. But all trumpets have the following characteristics in some degree: compass varying from less than three to more than four octaves; more or less narrow and cylindrical bore; more or less small and angular mouthpiece; more or less flaring bell; colourful and brilliant tone.

As with the horn, three main stages can be discerned in the orchestral history of the trumpet.

Orchestras of the later Baroque period normally employed a long *natural trumpet* of bent tubing to the total extent of about 7 feet, that being about the length required for the standard tonality of *D*. An 8-foot *C* trumpet was the early Baroque standard, and also remained in use; and there were shorter *E* flat and *F* trumpets (there is little evidence for a *G* trumpet before the nineteenth century). Various further tonalities (down to *A,* at lowest) were obtainable by crooks. But by far the most characteristic early long trumpet is that in *D*, which, possessing as it does an unusually long and narrow tube, is capable of an exceptionally extended upper range to its twenty-first harmonic, namely, *f'''*, four octaves and a minor third above its fundamental, and even to the twenty-fourth in rare instances (e.g. one by Michael Haydn). The fundamental is not feasible in practice; but from its octave, the second harmonic, upwards, the tone is excellent.

It is thought that the same player would never normally have been expected to cover the entire long (*D*) trumpet range. For very high trumpet parts, a fairly shallow mouthpiece perhaps facilitated the production of the extreme upper notes: in which aspect the trumpet had a specialized technique (only attainable by constant practice and unusual skill, which is harder to maintain if the lips are also used for lower notes). Lower parts were played on the same instrument with different technique. The parts (not the instruments) might be called Clarino; Quinta; Principale; Alto; Vulgano; Basso, etc. Tromba refers to the instrument.

The art of clarino playing was already declining in Mozart's time, towards the end of the eighteenth century. For a time, trumpet parts became comparatively simple, being limited to the lower register, where the natural harmonics do not lie so close together. To replace their difficult and now abandoned clarino register, a curious expedient was evolved: the easy, brilliant upper or clarino register of the clarinet (literally though misleadingly 'little trumpet'), then newly establishing itself in the orchestra, was used instead. It was soon found that the clarinet is happiest as a clarinet, while true trumpet tone can only be had from trumpets: which has not, however, prevented similar evasions in our own day, as when we misguidedly give Bach's trumpet parts to an E flat clarinet or a piccolo heckelphone.

The second main phase of trumpet history came with the early nineteenth-century addition of valves to the long trumpet (producing the *valve trumpet*). *Slide trumpets*, already ancient in Bach's time, had a considerable nineteenth-century vogue in England; but the valve mechanism won. Either method enables the gaps in the natural trumpet's scale to be satisfactorily filled. This was all to the good; but at the same time a further tendency set in which had less desirable results. To make the instrument easier to play, its standard length was shortened, and its fundamental pitch consequently raised. For a time, *F*, *G* or *A* flat, with crooks for *E* flat, *D* and *C* (yet lower by combining crooks) obtained; in the second half of the nineteenth century, the use of crooks went out of fashion, most orchestral players using the *F* trumpet uncrooked, and transposing their parts at sight where necessary.

Finally, early in the twentieth century, the *F* and *E* flat trumpets (the latter chiefly a military-band instrument) disappeared in turn, in favour of a yet shorter and higher-pitched trumpet in *B* flat or *A* (or both combined by a 'quick-change' valve), or often, even in *c*: instruments little over half the length of the early long trumpet in *D*. Of course, standing nearly an octave higher, they can play Bach, Handel and other high trumpet parts relatively easily, using their lower and middle registers. In fact, for Bach parts trumpets in *d* or even (for the celebrated and formidably lofty Second Brandenburg part) in *f* are now ordinarily used: which eases matters still further ('High D' and 'High F').

But what is gained in ease is unfortunately lost in quality. For as we have seen, it is precisely the long, narrow tube of the early trumpet which favours very high harmonics, not only as high notes, but also as brilliance and colourfulness of tone. To play high parts, the long trumpet must use its highest register, and this is difficult in the extreme. But it is by no means impossible. And the reward in sheer brilliance of tone is worth the effort.

The modern short trumpet, even in its high forms, is not to be belittled when the composer has specifically written to exploit its own virtues, as Rimsky-Korsakov, for example, was fond of doing (though not quite up to the modern extreme of a piccolo trumpet in b' flat, which is so short as to be in danger of sinking towards two-octave compass and tone quality, being a little shrill and bodiless). These virtues are great agility and certainty, coupled with a very excellent colourfulness and brilliance of tone. But they do not compensate for the lost advantages of the early long trumpet in music written for that instrument.

For this reason, repeated attempts have been made to recapture the assets without too many of the liabilities of the older instrument. One such attempt was Kosleck's so-called Bach trumpet in A (improved by Morrow), a fifth above the real Bach trumpet, and considerably more colourful and brilliant than the modern short trumpet, though less so than the early long trumpet, as might be expected from its intermediate position between the two. Except for its two valves, it is picturesquely made straight, instead of being bent on itself like an ordinary trumpet: but it is no more than a halfway compromise. A similar but shorter and higher Bach trumpet in d is also used: but this, though markedly brighter than the cornet-like modern short trumpet now fashionable, is itself a short instrument, lacking the noble qualities which only the long, narrow bore of the long trumpet brings.

Some years afterwards, true long D trumpets on the original pattern, with the justifiable addition of two valves for correcting the intonation, were reintroduced by Menke, together with an F trumpet for the Second Brandenburg; but without, unfortunately, being taken up. The obstacle was less the difficulty of the high clarino technique (which modern players have shown that they can master) than the economic problem of providing a livelihood for trumpeters specializing, as of old, on that technique. Nevertheless, the current fashion for Baroque music and Baroque-style performances is opening up new possibilities.

In 1961, an excellent narrow-bore trumpet at full Baroque length, made by Helmut Finke after the researches of Otto Steinkopf, was introduced by the trumpeter Walter Holy of the Cappella Coloniensis; it has side holes ingeniously placed which enable its off-pitch harmonies to be played in tune. This set off a new revival of interest. Among instruments in current use are a coiled Baroque *Jägertrompete* in C (by Finke and Steinkopf); a classical Baroque long trumpet in D with one double bend (by Adolf Egger in co-operation with the American trumpeter Edward Tarr; a more exact replica was next brought out by Meinl and Lauber in co-operation with Edward Tarr) and a short B flat trumpet with four valves introduced by Selmer and modified by others (including Egger and Tarr) which is the commonest in present practice for Baroque purposes.

It is to be hoped that the revival of the long Baroque trumpet, now so far advanced, will be taken up more widely. Edward Tarr is one of the most brilliant and musianly (as well as knowledgeable) among a small number of really excellent performers who are working to this end.

Meanwhile, the modern short trumpets, though not so brilliant as the true long trumpets, remain by far the most brilliant instruments in the symphonic orchestra, through which they can ring with magnificently stirring and exalted effect. They have, indeed, a more powerful kind of brilliance than the old long trumpets, whose tone is of a lighter character. Having all the advantages of agility and certainty, the modern trumpets can play freely in melody throughout their compass; and when supported by their near kith and kin, the slide trombones, they yield full harmony of splendid character and brightness.

CHAPTER II

THE HUMAN VOICE

Singing: a combination of two processes

The HUMAN VOICE, as we have seen, is a reed instrument; unless, indeed, you are whispering or whistling, in which case you do not use the vocal cords.

When you whistle, and also when you vocalize (sing wordlessly on a vowel or near-vowel sound) or hum (vocalize nasally with the mouth shut) you produce melody, but you do not enunciate. These practices, however, are not musically very important (vocalization is occasionally used in serious music). What is musically important is song, which is a combination of melody with enunciation.

The apparatus of vocal melody and the apparatus of verbal enunciation, though they are connected, are partially distinct. It will be simplest to take verbal enunciation first.

How language is enunciated

Language is made up of two chief classes of sound: consonants and vowels. A consonant is, roughly, the explosive sound with which a vowel is attacked, or concluded. For example you may start or end a vowel by bringing your tongue against your teeth, thus giving a 'dental' start or finish, such as D or T; or you may close the throat, thus interposing a 'guttural', such as G or K. There are also semi-vowels like L or M, which can be continued without leading to or following a true vowel sound (you can vocalize on L and hum on M).

Vowel sounds are continuous sounds into which two definite pitches enter, though you do not stop to think of them as such. The two pitches are produced in the two parts of a resonating chamber consisting of your mouth and throat, the relative sizes and openings of which you control by changing the position of the tongue and lips. The two pitches thus produced evoke, in turn, their own different upper harmonics; and the whole elaborate compound makes up one or other of the familiar vowel sounds. For example, you open your lips and raise your tongue, and 'ee' emerges; or you protrude and nearly close your lips, and 'oo' emerges.

If you adopt like positions, but merely breathe without setting your vocal cords in motion, you enunciate like vowels, but at a whisper. The whole of speech is possible at a whisper, thus showing that enunciation is controlled in the mouth, and not in the vocal cords, which merely reinforce it.

Melody can also be produced and controlled in the mouth, as in whistling. But melody combined with enunciation cannot be so produced: both the vocal cords and the control of the mouth are needed: the former to contribute the melody, and the latter to contribute the enunciation. Try 'singing' without the vocal cords, i.e. at a whisper: you can produce 'ee' on high notes and 'ah' on low notes; but not the other way about.

How vocal melody is produced

The pitch of the vocal cords can be varied at will, within a compass which generally extends over about two octaves, by varying their tension, and the pressure of air brought to bear on them. The necessary adjustments are involuntary, but can be improved by practice. This is part of what is called voice training. A further part is learning the best way of controlling the breath needed to excite the vocal cords, and incidentally to sustain life. Since a long vocal phrase may considerably exceed the duration of an ordinary breath, and, if loud and high, requires unusual volume and pressure, breathing must be exceptionally controlled and steady.

The quality of the voice, like that of other instruments, is governed by the upper harmonics, presented in this case by the vocal cords, and reinforced by the throat and head cavities. Both factors are largely determined by sex, age and personal idiosyncrasies; but within these limits, they can be controlled at will, and this control, too, can be improved by training.

Voice training is of an unknown antiquity. Medieval and Renaissance choirs were expected to sing with virtuoso accuracy and perfection. From the second half of the sixteenth century, we already have clear instructions for singing in the true *bel canto* technique. In the Baroque seventeenth and eighteenth centuries, voice training became almost an obsession: many obviously went to the opera to enjoy not so much the drama, or even the music, as the vocal acrobatics. In the romantic nineteenth century, operatic reforms, culminating in Wagner, necessitated a style of singing declamatory enough to match the emotional tension, and powerful enough to match the massive orchestration, of the new music-drama. This, too, was triumphantly achieved, though at some cost to pure *bel canto*.

Like most techniques, trained voice-production is capable of misuse. Folk songs can be hopelessly falsified by an inappropriate sophistication, which makes the song sound trivial, and the singer insincere. The sort of tone at which he has become an adept is quite unfitted for the purpose; and in acquiring it, he has overlaid his unaffected voice. A born folk singer, on the other hand, has his own skill, suited by nature and cultivation for his own folk purposes.

Our problem today with the vocal music of earlier centuries is not our usual one of adapting an excellent modern technique to the different requirements of the older styles. It is the special problem of recovering a consummate technique from a severe decline. The art of virtuoso singing is not currently in so sound a condition as it was even a generation ago. As we listen to the technically primitive gramophone recordings made on crude apparatus by the great singers of the beginning of the twentieth century (often in old age after their voices had long passed their best) we cannot help realizing how serious our loss in this repect has been. Only the very rare best singers of the present time can approach the effortless flow and prodigious accuracy which were by no means uncommon at that comparatively recent period, and which were the subject of innumerable ear-witness accounts at earlier periods. Most modern singers simply cannot do some of the things the older singers are known to have been able to do. The tradition is no longer fully with us.

There is only one fundamental tradition of great singing as the West understands it. This is the grand Italian tradition. All other good styles of singing have been based on it. The most important elements in it are a very forward voice-production, and a strong admixture of what singing-teachers call the chest voice, not only in the low notes but through the whole register. The forward production gives a carrying-power and an incisiveness beyond anything which mere forcing can achieve. The admixture of chest voice gives a richness and colour to the lower notes and a power and accuracy to the upper notes of which many modern singers have no real conception. Every note can be placed exactly in focus; and it is voice-placing such as this which reaches easily to the back of the largest hall through the largest orchestra. It does not sound particularly loud either from far away or from near by; but it carries and it cuts through clean and clear, as very little modern singing does. The vibrations are not exceptionally massive; they are exceptionally free, and that is the secret of good and telling tone on any instrument, the voice included. Only a few teachers of singing are in touch with this traditional technique at the present time, and there was some danger of its dying out. But recently there have been signs of a recovery, and admirable work is now being done to improve the situation.

The chest voice and the head voice must be capable of being joined very smoothly where they overlap. But in true *bel canto*, the lower notes are and should be chested very much more strongly than the present fashion allows; and this is one of the most necessary vocal reforms. The *castrato* voice, carrying into adult life a male treble voice of mature power and extraordinary beauty, can be heard on recordings made in 1904 by Alessandro Moreschi, probably not a particularly good specimen, but impressive all the same. The voice is not now available or in prospect. Our best modern substitute is usually a female soprano or mezzo-soprano or contralto, as required; or a strong male countertenor if one is available (see below); or sometimes a high tenor. The alternative of transposing castrato parts down an octave is musically very unsatisfactory.

How enunciation and melody are combined

Since, broadly, enunciation is controlled in the mouth, and melody and timbre in the throat, the judicious singer can range over his entire compass, and produce his utmost range of tone quality, without obliterating his words.

True, he must be at pains to sound his consonants effectively; but this has the added advantage of imparting articulation to what might otherwise be too uninterrupted a flow of vowel tone. As it is, Italian song always sounds comparatively soft, whereas German sounds comparatively rugged.

Again, the singer must sound his vowels from the best possible position of mouth and tongue; but this is usually the best position for singing them. Some nasal vowel sounds (conspicuous in sung French) are always a trifle acid. Worse, some vowels need formative harmonics not presented by certain notes in the human (especially the female) compass: in that event, enunciation and melody cannot be reconciled; and it is enunciation which goes to the wall, the vowel being inevitably falsified in the act of pitching the note. But for the most part, so far from conflicting, enunciation and melody enhance each other in a true marriage of the separate arts of poetry and music.

And what a marriage! We sometimes call music, metaphorically, a language. But poetry is literally language, with all the verbal power of narrating and describing, of evoking associations and visual images, of bringing before the mind a whole dramatic situation. Combine with this the musical power of conjuring up a mood and playing upon it, and you have, at worst, the most incongruous, but at best the most imaginative, of all artistic alliances.

Song may be unaccompanied, like most true folk song; or set to a mere supporting tissue of simple harmony. It may trace one from among a network of contrapuntal melodies, the rest of which are instrumental, as often in Elizabethan settings or Bach arias. It may carry the whole without necessary instrumental support, as in Palestrina; or with it, as in an oratorio. It may be matched with a complex, independent lute or harpsichord or piano part. It may be brought as Mahler brought it, into a great symphonic pattern. And finally, it may join with the drama, and sometimes with the dance as well: it may culminate in opera. In all these situations, it remains a colourful and satisfying instrument.

Modern uses of the voice will be found discussed towards the end of Chapter 17 below.

The Family of Human Voices

The family of human voices has four main members, two female and two male; their average compass being: *soprano*, *b* flat to *a″* or *b″* flat; *contralto*, *e* or *f* to *e″* or a little higher; *tenor*, *c* to about *b′* flat; *bass*, about *E* to about *e′*.

These limits are considerably exceeded in exceptional and highly trained voices. A *coloratura soprano* must ascend, with the utmost agility, to *f'''*, and higher notes have been attained. A fine *dramatic soprano* must reach *c'''* with full power, as well as possessing that ringing yet expressive timbre which is the mark of true soprano quality; a *lyric soprano* has a lighter version of the same quality. A *boy soprano* will cover about *a* to *a''*, with a certain cool innocence of timbre. A *mezzo-soprano* can reach almost as high as a dramatic soprano; but her most effective register (tessitura) lies rather lower, and her quality falls midway between soprano and contralto quality. It can be one of the most beautiful of vocal timbres. The true contralto quality is deep, rich and resonant, in complete contrast to the bright soprano timbre; indeed, it includes some of the most sombre of vocal tones, and can be peculiarly effective in opera. But it must be kept rather open and forward, and very well chested at the bottom, or it may tend to get too cavernous and fruity.

Contraltos are sometimes called altos; but *alto* properly means a male cathedral alto: this is a natural tenor or bass who has cultivated the art of using only part of his vocal cords, and of thus singing harmonics in a *falsetto* alto register from about *f'* to *c''*. A counter-tenor is a normal male alto of fine solo quality, such as was long neglected but has now been revived.

A fine operatic *tenore robusto* or *Heldentenor* (hero tenor) must reach *c''* with sureness and power, and his voice must have a special shimmering ring. A *lyric tenor* has a lighter quality. A *baritone* lies between a tenor and a bass, ranging from about *A* flat to perhaps *a'* flat. A *basso cantante* is a bass who excels in his high register, and tends to a light quality; a *bass-baritone* is one who has cultivated his high register and his low register equally, and has the necessary weight for such an operatic part as Wagner's Wotan; a *basso profundo* has an exceptionally fine and deep low register, and a massive quality; a *contra-basso* is that specialized bass found in Russia, capable of descending to the astonishing pitch of *F,*.

CHAPTER 12

THE ORGAN

The organ: many instruments mechanically combined

The organ is many instruments in one. In order to bring these many instruments within reach of a single player, machinery of considerable complexity is necessary, and this interferes in some degree with his direct control of expression. Nevertheless, effects are possible which no other means can offer; and when well designed and handled, the organ can be a magnificent instrument.

In essentials, an organ is a set of pipes, an apparatus for supplying wind under pressure, and a means of joining one with the other as required. The Romans and Byzantines had a rather elaborate form of organ (the *hydraulus*), with several sets of pipes; an apparatus for steadying the wind supply by water pressure; and a keyboard for joining the required pipes to the wind supply. The keyboard later disappeared, to be replaced by a cruder system of sliders; but reappeared in the twelfth century. The *pneumatic* organ as we know it was also known to antiquity.

The organ was of great importance in the Middle Ages, whether as a large and important *church organ*, in one case with as many as ten pipes to each note (this example needed seventy men to work the bellows); or as a small hand instrument (the *portative organ*), easily carried by a strap across the shoulder, and played with one hand while the other worked the bellows.[1] The *positive organ* was larger and normally left in position rather than carried; but it was transportable at need. The larger medieval organs were for mechanical reasons quite incapable of subtlety, and were valued mainly on account of their prodigious power and sheer raucous volume.

During the Renaissance, the portative declined in fashion. Its place was taken by the *chamber organ*, i.e. positive (a pipe organ about the size of a large bureau, or somewhat larger, and usually

[1] Plates 4, 9, 11.

149

with one or two sets of stopped wooden flue pipes of sweet soft tone, but sometimes with several sets of pipes of differing tones); and the *regals* (a beautifully snarling little reed organ with beating reeds as in the clarinet, but tiny pipes often hardly long enough to affect the pitch, though they affect the tone quality by picking out some high harmonics).

The harmonium

The regals, a more powerful instrument than its small size might suggest (at its smallest it was no larger than the tiny portative), is the forerunner of a not wholly satisfactory modern instrument, the HARMONIUM, with its smaller and less pretentious relatives, the *accordion* and *concertina*. But these three latter have 'free' instead of 'beating' reeds (closing the air-passage incompletely instead of completely); and no pipes.

The harmonium, and its softer variant, the *American organ* (which sucks air in, instead of blowing it out), have registers of different tone quality, contrived by different shapes and thicknesses of the tongues. The accordion may have a keyboard and studs for sounding the notes required; the concertina has studs alone, but it is the more virtuoso instrument. In both, the bellows are worked by the hands, while the fingers find the notes. These are excellent instruments in capable hands. The *mouth organ* is, in effect, a tiny accordion played with the breath, and can be made much more artistic than might be supposed.

The chamber organ

To return to the Renaissance: the portative, the chamber organ and the regals were alike in serving, on the whole, secular rather than religious purposes. When the Renaissance merged into the Baroque, the chamber organ became of still more importance. Throughout the seventeenth and eighteenth centuries, it stood in many homes. It was probably almost as common an accompanying instrument in seventeenth-century England as the harpsichord or the lute, not, it is true, for music in the lighter vein, but for serious fantasies, motets and the like.

Early in the eighteenth century, Handel wrote some fine concertos for the organ, which are very adequately served by a chamber organ or by a not very elaborate or powerful chamber organ, or a small Baroque church organ. Not every modern organ has stops of quite the right forward attack and transparent colouring to blend well with a rather small chamber orchestra such as Handel used. Haydn wrote a concerto, and Mozart wrote seventeen sonatas for the organ;[1] but in their day (the latter eighteenth century) the chamber organ, with its secular repertoire, had already begun to pass out of fashion. Dolmetsch revived it; and a very pleasing instrument it is. In recent years, it has taken its place again as one of the necessary instruments for a satisfactory performance of the earlier schools of music.

The medieval church organ

The great monastic *church organ* of the Middle Ages had multiple sets or 'ranks' of pipes, but no means of playing the ranks separately. If a key was pushed down, all the pipes attached to it came into operation. That was one main reason why the action was so heavy; the combined air-pressure built up a tremendous resistance to be overcome. The pipes attached to each key might include pipes of different scaling and proportions and perhaps material, giving different tone-colourings; they might also include pipes at a different pitch from the note in question, e.g. at the octave or double-octave; at a fifth plus one or more octaves ('quint'); at a third plus one or more octaves ('tierce'). The effect of these different pitches is to reinforce the upper harmonics corresponding to them: a quint rank will reinforce the third harmonic; a tierce rank will reinforce the fifth harmonic (see Fig. 18 on p. 14). Such ranks are called 'mixtures', and add very greatly to the colourfulness of any organ tone in which they take part. By an effort of attention we can quite easily hear them as separate notes in their own right, but we ordinarily hear them (like the upper harmonics which they reinforce) only as tone-colouring. The effect can be startlingly fiery.

The Renaissance church organ

By the fourteenth century, multiple keyboards (including a pedal board) were added to multiple ranks of pipes, as a means of playing

[1] Geiringer, *Musical Instruments*, p. 219.

M

on the different ranks not only in one vast and glorious mixture, but separately for distinct effects of tone-colouring. By the fifteenth century, there were added multiple stops, i.e. systems by which air can be directed at will into any desired selection from the pipes attached by a given key, thus giving much greater control over distinct effects. The variety of the ranks was also greatly developed. Some pipes, being narrow for their lengths, are rich in high harmonics, and yield a brilliant sound. Others, being wide for their lengths, are weak in high harmonics, and yield a veiled sound. If the exit to the pipe is stopped, the pitch drops an octave. If the exciting tone is made to overblow, the pitch rises to the second harmonic (i.e. the octave) in an open pipe, but to the third harmonic (i.e. the twelfth, or octave plus a fifth) in a stopped pipe. If the exciting tone is an edge tone (flue pipes) there tends to be less colourfulness caused by high harmonics than if the exciting tone is a reed tone (reed pipes, including regals with their very short resonating pipes). Reed pipes are generally conical; if they are made cylindrical, the pitch drops an octave. A number of such varied ranks might be attached to the keys of each keyboard; and devices (known as 'couplers') were also developed by which keyboards can be linked so that notes played on one will also operate the corresponding notes on another.

Organs of this refinement and complexity were first developed in North Germany; and Cecil Clutton, a great English expert on early organs, considers that by the late fifteenth century they were so far in advance of their time there that they have the essential character of Baroque rather than of Renaissance organs.[1] The typical Renaissance church organ was much simpler, and to judge from a fascinating tape-recording brought by Mr Clutton to a past meeting of the Royal Musical Association in London, much fiercer. The difference was in the 'voicing', which is a term for the fine adjustment of the exciting tone to produce the kind of attack desired. Forward voicing yields a comparatively explosive attack which incidentally favours high harmonics and fiery tone-colouring; mild voicing yields a comparatively reticent attack which moderates the high harmonics and the tone-colouring. This particular organ, a very rare survivor of Italian Renaissance work, had such forward voicing that it nearly

[1] Cecil Clutton, Ch. II, 'The Organ', in the symposium *Musical Instruments*, ed. Anthony C. Baines, London 1961, pp. 6off.

shot you out of the room. I have never in all my life heard anything more magnificent. It was certainly lacking in refinement; but it compensated for this by such a character and virility that it gave one new ideas about the extraordinary versatility and abounding potentialities of this most variable of instruments.

Quite such fierceness was excessive for average musical purposes. The organ reached its highest stage of development not in this Renaissance form (which must resemble the crude medieval form in this respect, and indeed inclines me to a more favourable view of what that crudity must have sounded like) but in the next stage, the Baroque organ proper.

The Baroque church organ

During the seventeenth century, and the first part of the eighteenth century, the organ received, besides several improvements in the wind-supplying apparatus, a number of new registers, notably (eighteenth century) narrow open flue pipes to simulate string tone. The tremolo stop (agitating the wind supply so as to give a wavy effect, very susceptible of abuse) and the swell (a shuttered box enclosing part of the organ, and permitting crescendos and diminuendos when opened and shut, as in some eighteenth-century harpsichords) were added; and couplers linking different registers were much elaborated. Wind pressure remained very low. The voicing was moderately forward, giving a much more virile attack than subsequently, though much less fierce than in at least some Renaissance organs. 'Mixtures' remained numerous and of strong tone-colouring.

There were many varieties of Baroque organ at different times and places. The best of them were about as good as an organ needs to be, with all the character and expressiveness a musician could desire. They are now in high fashion again, and excellent replicas are being built.

The modern organ

In the course of subsequent development, two tendencies set in, which reached their peak in the nineteenth-century organ. Many registers were included which did not greatly differ, but were rather intended to blend imperceptibly than to contrast decisively. And wind pressure was increased to meet new tastes and new demands on the air supply, until the action of the keys, when many stops were brought on, became almost as heavy and laborious as it had been in the strenuous medieval days; for the valve which lets air into the pipe must always be pressed open against the air pressure within; and the greater the pressure, the greater the resistance of the key.

To meet this latter difficulty (becoming really acute in the course of the nineteenth century when motors took the place of manpower for supplying air pressure, which could thus be raised beyond all precedent), an action was devised in which most of the work of opening the valve is also done by machinery, either pneumatic or electric, or a combination of the two. Of these, the most mechanically successful is no doubt the electric, which can be very light, and is instantaneous, while the console (keyboards and register controls) can be placed quite separately from the organ itself, being connected with it merely by electric cables: whence the peculiar freedom enjoyed by players of cinema organs, whose console became a species of electric lift. But the arrangement has other and more solid advantages, as when it is desired to join a modern organ with an orchestra, and the player and his console can be placed conveniently among the other players, where he can see the conductor easily. But high wind pressure had greatly changed the tone. Much of the old virility had gone, and a more mechanical character been substituted.

The nineteenth and twentieth centuries have also brought a number of other mechanical developments. One of the most ingenious is a system of combination pistons by which advance preparations can be made for blending several registers, which can then be brought into simultaneous operation at the touch of a single control. Or there is the double touch: press the key normally, and you sound a comparatively reticent register by means of an electric contact of the normal sort; press rather harder, and you make a second electric contact, bringing in another and louder register. Many good effects are thus possible, including a sudden accent on a single note; however, the effect, like so many mechanical substitutes for direct control of expression, is certainly a little out of character on this noble instrument. There are also special pistons for producing a sforzando accent; as well as a crescendo pedal operating a roller for bringing in and taking out a graded series of stops, much as a harpsichordist increases volume by bringing in more stops, and decreases it by taking them off again.

French organists and organ builders have tended to subordinate the solid, comparatively uncoloured diapason qualities to more dramatic colourings. In Germany, and on the whole in England, the diapason is still, and I think preferably, treated as the foundation. A certain dignified impersonality is in the nature of the instrument, and is not to be despised, still less exchanged for over-mechanical effects or freakish registration.

There is no 'sustaining pedal' on the organ, but none is needed. The foot (pedal) keyboard can always hold a long note or two at will, to bind the harmony together (this is the origin of the term 'pedal point', or 'organ point'). In general organ tone is more likely to be too much sustained than too little. No direct accentuation being natural to the instrument, phrasing on the organ, even more than on other instruments, depends on the minute but indispensable silences between one phrase and another: a good finger legato must, and can be, learnt; but its misuse is fatal. And it is remarkable how well a good organist can give the musical illusion of accentuation merely by leaving a silence of articulation before the note to which he wants to give this kind of prominence.

So long as organ keys were not power-assisted, not needing to be so because the wind pressure was kept within modest bounds, the player, by striking the key more smartly, could cause the pallet (air valve) to open more swiftly, so that the pipe responded more promptly, and a slight but appreciable accent resulted. This slight yet valuable resource was lost when high wind pressure and power-assisted actions (especially electric actions) became the rule. Thus the organ, always a comparatively impersonal instrument, has become more impersonal than it was when J. S. Bach played it and composed for it: while we have also tended to lose the old clear contrasts of tone in our new smoothly matched and graded registers. For these reasons, though a modern organ can render Bach finely when it includes suitable stops, and (yet more important) is played with understanding of the style, there has nevertheless been a determined attempt in Germany and America to restore the classical church organ as Bach knew it and loved it. Whatever their respective merits, the Baroque organ and the modern organ are very different instruments. Some large organs are now being built, however, to include some sections suited to romantic organ music, and others of a Baroque character suited to classical and pre-classical organ music.

The organist has certain special responsibilities from the special resources at his command. Even when the composer indicates his wishes in the matter of registration, organs differ so much that it really rests with the organist to use his judgement. This is much as if a symphonist left his orchestration to the conductor.

However, the worst heresy that can infect an organist is the ambition literally to imitate an orchestra. It is in keeping with the best traditions to give the organ a wide range of registers, and even to refer to them by their nearest equivalents, as geigen (violin), vox humana (human voice), oboe, trumpet and the rest. But to twist what should be a living instrument into a mechanized imitation of something it can never truly resemble is mere degradation.

Both among organ builders and among organists (often working in the closest co-operation) there has been an effective rebellion against the degradation to which the organ was largely being submitted a generation or two ago. It is hardly too much to say that the organ has been rescued and restored to its rightful place as not merely an impressive piece of machinery but an expressive one. For all its immense power and variety, the 'mighty Wurlitzer', for example, was a perfectly deadly affair, no longer much with us and in no way to be lamented. The new Wurlitzers are not pipe organs at all, but electrophonic organs: now a large and important family, to which attention will be given in a later chapter.

CHAPTER 13

PERCUSSION

How percussion is used in music

There is a wide variety of percussion instruments. Some yield a fluctuating fundamental, and upper harmonics too irregular to reinforce it to our ear or perception: the result is noise of no definite pitch. Others yield a sufficiently stable fundamental and a sufficiently regular harmonic series to result in tone of more or less definite pitch But both kinds have their uses in bringing out rhythms, colouring the tone, or even simply adding to the volume of sound.

In the symphonic orchestra, considerable restraint has been usual with the noisier percussion; but it is very valuable. Drums, cymbals, gongs and the like are capable of a tremendous crescendo from quiet beginnings to a powerful climax. Or they may be brought in at the last moment to bring already heated emotions to the boil: a single brilliant clash of the cymbals will often do as much. Soft drum-beats, again, may be heard throbbing through a lightly scored passage, or even playing fragments of melody unaccompanied. Barbaric splendour is by no means the only function of the percussion: indeed, the only percussion instruments to hold a classical position in the orchestra were the kettledrums, which can be tuned to a choice of notes definite in pitch, and beautifully musical in tone.

In music without harmony, there is less danger of obscuring the tonality by including overmuch percussion. Hindu orchestras have been brought to Europe and America, in which a leading part is taken by complete sets of drums, bowls, bells, clappers and the like, some beautifully clear in tone and definite in pitch; others less so, or not at all. An Oriental drummer's judgement and sheer manual dexterity may equal those of a superb concert pianist. Many native orchestras consist of percussion instruments alone, in a combination of different tone qualities and rhythms so intricate as to effect what in Western music we should call counterpoint. The finesse, the virtuosity and the musicianship of such performances are among the many features of Oriental music which in recent years have become acclimatized into Western music. *Avant-garde* composers not interested in traditional harmony are exploiting every sort of percussion with the greatest scope and skill.

Membrane percussion

The KETTLEDRUM[1] is now usually employed in sets of three, which may be tuned to a choice of three notes, normally ranging from about E to g (but four kettledrums is by no means extreme). The tuning can be changed during the course of a composition, provided the drummer is left a few bars' rest in which to make the change. Since composers are not always as considerate as they might be, the drummer may at times be seen very rapidly at work making the necessary adjustments in the tension of his vellum, by tightening or loosening the screws which hold its outer hoop in position. Numerous devices have been patented for quick changes of tuning by a single screw (*machine drum*) or by means of the feet (*pedal drum*), the best of which are reasonably satisfactory. Pedal drums, though not ideal either for tone or for intonation, are now becoming standard; they have been much improved.

The pitch of the kettledrum does not only depend on the tension of the vellum, but also on the diameter of the drum. Standard diameters are 29 in., 26 in., and 23 in. or thereabouts, though 30 in. and 19 in. would not be too extreme for a low *D* or a high *g* or *a*. (Schubert and Mendelssohn asked for *f* sharp: Elgar for *g*; and even higher notes are not unknown.) The shape of the shell affects the internal reflection of sound vibrations and the resonance of the contained air very greatly, as can be heard in various designs favoured by different makers and players.

The quality of the tone also depends on the fineness and crucial uniformity of the vellum – what a tympanist will call a 'good head'. It is also affected by the material used for covering the stick heads. Piano felt soft or hard is standard, but composers (e.g. Berlioz) have indicated wooden sticks for special effects. A bigger, tighter head and a smaller, slacker head yield different timbres for the same note. The player's skill can make a radical difference in the beauty of the

[1] Plates 30, 35.

tone, and will give him considerable control over its character. The exact manner of his stroke, and the exact place at which he strikes, are both very critical factors.

The *side-drum*,[1] the *tenor drum* and the *bass drum*,[1] unlike the bowl-shaped kettledrum, have a vellum at either end; they are quite indefinite in pitch. The side-drum has a set of catgut strings or metal spirals tightly stretched across the opposite end to that which the player strikes: these rattle against the parchment, giving a dry, crisp sound; they are called snares, whence the alternative name of snare-drum for this instrument. The tenor drum is not common in the orchestra; but the bass drum is frequently employed when a deep, thunderous sound, either loud or soft, is wanted. It can be extraordinarily impressive.

The *tabor* is a double-parchment drum of varying size (but usually small) which can be tuned to a note fairly definite in pitch, though not nearly so definite as the kettledrum. It is the time-honoured associate of the three-holed pipe, as we have already seen; and was, furthermore, a virtually indispensable member of the Renaissance dance orchestra. In all revivals of Renaissance court dances, it should take its part; and it would likewise be invaluable for country dances, drum rhythm being desirable in the accompaniment of almost any dance.

The *tambourine*[2] is a small, flat drum open at one end, and carrying tiny round metal plates, known as jingles, round its edges: it is struck, shaken, or rubbed with the thumb. *Bongos* are single-headed drums played with the fingers; *tom-toms* or *timbales* are larger and played with drumsticks.

Solid percussion

This category (solid percussion) and the next (hollow percussion) tend to merge one into another, since the solidity may be modified by gradual degrees into a hollow form, and the same instrument may often be found with or without some degree of hollowness. The effect is to introduce some degree of resonance from any air thus contained. The degree of resonance increases with the degree of hollowness;

[1] Plate 30 (showing a single-headed bass drum, peculiar to London orchestras).
[2] Plates 6, 9.

but it would in many cases be pedantic to class different variants of what is essentially the same instrument into different categories. Moreover, several instruments of which the tone-producing portion is itself in solid shape may have, or may possess variants which have hollow resonators linked or linkable with them.

The present section, therefore, ought strictly to be headed: more or less solid percussion, with or without some structural or auxiliary hollowness of form. The following section ought strictly to be headed: decidedly and essentially hollow percussion, having a solid substance (as opposed to a membrane) for its tone-producing portion.

Thus the *cymbals*[1] are a pair of brass plates, mainly flat but with slight cup-like indentations in the centre, and normally quite indefinite in pitch; they can be clashed or jangled together, or one can be suspended and struck or rolled upon with drumsticks. But there are also small and decidedly cup-shaped cymbals, which can be tuned to quite clear, high notes of definite pitch. The large, orchestral cymbals have a vibrant power which can add greatly to the emotional quality of an orchestral score; but they were sparingly used in classical tradition.

The *triangle* is a metal rod left open at one corner, played by being struck with a straight rod of the same material. A roll can also be executed in one of the corners. Its tone is much lighter and more tinkling than the cymbals; it has a comparable emotional effect, but in a higher register and lighter timbre. It sounds too like a telephone bell to be much favoured today.

The tone of the triangle is a product of numerous high partials, all close to each other in pitch, and all of roughly equal strength. While it is of quite indeterminate pitch when heard alone, it always appears to belong to the prevailing tonality of the orchestra; for this reinforces the appropriate partials; while the mind itself tends to pick them out from the whole ringing mass, just because they are appropriate. This is also true of many other comparable sound-producers in use today.

The *tuning fork* is a U-shaped steel bar with a very prominent fundamental harmonic, which is heard almost pure, because the only upper partials are very high and distant, and quickly die away, though they are very complex and discordant while they last. Much the same, though in lesser degree, is true of the wooden bars of

[1] Plates 6, 9.

graded lengths and pitches, struck with two beaters held like kettle-drum sticks, which form the *xylophone* with its dry resonance, extra-ordinarily effective when well used; commonly resonators are placed beneath each bar, in which case *marimba* is the more proper name, or *marimba gongs* if the bars are of metal. But *marimba* is also used to mean a larger, four-octave instrument. (More beaters may be used.)

Castanets are a pair of hollow wooden clackers shaken together to produce a rhythmic rattling sound. *Wood blocks* are rectangular blocks of wood, or sometimes of plastic, in which slight resonant cavities are cut in the form of a slit or slits. The resonance is not great, and the tone made by striking the suspended blocks with wooden sticks (snare-drum sticks, or mallets as used for xylophones) is dry and crisp. The pitch varies with the size (usually $6\frac{1}{2}$ in. for the highest, $7\frac{1}{2}$ in. for the medium and 8 in. for the lowest of three blocks) but is fairly indefinite. *Temple blocks* are more or less round and hollow and of moderately definite pitch, customarily tuned to suggest the five notes (or some of them) of a pentatonic scale; but no attempt is made to notate them as exact pitches. The smaller are the higher, the larger are the lower in pitch. Since the resonant cavity is proportion-ately greater than in ordinary wood blocks, the timbre is a little less dry and more sonorous. Temple blocks may be played with wooden sticks or with felt-covered sticks of the desired hardness. The *claves* are a pair of short sticks, struck together, but in such a position that the cupped hollow of one hand provides a slight resonator: the pitch is quite indefinite and the timbre very dry and sharp. *Maracas* are hollow gourds, usually held one in either hand, and containing dried seeds (or shot) which rattle inside when shaken. The *guiro* is a larger gourd with notches cut into it, across which a stick is scraped. All these instruments are liable to variants of form and technique. Their importance is considerable in the new music of the *avant-garde*, where they are valued for their subtleties of timbre as much as for their rhythmic qualities.

Rattles of various kinds may be used. The loudest is swung around its handle, which causes a thin tongue of wood to pass over the teeth of a wooden cog at any speed desired, setting up a fiendish clattering. The *wind-machine* is a barrel covered with silk, which swishes against a cross-piece of wood or card as the barrel is revolved: the faster, the swishier and higher in pitch. Richard Strauss en-countered much stuffy opposition for introducing it in one humorous variation of his *Don Quixote*, where it takes a very minor share in the orchestral sound.

The *anvil*, struck with a hammer, has had a fluctuating orchestral existence. Virdung notes it (1511); Martin Agricola includes it in his list of instruments (*Musica instrumentalis deudsch*, 1529), but rather as a compliment to his classical Greek model, Pythagoras (who was always associated with it), than from conviction. However, Auber, Berlioz, Verdi, Wagner, Gounod, Bizet and other operatic composers have included parts for anvils, often a pair tuned a third apart, the pitch being fairly definite. It must be confessed that orchestras tend to substitute a mere steel bar, unless the anvil is to appear visibly on the stage.

In Wagner's *Rheingold*, six little anvils, six larger anvils and six very large anvils are scored for, eighteen in all, though unfortunately financial considerations usually intervene to cut down this imposing force. The anvils gradually permeate the orchestra as Wotan and Loge reach the cave of the wretched labouring dwarfs. The orchestra leaves off, and they are heard alone, with strangely moving effect; the orchestra re-enters, and the anvils die away, as the gods pass on: the whole scene being as vivid as if the eye beheld it, although the curtain remains down the while.

The *glockenspiel* is a row of metal bars of graded lengths and pitches, struck with two wooden hammers held like kettledrum sticks. The tone is pure, light and ringing, with an unearthly, fairyland quality which would soon cloy, but is extraordinarily effective on the right occasion. The pitch is quite definite. There is a variety with steel tubes in place of plates, known as the *tubophone*, and popular in dance music. (For the keyed version see p. 164.)

The *vibraphone* was a new invention popularized for dance music round and about the early 1920s, but recently given extreme prominence in the music of the *avant-garde*. It has bars of metal graded by length and pitch, and lying horizontally, as in the glockenspiel. Beneath the bars stand, vertically, tubular resonators closed at the bottom, and tuned for sympathetic vibration with their respective bars. In between, vanes are mounted on a horizontal shaft revolved by a motor which can be instantly turned on and off. Each bar and resonator has its own vane. When in motion, the vanes alternately open and occlude the tubes. This cuts their resonance in and out, making a very conspicuous pulsation in the sound, which they also help to prolong. The speed of motion can be controlled, and this varies the speed of pulsation. Stopping the vanes stops the pulsation. There is also a felt-covered damper which can be applied to silence the bars, under which it lies, and on all of which it acts at once; it is controlled, as in the piano, by a pedal. The usual compass is three octaves from f to f''' (wider compasses are also built). Sticks can be used with or without coverings of different hardness, felt being common. The sticks can be held one in either hand, or for playing simple chords, two, three, or even four in either hand. The instrument is better adapted to melody than to harmony, excepting for slow chords sustained by the action of the vanes and the resonators. Rapid melodies can be played with the vanes stationary, or with the dampers operative, unless an atmospheric effect is desired from undamped figuration, with the tubes building up the sound.

Hollow percussion

The *bell* has somewhat peculiar acoustic properties. You hear two prominent partials: the strike tone, and the hum tone about one full octave below; together with a mass of moderately unstable and irregular further partials, which are much more prominent, as notes separate in pitch, than is ordinarily the case. The strike tone *appears* to be the fifth partial of a rather unusual series: the ear misjudging it for the octave below, and accepting it as the fundamental of the series. That the strike tone is in some sense aural perception is no longer doubted: the most likely explanation is that it is a perceptual effect, possibly a difference tone created subjectively by the ear from two objectively existing partials. The hum tone, which both can and should be the exact octave below, is the actual first or fundamental partial, though English bell founders call the strike tone the fundamental, since it is the note which the ear accepts as the effective pitch of the bell, when tuned on the English principle.

The best and sweetest bells are tuned, most skilfully, by removing metal from the correct places, in order to bring their partials into as harmonious a relationship as possible. Care is taken to secure uniformity of thickness elsewhere, so as to avoid the unpleasant beats resulting from the nearly but not quite identical series of partials which accidental unevenness or 'loading' introduces. (Big Ben gives prominent beats, as every English radio owner knows; but these are due to actual cracks.)

The most accurately tuned bells, especially in their smaller sizes, will still give a somewhat confused sound, not suitable to much traditional orchestral use. They were occasionally employed to good effect, the ear no doubt assisting by picking out chiefly those partials which suit the prevailing tonality (just as it does when listening to the triangle). They are, however, more often replaced by what are called *tubular bells* (hollow steel tubes of graded lengths and pitches), apparently in the expectation of a more strictly harmonic tone: but analysis shows that they are in fact more inharmonic. The true bell shape is the outcome of many centuries of skilled empirical craftsmanship, supported of late by scientific research; and it is certainly not to be improved upon by a simple tube.[1]

One such tube of quite exceptional magnitude is sometimes used to yield a bell or gong tone of great depth and resonance, at once noble and horrific in an orchestral ensemble. The *gong* (tam-tam) proper is a special variety of very shallow bell, and largely shares its qualities. It is now much used, and in many sizes.

Other materials may be used for bell-like or bowl-like objects of more or less definite pitch, such as are exploited with peculiar effectiveness in the East, and now in the modern West as well. Glass, if thin, is highly resonant and tunable; pottery rather less so, but tuned pottery bowls in graded pitches have a subtle role in some Eastern orchestras. *Musical bowls* are a recent importation into Western music, but *musical glasses*, played not by percussion, but by the friction of the wetted finger, were all the rage at the end of the eighteenth century, though they would perhaps be regarded as an eccentricity today.

The tone and volume of bell-like instruments can be largely controlled by varying the point of percussion, the hardness of the striking implement, and the force of the blow. The pitch, so far as it is definite at all, is fixed, depending on size and weight; except that in markedly asymmetrical structures, it will vary with varying points of percussion. The beauty of tone depends not only on good tuning, but equally on an adequate weight of metal for the note produced.

Keyboard percussion

Keyboard mechanisms have been added to certain percussive instruments, notably the glockenspiel: this then becomes an extremely

[1] By far the best available general account of the properties of bells will be found in Lloyd, *The Musical Ear*, iv.

versatile and agile little instrument, of a certain innocent, but, when well used, incredibly touching charm. When a resonator of wood is attached to each steel bar, the instrument is commonly called the *celesta*; it is then normally larger in size and deeper in pitch, with a rather fuller but still quite unearthly tone (the Silver Rose scene in *Der Rosenkavalier* is an excellent example of its beauty when well employed). Glockenspiel is the generic title, broadly speaking: it means literally 'bell-play', and the instrument used by Mozart in the *Magic Flute* and by Handel in *Saul* had small bells, not bars. It was, in fact, a small orchestral adaptation of the carillon, or set of bells (often of good size) with a suitable keyboard: an instrument of great beauty in its own very individual fashion, of particular importance on the European continent (and some in America).

The *dulcitone* is a series of graded tuning forks played with keyboard-operated hammers. Its excessively pure tone makes it rather dull; but it is cheap, it is handy, and it is always in tune: and it has had some use as a miniature substitute piano. A rather beautiful instrument has also existed in which the tuning forks stood in glass tubes, acting as resonators.

CHAPTER 14

ELECTROPHONES

Melodic electrophones

The *aetherophone* (thérémin, théréminvox, etherophone); the *electronde*; the *trautonium*; the *ondes musicales* (martenot, ondium martenot); the *croix sonore*; the *hellertion*; the *dynaphone*; the *Wurlitzer electronic piano*: these are or have been more or less melodic electrophones, capable of infinite gradations of pitch, so that quarter-tones or any other desired microtones can be obtained, for which purpose some of them were originally designed. The *spherophone* has a keyboard of more than ordinary multiplicity, with this end in view; but only melody is obtainable. The *emicon* has a keyboard, but again only melody is obtainable. There are frequently means for varying the quality of tone.

None of the above has now much, if any, importance. The *Hammond Solovox*, however, though no longer in production, had until recently a great run in popular use, both by amateurs and by dance bands. It has a small keyboard which can be clamped to a piano, with the idea of playing a solo melody on the organ-like Solovox, accompanied by harmonies on the piano. The sources of vibration are vacuum tubes. There is one master oscillator controlled through three octaves (the total range of the keyboard), synchronized with frequency dividers producing lower octaves. There is thus a choice of octave pitches, marked: soprano, contralto, tenor, bass. These are selectable singly or in combination. There is a knee-operated volume control, a vibrato, and built-in delay to the attack. The variety and expressiveness obtainable are not extensive, but considerable for so relatively simple and inexpensive a piece of electronic apparatus.

A much more extensive and ambitious melodic electrophone is described under the name of *Thyratone* by Richard H. Dorf, its designer, in his valuable book, *Electronic Musical Instruments*, 2nd ed., New York, pp. 213–230.

166

Harmonic electrophones

By this I mean electrophonic instruments capable of harmony, which is the normal implication of a keyboard. The *partiturophone* was a development of the spherophone. The *Givelet-coupleux organ*, the *rangertone*, the *orgatron* and others are, or have been, instruments designed to cover electrically much the same ground as the organ proper covers by pipes: hence they are sometimes called pipeless organs. Of these, the Compton organ, the Hammond organ, the

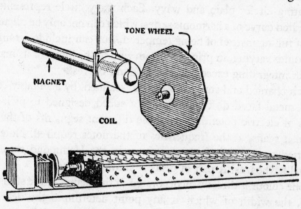

Fig. 26. Hammond electronic tone generator

Baldwin, the Conn and the Allen electronic organs and certain others are by now extremely well-established instruments.

The Hammond organ. Here, the tone is generated magnetically. A number of metal wheels, bumpy in shape, revolve at different but constant speeds, so that the bumps of each approach a permanent (but wound) magnet the requisite number of times per second to induce an electric impulse of the frequency of the note required. When a note is wanted, this impulse is admitted to the amplifying circuit by a contact resulting from pressing the appropriate key. The keyboards are normal.

Tone colour is additive, by introducing in variable strength a selection from a choice of eight further tones from the harmonic series. Their generators are not additional, but 'borrowed' from other notes of the keyboard; hence they are all, unlike true harmonics, tuned to equal temperament (see Appendix IV). Within the limits

N

imposed by this slightly inharmonic tempering and by the comparatively restricted range of partials provided, an excellent variety of tone-colourings can be compounded. There is a slightly blatant assertiveness about the Hammond organ which fits it better for some musical purposes than for others.

The Compton electric organ. This is a much subtler and more remarkable electrophonic imitation of the pipe organ. Here the tone is generated electrostatically. There are a number of fixed non-conducting disks, coated in electrically charged metal except where scored by insulating circles plain and wavy. Each wavy circle represents the integrated curve of a harmonic series, which can not only be calculated in just tuning instead of being tempered, but can include a range of harmonics varying, in principle, from zero to the limits of its maker's skill in integrating exceedingly compound curves.

Each charged and stationary disk is 'scanned' by a suitably corrugated metal-faced disk revolving at a speed designed to pick up a series of electric potentials from the different segments of the disk which it scans, at the frequencies of the notes required. Notes are admitted to the amplifying circuit, as in the Hammond organ, by normal keyboards. A pair of disks is shown in Plate 37.

Tone colour is directly incorporated in the shapes of the stationary rings, the width of which at any point determines the degree of potential picked up by the revolving corrugations of the scanning disk. As with any other organ (including the Hammond organ) the tone-colourings required are controlled by stops.

On the Hammond it is also possible to compound individual tone-colourings by graded drawbars; but the total choice, though immense in theory, is limited in practice, since no harmonic above the eighth is available. The Compton organ already employs the first thirty-two harmonics, and it is hoped to carry the series to the first 164 harmonics at a later stage.

The range of subsidiary devices incorporated is also somewhat greater than in the Hammond organ, and includes a particularly effective mechanism for imitating the far from instantaneous build-up and die away of normal organ tone.

The Baldwin organ. This is in the strict sense an electronic organ, since its sources of vibration are transistors (replacing the earlier vacuum-tubes) with frequency-dividers; and its tone-colourings are got by subtraction from sawtooth waves by means of selectable frequency filters. There is a frequency oscillator for vibrato when desired. There is a general volume control, and a pair of loud-speakers with their amplifiers, set in different places, either or both of which can be selected; this makes it possible to simulate the effect of an echo organ. Ingenious gradual-contact switching prevents an unnaturally abrupt attack when the keys are depressed.

A still more ingenious set of circuits gives a choice of square waves compounded from the initial sawtooth waves: the sawtooth waves, including both odd and even harmonics, are the foundation of tones resembling the diapason registers of a pipe organ; the square waves, mainly confined to odd harmonics, are the foundation of tones resembling the stopped registers. The specifications are deliberately and successfully modelled on those of a large and varied pipe organ, both in the choice of registers and in the resources for coupling them. A deliberate attempt has been made, moreover, to include sonorities appropriate for different styles of music, the Baroque included. There are many models.

The *Allen organ* at its biggest has the valuable distinction of em-ploying an individual transistor (originally vacuum-tube) oscillator for each note of each register, in the same manner in which a pipe organ may employ an individual pipe for each note of each register. Some compromise is admitted, however, in most models, as it is in most pipe organs, to save impracticable demands on complexity, space and money. The larger models of the Allen organ are, as it is, exceptionally complex and expensive but justify this by exceptional musicianliness of sound. Because of this characteristic principle of individual tone-production, each fundamental can be tuned to the desired volume while retaining its content of upper harmonic un-impaired. Both attack and decay are controlled to give an envelope of the slight gradualness normal in pipe organs, and a convincing 'chiff' can be introduced.

There may be a mechanism (rotating speakers) to increase an effect already present in part from the individuality of the oscillators: vibrations reach the ear not perfectly in phase and pitch, which is the general disposition of electronic sounds, but more or less out of phase, and very slightly spread in pitch, which is normal to pipe organs and other traditional sources of multiple vibrations (such as the string section, and indeed the entirety of an orchestra). This effect (called 'chorus effect') is musically of the greatest value in giving a natural vitality far pleasanter than too accurate a mechanical perfection. It is one of the ironies of electronic sound-production that quite elaborate steps may have to be taken in order to diminish an exactitude which comes more naturally and on the whole desirably to machines than to human beings. (Comparable mechanisms, especially the Leslie Organ Speaker, are incorporated in many other makes.)

The *Conn organ* shares much of the principle of the Allen organ, but on a somewhat simpler and less ambitious mode of application, rather less expensive to put into effect. The newest *Wurlitzer organ* is a frequency-divider electronic instrument of considerable complexity; its predecessor was an acoustic electrophone, and belongs in the section next below. The *Minshall organ*, now discontinued, was remarkable in its day for a particularly ingenious and economical feed-back system of tone-generation, with master oscillators and frequency dividers, and a printed circuit for further economy.

Acoustic electrophones

The electric Wurlitzer organ was until recently an electronic organ in all respects except for the exciting tone which is the initial source of vibrations: this is acoustic, since it consists of brass reeds kept in continuous vibration at low air-pressure, and contained in sound-proof material so that no sound is heard from them directly. Each reed forms one capacitator plate, of which the paired capacitator plate can be chosen from screws or strips of metal in different positions relative to the reed, giving different harmonic contents, including numerous mixtures. There is an admirable vibrato effect by phase-modulation, which gives the same fluctuation of frequency (and therefore of pitch) by purely electronic means as the Allen organ produces mechanically by rotating the source of sound towards and away from the hearer's ear (the 'Doppler effect', caused by alternate shortening and lengthening of the effective wavelength).

The *electric piano* may take either of two forms. Electromagnetic pick-ups may be placed over the (metal) strings of a normal piano, and the electronically amplified (perhaps modified) sound allowed to blend with the acoustically amplified sound from the sound-board; the harmonic content of the initial exciting tone depending upon what point of the string (a node, an antinode or intermediately) the pick-up stands closest to in its position. Or the sound-board may be removed or damped, preventing any acoustic amplification of the small amplitude exerted by the strings themselves, so that only electronically processed sounds are heard.

Various techniques not normal to the piano can be brought into use: for example, raising the dampers (by the pedal) and rubbing the covered strings with the finger-nails, or plucking a string with the finger, thus causing small but unusual sounds the volume of which can be amplified electronically at will. This is an extension of what can already be done on the *prepared piano* ('prepared' by inserting screws or other intrusive objects, etc.), which is in turn made more effective by electronic amplification.

The *electric harpsichord* can be contrived for similar electronic manipulation, with the different envelope and harmonic content introduced by using a plucked string, instead of a hammered string, as the exciting tone.

It is just as possible to 'prepare' a harpsichord for special effects as it is to 'prepare' a piano; but it is not, for example, possible to lean over and sound the strings with the fingers, while keeping one foot down on the damper-raising pedal, for the sufficient reason that there is not, on the normal harpsichord, a damper-raising pedal. What is ordinarily meant, in dance bands and *avant-garde* ensembles, by the electric harpsichord, is a small instrument having plucked strings but designed expressly for use with electronic processing. (There are also electronic imitations of piano and harpsichord.)

The *electric violin* does not seem to be of current importance.

The *electric bass*, on the other hand, is in considerable demand. It can be built with a vestigial body, but with strings of normal length and tunings, though necessarily of metal or metal-covered. But this, even as amplified, has a poor and unsatisfactory resonance. It is much better to apply the amplification to a normal double bass, complete with its own fine and resonant body. Because of the power of electronic amplification which can be applied at will, the lightest harmonics may be given an impressive resonance, and an ordinary pizzicato may range from a whispered menace to a thudding boom.

The *electric guitar*, both in its Spanish forms (played traditionally much like a lute) and in the variant commonly known as *Hawaiian guitar* (played traditionally with much vibrato and portamento), has become an immensely popular instrument in dance bands and quite common in *avant-garde* ensembles. It appears both with a normal body, and with a vestigial body quite inoperative for acoustic amplification. As with all electromagnetic amplification of string instruments, the point of the string to which the pick-up is adjacent influences the harmonic content picked up (broadly, the nearer the end, the sharper the sound, and the nearer the middle, the mellower the sound; but much also depends on the exact adjacent node or antinode, if any). Some electric guitars are equipped with a choice of pick-ups selectable at will for immediate variety of tone-colouring. The point of the string at which it is plucked also continues to influence the harmonic content. The instrument, when well used, has a haunting quality for all its new electronic brashness.

Portable apparatus for electronically modifying, to an extraordinary extent, the sound of clarinets and many other conventional instruments are developing at a phenomenal rate and often with startling results, especially when, among other things, the volume is vastly amplified: 'magic boxes' of the utmost potency.

Electronic synthesizers

Many radio or recording studios are now equipped with apparatus for synthesizing music electronically, as well as for processing sounds of other than electronic origin (as in concrete music). There is a particularly large and elaborate specimen at Columbia University, New York, where much experimental work of the highest subtlety has been carried out in recent years, though newer methods have now virtually superseded it.

Work can be done with relatively simple equipment, such as an individual composer interested in concrete music or electronic music or both might expect to piece together at his own expense. (An ordinary tape recorder, or better two, can be used to produce electronic music.) But a limit to such private equipment is very soon and emphatically encountered; and for this reason, access to professional equipment on a much larger scale becomes urgently necessary. Most of the important electronic developments made by contemporary composers have been possible only because of the welcome given to them by the big institutions interested in such developments; and co-operative work along these lines seems to offer the most promising future to electronic music. It is for electronic composers to justify their cost in expensive studio time by offering musical experiences which are really felt to be worth while in an artistic sense; but that, after all, is no different from the conditions on which we judge the success of any other variety of music or instrument of music. It already seems likely that electronic music will go on developing, and is here to stay.

PART FOUR

INSTRUMENTS IN CONSORT

CHAPTER 15

CHAMBER MUSIC

Which instruments are suited for solo music

Keyboard instruments like the clavichord, the harpsichord, the piano and the organ, because they can play so easily in full harmony, are as much solo instruments as they are consort instruments (a 'consort' is simply the good old English word for any grouping of instruments playing together in a united ensemble). Indeed, the clavichord, with its tiny voice, is of no practical use for consort purposes. Hence these instruments, whatever their other uses, each possesses an extensive and magnificent literature of solo music.

Some plucked instruments, including the lute and the guitar, are equally suited to play solo music unaccompanied. Bowed instruments are occasionally used as instruments of full harmony, without accompaniment: J. S. Bach's famous and difficult unaccompanied violin suites and 'cello suites are the most extreme examples. But this is forcing the nature of most bowed instruments, and is only successful as a rare *tour de force*.

However, instruments whose natural bent is melody rather than harmony can play unaccompanied music provided that this is genuinely designed to be heard as unharmonized melody.

On the whole, music of this latter kind has not been written by sophisticated composers in our Western tradition, for the simple reason that if you are accustomed to write music based on harmony, you will find it very nearly impossible to write melody which is genuinely free from all suggestion of harmony. Your melody tends to suggest harmonies by implication, even though they are not played. For centuries, the shapes of our Western melodies have been so influenced by the chord progressions which carry them that even if these progressions are not added as chords, they are added mentally. But in the new music of the mid-twentieth century, chord progressions may be entirely excluded, and unaccompanied melodies can now again be composed which exist in their own right, without suggesting any implication of harmony.

The great Eastern traditions always have been melodic and rhythmic but not harmonic. Even where a considerable amount of harmony is heard (which is quite often the case) it does not go anywhere progressively. It does not operate at all as progressive harmony; it operates as colouring and atmosphere. This method of using harmony which is colourful but not functional has been extensively taken over, like many other features of Oriental music, into the new music of the Western *avant-garde*.

Previously, the only important Western tradition partly to survive which uses melody without a thought of harmony is folk melody, of which the early periods were devoid not only of actual harmony but of harmonic implications. Adding harmony to it for modern use is possible, with a sort of humble skill which does not seek to be too pretentious. But with the way our own modern music is developing, we may come more and more round to the idea that early, melodic folk tunes can best be left as unaccompanied melody after all.

Almost any instrument of melody lends itself to such genuinely unaccompanied and independent solo music, if the composer knows its idioms well and composes for it with insight and imagination. A great favourite at the present time seems to be the unaccompanied flute, with or without the latest techniques (including chords, key-clicks voiced or unvoiced, etc.). The instrument, however ingeniously manipulated, is relatively limited in its resources; but turning limitations into advantages has always been part of a creator's skill.

Accompanied solos

There is another class of music illogically but quite understandably spoken of as solo music. This is music in which one melodic instrument (voice; violin; viola or violoncello; treble or bass viol; recorder flute; oboe; clarinet; horn; or what you will) has most of the interest, while another instrument fills in the harmony with an accompaniment of subsidiary interest.

This category ranges from quite simple songs depending for their beauty almost entirely on their expressive melody, to very ornate displays of virtuosity on the violin, the viola da gamba or some other instrument capable of dazzling feats of technique. The pianist may display his virtuosity unaccompanied; the violinist ordinarily requisitions a discreet accompanist: that is the only difference between what is in either case essentially a one-man display.

But whenever the partners share the musical interest on a more equal footing, it becomes misleading to speak of solo and accompaniment. Thus this class of accompanied solos very quickly merges into the next class of chamber-music partnerships. For even an accompaniment whose function is entirely subsidiary needs to be given a reasonably satisfactory musical shape, however simple. And the more complete in itself the accompaniment becomes, the more nearly it is likely to approach the leading melody in interest.

Chamber partnerships

When all concerned have parts roughly equal of interest, two broad methods, or a combination, have long been possible. You can give each performer the same melodic themes to interweave in turn after the fugal manner (not by any means necessarily in the actual musical form called fugue). Or you can give one performer a melody of his own, and the other performer or performers more fragmentary figures, or perhaps an equally tuneful melody, but not the same melody (which does not by any means preclude their taking the chief melody turn and turn about). Or you may use both methods in different parts of your composition. And, indeed, the distinction itself is not a rigid one: there are countless border-line cases.

But broadly speaking: while all concerned are simultaneously playing tuneful melodies, which combine together to form the harmonies, your music is of the kind called contrapuntal. While one player has a tuneful melody, but the others have, at least for the time being, more fragmentary figures, or simply chords, your music is not of the kind called contrapuntal. And between these two extremes, the more you give your players tuneful melodies at the same time, the more contrapuntal your music is: for counterpoint is a matter of degree.

The degree of counterpoint to which a composer is addicted will depend on his traditions and predilections. But the question is also bound up with the instruments for which he writes: for, although their limitations are very elastic, and can cater for an immense variety of needs, different instruments do lend themselves most naturally to different styles of treatment.

What instruments best suit what styles of music

We have already considered the reasons for some of these differences. We saw, for example, how the clavichord and the harpsichord have both a sufficiently transparent tone to make contrapuntal music, woven of several strands of melody at once, sound clear and easy to follow: though the clavichord is on the whole more suited to tender and expressive moods; the big harpsichord to brilliant and bravura moods; while the little harpsichord or virginals stands midway in this respect. The piano excels in rather different directions: it has its expressive and its bravura aspects; but it is markedly inferior in sounding contrapuntal music translucently. It is, perhaps, at its best in romantic situations calling for dramatic contrasts and a rich and rounded surge of tone, in which it is all the better for the finer details of the inner parts not to stand out too clearly.

And naturally, the qualities most proper to these instruments in their solo music likewise influence their most characteristic treatment as instruments of accompaniment. Harpsichord accompaniments are quite often contrapuntal: for example, Bach's sonatas for viola da gamba and harpsichord, or for violin and harpsichord, are really trios, in which the bowed instrument plays one thread of melody; while each hand of the harpsichordist simultaneously plays another thread; and the three systematically interchange their melodies from time to time. This is real chamber music in the fullest sense.

Piano accompaniments are less apt to weave independent melodic strands, and more apt to use short, rhythmical figures, full chords, chords broken up into arpeggios up and down the keyboard, or into other, more tuneful figures: and many characteristically 'pianistic' effects. (But 'broken chords' are also very telling on the harpsichord.) I do not necessarily mean that such piano parts are less independent: in a sense, indeed, they are more independent; they may use quite separate material, instead of exchanging the same material in turns. Many of the finest songs are written on this pattern. Violin sonatas are more usually so designed that the violin and the piano have each the main tunes by turns: but only comparatively subsidiary and fragmentary material (largely broken chords) when it is the other's turn. This, of course, is quite a different pattern from the threefold melody of the Bach sonatas: but it is just as genuine a chamber partnership, since neither partner monopolizes the interest.

The lute, again, both as a solo and as an accompanying instrument, has its own special brand of sketchy but expressive counterpoint and full but delicately ringing chords. The viols suggest a more contrapuntal style than the string quartet of violins. And so through the whole range of diverse instruments: each has its special features, which include both its virtues and the defects of those virtues.

Good composers have always known how to exploit to the best effect the peculiar virtues of the instruments for which they write: and to a very substantial extent their style is modified to fit them. This is no slavery: it is mere common-sense co-operation. When the composer conceives a different effect, he does not try to force it on the instrument (though sometimes he may see possibilities in it that others had not thought of); he uses another instrument: or if no suitable instrument exists, he harries the instrument-makers, as Wagner did, to evolve one suited to his novel purpose. Changes in instruments and changes in musical idiom go hand in hand: sometimes the one leading, sometimes the other; and both profoundly influenced by the changing climate of the age itself.

What instruments sound best together in chamber music

We have already noted in passing that the same chord may sound smoother on some instruments, and harsher on others: the cause being that concordance and discordance depend on the degree of beating among the high harmonics; which in turn vary in strength on various instruments. Our use of 'tempered' intervals in place of acoustically just intervals (for necessary reasons, discussed in Appendix IV) makes this problem still more acute, especially on the organ, where you can produce the most fiendish racket of beating high harmonics from a very moderate progression of chords, by injudicious indulgence in your mixture stops, heavy tuba stops and the like.

On the whole, the smoothest and purest effects are produced by keeping your instruments in single families. That is perhaps why the most intimate of all chamber music has traditionally been written either for a single instrument such as the lute, the clavichord, the harpsichord or the piano; or else for a single complete family, such as the consort of viols or the string quartet of violins. And there is no doubt that such severely limited means do afford an austere beauty of tone and an undistracted inwardness of expression which no other form of music can rival. Indeed, there are no sounds more lovely, even sensually: but, of course, their variety and range of contrast are inherently restricted. That is their very appeal: but there is another kind of appeal, likewise very strong, in the almost infinite variety of tone-colouring to be effected by combining instruments of different families. And in this lies endless art.

> Some *Consorts of Instruments* [remarked Francis Bacon in 1626] are sweeter than others; (A thing not sufficiently yet observed:) As the *Irish Harp*, and *Base Viall* agree well: *The Recorder* and *Stringed Musick* agree well: *Organs* and the *Voice* agree well, &c. But the *Virginalls* and the *Lute*; Or the *Welch-Harp*; and the *Irish-Harp*; or the *Voice* and *Pipes* alone, agree not so well; But for the *Melioration* of *Musick* there is yet much left (in this Point of *Exquisite Consorts*) to try and enquire.[1]

Much has been 'tried and enquired', both successfully and unsuccessfully, since this passage was written, in the Golden Age of English music. Many combinations have been written for, with excellent effect on, special occasions; others have become standard groupings, the vehicle of very diverse styles of music.

When a composer writes for some small group of instruments which do not form a standard combination, he probably does so either because on some particular occasion or occasions precisely that selection of instrumentalists happens to be available for his use; or because he conceives the notion of trying out the particular potentialities of some one instrument in such a setting; or because he has some music in his mind for which the most expressive medium strikes him as being just that one unusual combination, and none other.

Bach's orchestral scorings offer a fair instance of the first case: which does not imply that they are in any way less exactly and imaginatively scored to suit the instruments in question than they would have been if an unlimited choice had been available. Brahms's Trio for Horn, Violin and Piano illustrates the second class: the composer, a horn player himself in his youth, retained an especial affection for the instrument, and composed this lovely work to exploit its most characteristic effects (incidentally, he insisted on a natural horn, considering that the valve horn relieved the player not

[1] *Sylva Sylvarum*, Cent. III, No. 278. Cited from ed. of 1658 (1st ed. 1626).

only of many special difficulties but also, unless he were unusually conscientious and imaginative, of many of the special beauties associated with them). The third case might be exemplified by Schubert's pastoral song, 'Der Hirt auf dem Felsen', with an obbligato part for the clarinet, which is quite indispensable to the whole mood and texture of the piece. But in not one of these examples should the music be considered apart from the special characteristics of the instruments for which it is designed.

Of the standard combinations, only the most familiar can be instanced here. Many of them are based on the piano: voice with piano, violin with piano, and so forth. Now the piano is never the instrument to blend imperceptibly with other qualities of tone, and least of all with highly colourful tones like the voice or the violin. This is not necessarily a defect: but it is an unavoidable feature for the composer to take into account. The piano can either take its own way on a footing of equality, or it can fall unobtrusively into the background: it cannot merge with its companion as if into one single instrument.

Hence it is that so many chamber works in which the piano is more than a mere servant have an air of friendly rivalry rather than reposeful team-work. This is less noticeable with the voice than with the violin, but never wholly absent. If anything it is still more conspicuous when a string trio or quartet joins with the piano: these are forms in which great care is needed to prevent friendly rivalry from degenerating into open conflict. But as so often, the very difficulties can lead to peculiarly strong and satisfying results when their divergencies are sensitively reconciled.

Both the lute, in its quiet way, and the harpsichord, after its more brilliant fashion, are unusually good mixers. Although the lute has a much sharper attack than the voice, these two make a beautifully matched combination of tone qualities (but the singer must produce an appropriately pure and unforced tone, and the lutenist must be capable of a really full and singing tone). The harpsichord will also enter into a not very much less intimate union with the voice: while its capacity for merging with the bowed strings, whether viols or violins, is more remarkable still. The bass viol with the harpsichord and the violin with the harpsichord offer two of the most natural and pleasing blends available. Harpsichord and violin music possesses quite a different atmosphere from piano and violin music: the one a fusion of closely united partners, the other a balance of strongly contrasted partners.

Unmixed families in chamber music

Of the unmixed families used in chamber music, the chief tradition-ally is the string quartet of violins (violin I, violin II, viola, violon-cello). The very fact that, as we saw, this ensemble lacks one origin-ally normal member of the violin family, to wit the tenor violin, gives it a peculiar quality of brilliance: for the three upper instruments are all grouped together in a comparatively high register, upon a bass which stands considerably lower; and when chords are spaced in this fashion, they are likely to produce a brilliant effect.

Of course, closer spacings are physically possible on these four instruments: but this is less in evidence in well-written string quartets (note, by the way, that 'quartet' can refer either to the in-struments or to the music – or even to the players). Indeed, the loss of the tenor violin was probably the result of pursuing this particular effect of brilliance.

The string quartet as it actually settled down (two violins, viola and violoncello) is in every respect a satisfactory combination of instruments for intimate chamber music. This does not mean that it covers every possible variety of string sonority; the combination of viols next to be described has different qualities, and for its own particular kind of scoring is actually superior to the violin quartet. In a more general sense, the violin quartet is superior to the consort of viols, since it is more versatile. But each of the two sonorities is beautiful in its own kind.

The sonority of the string quartet stands high among all the many diverse and glorious sounds of music. It has a certain chasteness, so that it never oversates the listener, yet it is rich enough, too, to be endlessly satisfying. It is equally capable of warmth and of coolness, of brilliance and of contemplation, of passion and of serenity.

From Haydn and Mozart to Schoenberg and after, from the age of the stagecoach to the age of the jet aeroplane, the string quartet has kept its pride of place at the very heart of our musical experience. The string quartet is a quiet voice, by the side of our great symphonic orchestras, and in variety of sound not difficult to surpass. Yet most great composers for the past two hundred years have given it fine music, and some have put into it thoughts hardly equalled, if at all, elsewhere in their life's work.

And we in the audience, too, answer to these glowing sounds with a richness of response out of all proportion to their mere volume. What has this small group of well-balanced instruments to offer which pleases us so differently from the full orchestral sonority, but pleases us as much, and in some moods more?

It seems that quietness and intimacy have an eloquence which moves us in some region where power and bigness do not reach. Four strings have neither the scope nor the colourings of a hundred various instrumentalists. Yet no single instrument has more variety and beauty of tone and articulation than a fine violin, viola or 'cello: few have as much. And what is beautiful alone becomes supremely beautiful in combination. The warmth and the glamour, the subtle blending, the infinite satisfaction of a good string quartet is, after all, one of the best sounds known to man, and those who love it never grow tired of it.

Before the rise of the string quartet of violins in its present form, a comparable role was taken by the consort of viols, which, after a silence of more than two centuries, is now being heard again for the sake of the fine and serious music (particularly the early seventeenth-century English music) composed for it. This family, as we saw, was not lacking in any normal member; and its most characteristic music is not spaced unevenly, with three high instruments to one low one, as in the violin quartet. Hence it does not share the peculiar brilliance which this feature lends: the lower registers tend to be as well filled out as the upper ones.

The rather sharper and clearer tone of the viols is not only, as we have seen, an asset in making contrapuntal melodies in the inner parts easier to follow: it has also the effect of making the lower intervals in an evenly spaced chord somewhat brighter. There is less risk of their sounding thick and muddy.

Again, the viol consort at the best periods, though it might range from two to seven in number, was at its most standard a group, not of four instruments like the violin quartet, but of five. And of these five, much the most normal arrangement was to include two treble viols, whose parts often cross and recross until it is an open question which is Treble I and which is Treble II. This effect is also one of extraordinary brilliance, though for different reasons and in a different way.

Both the consort of viols and the quartet of violins make, in addition, a wonderful setting for a solo voice: the former matching it more closely, so that voice and viols can pursue their own contrapuntal melodies in equal partnership; the latter standing rather more apart from the vocal line.

A very pleasant and effective grouping on the borders of chamber music consists of a small orchestra of violins in all sizes: what we call a string orchestra, or sometimes, more loosely, a chamber orchestra (a term which may, however, cover a small orchestra including a contingent of wind instruments). Besides first and second violins, violas and violoncellos, the string orchestra has always included one or more double basses (originally, as we have seen, true violones). The number of players to each part should not be very large, or the chamber-music quality is speedily destroyed. The family of viols has never been used in this way as a standard form, though viols took their share in many of the highly various and colourful small 'occasional' orchestras of the seventeenth and eighteenth centuries, along with lutes, keyboard instruments, and wind instruments of every species.

The remaining chamber family of prime importance is the human voice itself, in all its registers. This is heard at its purest when there is a single singer to each part (for example, soprano, alto, tenor, bass), just as there is a single player to each part in a viol consort or a violin quartet. When the singers are as good and as well practised in the subtle art of keeping perfectly together in time, style and expression, the result is an ideal means of rendering the finest madrigals and other music for such a combination. But it is also quite legitimate to use two, three or four singers to each part, or (though this needs a judicious touch) to back the voices with instruments playing the same parts in unison (violins, viols, recorders, cornetts, trombones and other instruments were thus used in vocal counterpoint).

For sacred music intended for cathedral, church, or even private chapel, a rather different vocal group is commonly intended, in which the upper parts are sung by boy sopranos, and adult male altos using their 'falsetto' register in the manner already described. The effect is not radically different: it is, perhaps, a little cooler and more other-worldly; but no kinds of early music were ever sung, at the time, with a white or unimpassioned quality of tone. Modern choirs are often far too refined in early music; whether secular or ecclesiastical, it all got and urgently needs the full operatic robustness of the *bel canto* technique.

As with the madrigals, or those sacred motets for mixed voices of either sex designed less for church or chapel than for domestic piety and pleasure, the singers, at the most, must not be too numerous if they are not to pass from the intimacy proper to chamber music into the atmosphere of the concert hall.

CHAPTER 16

PUBLIC MUSIC

Public music broadly distinct from chamber music

There is, of course, no rigid distinction between chamber music and what, for want of a better word, we may call public music (chamber music is often heard in public, but, on the whole, is not primarily designed for that use). To a considerable extent, the same instruments serve either purpose. Yet there is no mistaking the difference in mood and manner between a typical string quartet and a typical symphony. (Chamber music is *mainly* 'one to a part'.)

In the case of public music, the trappings of outward splendour and display take a much larger share. It is in the very nature of music intended primarily for public performance to include an element of bravura. This does not imply any lack of sincerity: it is simply that striking effects are on the whole more appropriate than reticence. The music may be just as thoughtful, but the thought is likely to be conceived on broader lines. That is why the instruments chosen to convey it are frequently the richest and most colourful combinations obtainable. And conversely, if you choose to employ the wealth and variety of a full symphonic orchestra, you will not ordinarily write for it in the same pure lines and restricted colourings which are offered by the string quartet: you will make the most of the dramatic contrasts and excitements peculiar to large-scale orchestral music. You will make good use of all your available instruments severally, and at least to some extent jointly.

It is important to bear this general difference between the functions of chamber music and public music in mind, even though the two merge together at their nearer boundaries, so that some works scored for full orchestra nevertheless possess a texture reminiscent of chamber music, while many works for the solo piano, and many piano trios, quartets and quintets, are conceived in virtually symphonic terms. Half the secret of good instrumentation simply lies in

choosing the truly appropriate instruments for your mood and purpose; the other half lies in the skill to use them to their own best
effect, letting their special character and the character of the parts
you write for them react upon each other as you proceed. For each
phrase as you conceive it you will select the instrument best fitted to
express it; for each instrument you choose to bring in you will mould
your phrase to make the most of it. The two aspects cannot properly
be conceived apart from one another.

The symphonic orchestra and the wind and brass bands

Roughly speaking, the symphonic orchestra is a development of the
past two hundred years. There were many admirable orchestras of
much earlier dates: but they were not symphonic orchestras; they
were occasional orchestras – assembled for a given occasion, or at
most a given locality; and they were based on no standard pattern.

What we should call the orchestras of the Renaissance centuries
were what an Elizabethan would have called 'broken consorts', by
which he meant any grouping of instruments not all of one kind
('whole consort'), but of diverse kinds together. Many of them were
in effect chamber orchestras with a kernel of bowed strings (both
viols and violins), an often very strong contingent of wind instruments (flutes, recorders, cornetts, shawms, trumpets, trombones and
others), frequently an equally remarkable array of plucked lutes and
harpsichords, probably a drum (certainly if dance music was in
question): but the whole subject to wide variation as taste or opportunity dictated. This does not by any means imply that they were
casual assortments: all the evidence goes to suggest that the taste
which assembled them was both imaginative and sensitive, and that
the opportunity was often highly prodigal. Many such groupings
were assembled on a scale and conceived in a spirit which were no
longer of the chamber, and might very loosely be termed symphonic,
so long as we remember that while they were imaginatively and
sensitively exploited, they were not systematically exploited. Hence
it is that the best word for them, without disparagement, is 'occasional' orchestras.

During the seventeenth and eighteenth centuries, a substantially
standard orchestra evolved, based on a strong and regular contingent
from the violin family. The wind department was much less stable;
but from the late seventeenth century onwards, flutes, oboes,

bassoons, trumpets and one or two others might normally be present, as well as a keyboard instrument (usually a harpsichord, or when suitable an organ, or both) and drums. The orchestra was more often led by the first violinist or the harpsichordist or both than by a conductor beating time with a baton or a roll of music-paper. But conducting with a baton can be demonstrated as far back as the sixteenth century. The average numbers were much fewer than in our present symphonic orchestras: perhaps round and about forty, as opposed to some sixty to a hundred or more. But what still chiefly prevents our regarding them as symphonic orchestras in the modern sense is not their size, but the manner in which they were used.

The commonest rule (it was not, of course, invariable) was to play long passages, or even whole movements, in one instrumental colouring or blend of colourings: then to change to some other colouring for a contrasted effect. But that is the exact opposite of the typical symphonic method evolved during the past two centuries, especially the late nineteenth. There are, in this method, occasions for continuing a fairly lengthy passage with the instrumental colouring unchanged; but they are exceptional. In the ordinary way, the blend of instruments is changing continually. Even a single chord may require a special shading or distribution of emphasis: and much will depend on which instruments you cause to play each several note of it. Or half a phrase may be given to one group; the other half which balances it may be passed to a different group. In such ways a subtle nuance is imparted to each thread in the whole shimmering network. This art of systematic orchestration for its own sake, which has been carried to the utmost finesse by recent generations of composers, is an essential element in what we call symphonic composition; and unlike most basic musical resources, it is a fairly new development.

The modern orchestra, like the eighteenth-century orchestra, has a solid foundation provided by the violin family, which varies only in the number of players allotted to each part. Flutes, oboes, clarinets and bassoons; trumpets, trombones, horns and tubas; kettledrums: these are all equally standard members; while further wind and percussion instruments, harps, etc., are, up to a point, regarded as reasonable requests. The one regular eighteenth-century instrument to vanish is the keyboard instrument: otherwise, the modern symphonic orchestra is nothing but a greatly expanded and systematized eighteenth-century orchestra, differing chiefly in the manner of its use, and in being now almost invariably controlled by a conductor, on whom falls primary responsibility for interpreting the composer's wishes with fidelity and imagination.

Besides the symphonic orchestra, there are other combinations in regular modern use. These are the brass and wind (military) bands. As their names imply, they are based not, like the orchestra, on the violin family, but on brass instruments of different kinds, with which may be mixed a larger or smaller number of other wind instruments from the reed and flute groups.

A good brass band, unalloyed with the sound of any other instruments, is the warmest and silkiest, the mellowest and most powerful of all the sonorous consorts of music, better known in Great Britain than in other countries (especially the Northern regions). Nearly all the music actually composed for brass band is light in content, and much of it, unfortunately, is trivial. A further large part of the brass band's repertoire, probably much the largest, consists of music arranged from symphonic or operatic or other originals, with an effect very nearly as filtered-down as when the organ imitates the symphonic orchestra. In such a role, however, the brass band, and still more the mixed band, have enjoyed very wide popularity as an unexacting kind of public music-making particularly suitable to the open air. But while the brass band would never, from its limited constitution, be a means to very complex or diversified forms of music, for which it lacks a sufficient range of contrasts, nevertheless it is fully capable of combining depth of feeling with brilliance and richness of sound. The use of brass consorts by Giovanni Gabrieli and his early Baroque contemporaries illustrates its noble possibilities in one direction; another direction may be discovered in the sustained and colourful brass band music occasionally written for it by such twentieth-century composers, for example, as Vaughan Williams (an unforgettable experience).

There has been a vast development in America, starting after the Civil War and renewed in the 1920s, of mixed wind bands of great size in which an already large array of brass instruments is combined with powerful rows of massed flutes, oboes, clarinets and other woodwind, and with timpani, and commonly (though a little incongruously) string double basses. In American high schools and colleges, bands of this nature, though not necessarily of this size, account for a very high proportion of music-making and are really something of a phenomenon. One remarkable variant is the marching band, which, equipped with splendid uniforms and drilled with full military precision, parades and counter-parades and executes manœuvres and patterns of almost ballet-like elaboration, particularly in the intervals of ball games and on similar athletic occasions. Many band directors strive intelligently and enthusiastically to raise the standards of music performed. Some of the most interesting of this has been provided by contemporary composers of a certain stature; but the greater part consists either of arrangements, or of sincere but mediocre compositions often of a depressing conventionality, and at the worst of a banality that must be heard to be believed. Many arrangements are now being made, with very fair success, of Baroque music, which on the whole transfers considerably better and more convincingly than nineteenth-century opera or twentieth-century musicals; but an immense opportunity lies open for contemporary composers willing and able to put genuine gifts of originality at the disposal of an art necessarily popular, but not necessarily trivial. When it is well done, it is warmly welcomed.

Concertos of solo and orchestra

The symphonic orchestra is not only heard alone, but in various further combinations.

Some of these take the form of concertos. It was an eighteenth-century practice, under the name of concerto, to alternate passages for a string orchestra with passages played solo by the leading two violins and violoncello; a beautiful effect, but rather different from our present type of concerto, which was, however, more nearly approached in other cases, as, for example, in some of Bach's Brandenburg Concertos; or his incredibly glittering Concerto for four harpsichords based on a four-violin concerto by Vivaldi; or his romantic Concerto for two violins.

Our present type of concerto was becoming standardized in the period of Haydn and Mozart. Here, a normal symphonic orchestra is joined with one or more definitely solo instruments, whose role it is to display a high degree of virtuosity. At times the soloist may be silent, and at certain conventional points the orchestra may leave the field to the soloist alone for a culminating display (originally improvised), termed a cadenza. But for the most part the two partners do not alternate, but combine. The main themes will be heard sometimes from the orchestra and sometimes from the soloist; but there are certain to be long and important passages in which the soloist is engaged in weaving an intricate web of ornamentation and variation over a plainer statement by the orchestra.

It is clear that some instruments are much better suited than others for this bravura role: and much the most customary are either the violin or the piano. The result in these two cases is rather different. A solo violin is like a member of the orchestra itself, promoted to a virtuoso status, and set off against its fellows, without losing its close kinship with them. What the orchestra sounds broadly, the solo violin echoes or embroiders in its own fine and subtle tones. The partners are complementary, blending naturally with one another.

But a piano is not a normal orchestral instrument: it is quite distinct from any such, even from its nearest orchestral relative, the harp. As we have already seen, it is not of a nature to blend readily with other instruments. Introducing the piano as your solo instrument is like inviting a distinguished guest to rule your ceremonies for the occasion. The partnership, though it can be remarkably effective, will have rather more friendly rivalry about it, and rather less of a purely family character. There may even be times when the rivalry does not seem particularly friendly; concertos such as have been facetiously styled less for 'Piano with Orchestra' than for 'Piano against Orchestra'. Even such a contest may have its exhilarating qualities; but as a whole the proper ideal for a concerto is partnership, not competition.

Concertos for other instruments afford opportunities of various kinds. The violoncello makes a very rich and mellow soloist: the harpsichord a very sparkling one. No instrument which is suitable for a bravura solo role at all is an impossible soloist for a concerto: but some require a more tactful setting than others, and only those with a certain aggressiveness in their disposition and a certain volume of tone at their disposal can hold their own with a full symphonic orchestra freely handled.

Opera and symphonic song

The human voice and the orchestra combine in a number of important ways. Some of these involve one or more solo voices, others employ a large choir, and others again may make use of both.

When a large choir is composed for, it is customary in our present tradition, though by no means invariable, to support it with an independent part for a symphonic orchestra. In such a case, the choir has normally been given (just as it has when singing alone) comparatively broad melodies and straightforward harmonies of the kind which it can most effectively perform, while the orchestra is allotted whatever finesse and elaboration is required. But far more fragmentary idioms are now usual with the *avant-garde*.

An opera is a combination of these resources with a drama conducted through the words and actions of the singers. The first operas (turn of the seventeenth to eighteenth centuries) were an attempt to give the most faithful possible musical expression to the words and action. Thus the singers were given not much formal melody, and a great deal of tuneful declamation closely fitted to the rhythms and inflections of the speaking voice. But later, at the turn of the seventeenth to eighteenth centuries, this original ideal was obscured by a desire to exploit what may be called the instrumental qualities of a perfectly trained voice singing very ornate and formal melody indeed, until many operas became little more than stage concerts in costume, with a rather over-formal plot to justify the scenery. Not that this plot was necessarily lacking in dignity and effect: but no one doubted that it was the star singers who were the centres of attraction.

There has since been a partial revolt against this conception: a revolt of which Gluck was one of the most conspicuous pioneers, in the eighteenth century, and Wagner, in the nineteenth, the final engineer. Wagnerian opera is, from one aspect, a revival of the earliest operatic ideal of an informal flow of declamatory melody closely expressive of the words and action. But Wagner's solution to this difficult problem, though not more expressive than Monteverdi's, is much richer and more elaborate, being, in fact, the very apex of nineteenth-century romantic art.

Wagner never abuses the vocal resources which his novel demands did so much to develop in new directions; nor, unless improperly conducted, does he bury his singers with an overload of orchestral accompaniment: but he causes them to share much more intimately in a closely knit orchestral texture than had previously been attempted. He thereby made opera symphonic in our modern sense and in doing so evolved new uses for the solo voice. A choir or chorus has also still a share in the developed Wagnerian opera, though a much less prominent and artificial one than in some other operatic styles.

Orchestral song is very close to opera. Beethoven, besides writing one clumsily moving opera (*Fidelio*), brought solo singers and chorus into the last movement of his Ninth and last Symphony, with the aim, not quite successfully achieved, of a sublime hymn of joy and goodness. Mahler, a supreme Wagnerian conductor who yet wrote no opera, followed this example in certain of his symphonies, as well as composing song cycles for solo voices and orchestra which tend (especially his masterpiece, *The Song of the Earth*) to be symphonies in fact if not in name: but here, though there is neither stage, scenery nor plot, the music is essentially dramatic, with every dramatic resource of harmony, instrumentation and impassioned declamation. And such has also been the case, to some extent, with oratorio: for this is, virtually, unstaged opera.

CHAPTER 17

THE NEW MUSIC

A contrast of styles

As I bring this now renewed book once more to a conclusion, in 1970, we stand confronted not only with much that is essentially unchanged and traditional, but also with much that is greatly changed and greatly changing.

For on the one hand, our fine symphony orchestras, our famous opera houses, our noted choruses and bands continue to provide even bigger audiences than before with feasts of music often as traditional as if Richard Strauss still ruled and not one electronic murmur had been heard across the land. Ironically, by means of recordings on disk and electromagnetic tape and broadcasts over the radio, more traditional music is being consumed by more varieties of audience than could ever have been reached by traditional means alone. And on the traditional side alone, more varieties of music are being consumed. From medieval plain-chant to Strauss and Mahler is already an unprecedented variety of music for any one generation of performers and listeners to enjoy. Every century of that long traditional development is represented on disks, often thickly represented by best-selling disks. It is an odd claim, made unthinkingly by some champions of new music in our time, that traditional music is dead and superseded. Perhaps it never gave so much pleasure to so many.

But on the other hand, there are composers, performers and listeners so dedicated to new music that for them, in their small though influential numbers, traditional music must seem at times the most distant and irrelevant of worlds. Only a few of them, perhaps, would if pressed maintain sternly that the traditional pleasures are gone for ever, or ought to be gone. Most of them still take keen delight in the music of the past, and some of them are even keen performers of it, or at the very least see nothing wrong for other people in a keen enjoyment of it. An enthusiasm shared between modern music and Baroque music seems a particularly frequent combination, though it does not always go with a genuine understanding of Baroque music. It is the genuinely romantic aspects of Baroque music which are most liable to be either unfeelingly disregarded, or sentimentally misinterpreted; for the romantic ingredient in music is currently under a heavy cloud of suspicion and misunderstanding. Nevertheless, the new music is in many cases as romantic as ever Strauss and Mahler were, although the tremendous difference in scale and means is apt effectually to disguise the fact.

In between, there are composers, and not only elderly composers, who whatever their sympathetic understanding of the *avant-garde*, are not of that company in either their theory or their practice. Some of these, of course, are essentially mediocre and essentially old-fashioned, even when they borrow some of the superficial eccentricities of the *avant-garde* in a calculated endeavour to be thought up to date. They may achieve much success in pleasing audiences only too grateful to be able to feel in the fashion without the pains and difficulties of genuine new experience. They may do this without conscious insincerity, since they are clearly not capable themselves, for all their talent, of new experience. But those who are capable of new experience, whether as composers, performers or listeners, are not so easily deceived. They have a harder time of it, but much more rewarding. Most of the genuine new talent is going into the new music today; but some of it is not, and there is a genuine middle party whose work is not only sincere, but deeply valid.

Tonality: a force of nature

Revolutions usually overshoot the point of equilibrium and return to it at a later stage. It is quite possible that in fifty years' time, the cleavage which now seems so incurable between our traditional music and our new music will have cured itself, and our present somewhat schizoid situation be thereby remedied. The young men who now need to swing so far away from the influence of Strauss and Mahler, or even of Schoenberg and Webern, will be replaced by other young men in no such need of extreme measures to secure their own individuality.

So much of what we mean when we speak of traditional music is merely using another name for the implications of our objective universe in the matter of acoustics. Tonal relationships are not arbitrary, and never were. They are bound up intimately with the physical properties of pendular motion and its consequences in the Natural Harmonic Series. We have no need to discover and have very little possibility of ever discovering the historic or rather prehistoric connections between the properties of vibrating bodies and the raw materials of tonality, as subsequently rationalized in the form of scales and temperaments. But anyone who thinks of tonality (in its widest meaning of direction or hierarchy between tones) as an arbitrary system, replaceable at will by another arbitrary system no better or worse than the last, is singularly obtuse in the face of the great facts of nature. Pendular (periodic, harmonic) motion and its acoustic consequences are among the great facts of nature, and the uses made of them by musicians of different cultures are among the great facts of art.

Those who wish can leave tonality more or less alone for a while, concentrating rather on timbre and rhythm and indefinite sounds with little or no tonal involvement; and some, though far from all of the new idioms today are along these lines. But the tonal forces remain just as much at our disposal as the forces of gravity or the forces of electricity. When the Bulova Watch Company wanted to design a revolutionary new watch without a balance wheel or hairspring, they did not try to dispense with pendular motion. They employed it again in the particularly cunning form of a miniature tuning fork electrically excited from a tiny battery. You can hear the tone of it humming away most musically when you put the watch to your ear; and the watch keeps time to phenomenally fine limits. Force of restitution equals force of displacement: that is pendular motion in the miniature tuning fork, as it is in the 39 in. seconds' pendulum of my long-case clock. New methods, old principles is a familar story in the arts and the sciences alike, and our musical successors will probably be reading the next chapter of it well before fifty years have passed from now.

But meanwhile? Meanwhile we are confronted with these remarkable contrasts between a traditional orchestra and an *avant-garde* ensemble, between traditional *bel canto* and *avant-garde* voiceproduction, between traditional textures in choral music and *avantgarde* textures. The contrasts are so wide at times that it is small wonder if some timid souls convince themselves that the former are music, but the latter are – well, what? Of course they are music too, but there are timid souls, convinced that music has been destroyed, in every generation in turn, and if, as it does seem fair to grant, they have rather more excuse this time, they are certainly just as wrong as ever.

The younger generation are making music to the top of their considerable talent; and if it does not sound like music to some of the older generation, the more loss to them. No one is diabolically gifted enough to destroy an art; nor godlike enough to create it anew. The new music is not as new as that. The new music is still music.

The ensembles of the new music

The new ensembles are still musical ensembles, and very interesting they certainly are. We in the audience may see a stage clustered with stands and racks and scaffoldings bearing gongs, cymbals, bells, tubes, rods, blocks or any other manner of smiteable or swipeable object. There may also be an assortment of electrical apparatus and electrical cables. There may well be a concert grand piano, incongruous in its conventional, shiny black case, and deceptively reassuring in its outer appearance but for a tell-tale wire or two; for who knows what unconventional preparations and electrifications have been arranged inside? And if, presently, a violinist or a cellist or a flautist or a clarinettist or a trumpeter or a trombonist comes on stage, we see the same apparent familiarity, but may perhaps be in for not much less of a surprise when the music begins.

There is, next, quite likely to be an xylophone, and very likely to be a vibraphone. Drums and rattles may be both numerous and various, not only in different shapes and sizes, but in different strategic positions; for strategic placing is important where each performer may need to attend in turn to different instruments, and each instrument may receive attention from different performers. This is all bound up with the nature of the music given to these diversified ensembles; for on the whole, no one sound is continued for long at a time, and often its entry is of the briefest possible. To avoid an uneconomic multiplication of performers, some very agile twisting and turning about, and even smartly crossing the stage, is to be expected.

P

But not too smartly, on account of the electric cables. As the performers arrive on the stage, they pick their way through necessarily with a more leisurely dignity than under conventional circumstances, and also with a more casual air. Even before they begin to perform, we are commonly given the impression that this is no solemn ritual in the temple of art, but a more or less spontaneous series of occurrences which the performers happen to be going through and we happen to be overhearing. Or, perhaps, we may be drawn into involvement by more forceful measures, as when brightly coloured lights are flashed across the audience, or fragments of a film or films are projected or superimposed across the walls and ceiling, or performers appear unexpectedly within the audience itself. Such a performance merges into one of the fashionable happenings in which the young try to express their sense of oneness with the stream of life and their willingness to let happen what may, and to take it all as meaningful and valuable in ways for which they need assume no conscious responsibility. As a reaction from living too consciously in the head and the will, this extreme, though not less one-sided, has its own validity.

Space as well as time is brought to our attention in some performances of the *avant-garde*. It is as if there may be currents of movement in both kinds of dimension at once: related movements. Whereas a conventional string quartet forms a concentrated little group in the middle of the stage, and even an orchestra is ordinarily as closely assembled as its numbers allow, the performers at a new music concert may start in scattered groupings as far apart as the stage allows. Sounds reach us from different quarters, and we are made aware of space as an element in the structure of the music.

Presently there may be interchange between the groups, and our visual and aural perception of the spacing changes too. As the music unfolds in time, it also circulates in space, and we are offered a multi-dimensional experience.

There is a certain breaking down of boundaries. The visual movement brings in a touch of ballet, yet those who move are not dancers but musicians. When singers are on the stage, and involved in both the movement and the music, we get a touch of opera; if there is a chorus, it must then be stage-managed like an operatic chorus, and hopefully the cables are not too extensively entangling. At an opposite extreme, cables and loud-speakers are the chief or the only visible performers.

Multi-channel tape-recordings may reach us from the four quarters of the hall, and we are surrounded by aural space with nothing human visible, or perhaps one lonely singer in an otherwise electronic emptiness.

The combination of recorded sounds with live sounds can be graded in many ways, and even the live sounds can be left to reach us directly, or carried to us through many varieties of electronic modification. The confrontation of human (vocal or instrumental) sounds with electronic sounds, however cleverly it is done, nevertheless tends to feel uneasy, as if two worlds not really quite belonging to one another were focused into an unnatural alliance. An unholy alliance, some would say; for indeed, what has all this machinery to do with art?

The answer is that the artist is still there even if he is not seen to be there. And the machinery is there because an artist has willed that it should be there. The machinery is doing more or less what the artist has willed that it should do; for even where a computer has been instructed to produce random sounds of its own assembling, somebody deeming himself to be an artist has given it the elaborate instructions to produce random sounds.

Even these random sounds, seemingly so abstract, yield a vivid picture of what the world is like for that artist. In so far as he experiences the world as a random chaos, he paints it so. Autobiographically, as all artists do; though not many artists, even in the unconscious, experience the world predominantly as a random chaos. Most artists, even when including an aleatory element of chance (if that is what it really is), are willing to take considerable responsibility for making or finding an order in the chaos. It is a human need.

The untraditional ensembles of the new music are there to be used in untraditional ways. For instruments, and instrumental ensembles, do not change without sufficient cause. Technical and musical developments go hand in hand. Electronic developments have proved extremely suggestive to composers; composers have put equally suggestive demands to electronic engineers, and had them satisfied. Performers are quick to take advantage of what makers improve; makers are ingenious in improving what performers press to have improved. All such influences are mutual; and by and large we find instruments evolving as music evolves, in keeping with the spirit of the times.

A mosaic of small musical events

The spirit of our times favours a lowering of formal thresholds, an uninhibited expansion of resources, a blend of previously incompatible extremes, and a fragmentation which facilitates this breaking down and reuniting of elements.

The sonorities of the new ensembles are textures commonly built up of much smaller fragments of sound and pattern than the traditionally symphonic texture. For the sonorities of Strauss and Mahler, though often combined from innumerable small strokes of orchestration, are like paintwork covering a vast canvas continuously yet with the richest diversity. The new sonorities are more often broken up with silences and discontinuities, like a canvas left unpainted in places for deliberate effect. The patterns of musical events are often more disjointed, and made up from briefer units less similar to one another. Melodic intervals, when present, are often far wider and more abrupt, or alternatively, clustered very narrowly. Rhythms are at once more explosive and more evanescent, or alternatively, obsessive in their persistence.

Things tend to come and go in the new music with calculated unexpectedness. No sooner is some anticipation of sequence or repetition built up than it is swept aside, unless, alternatively, it is taken up into an obsessive persistence no less calculated than its unforeseen cessation.

The sounds themselves, though sometimes very loud and sometimes very soft, have almost always a certain tenuous and insubstantial quality quite unlike the strong and steady flow of so much traditionally symphonic sound. If only because they are mostly so soon interrupted, the new sounds hardly ever build up a traditionally symphonic momentum. It is more the way of the new music to seek a distinctiveness in the musical events than to seek an obvious symmetry or even an obvious continuity.

Yet the hidden organization of these events may itself be complex and continuous in the highest degree. And in practice, the failing most commonly encountered in the new music is not merely disconnectedness; it is monotony. It is the sense of not getting anywhere in particular with all this fragmented variety, and thus of having no particular interest in what happens next. The factor most in need of development to meet this failing, and to rivet the interest of the listener more securely, may well be the factor of obvious, recognizable and potent form. Some of the newest music is on these lines.

New uses of the voice

The treatment of the voice in new music is one of its most striking innovations. Wide leaps, beyond the octave, are in common demand, and require great certainty of vocal technique. Comparatively little use is made of that sustained and mellifluous cantilena which is and has been at least since the sixteenth century the foundation of *bel canto*. Instead, a mixture of extremes is produced, some of them outside the traditional scope of singing and more in the nature of ordinary speaking, of shouting, of whispering, of moaning, of shrieking (but not, somehow, very often of laughing) and all blends of these, including that expressive variety of Sprechstimme (speech-song), half-way between speaking and singing, which Schoenberg developed on the full scale so movingly in his *Pierrot Lunaire* (1912 – so long ago). All this, or any of it, may be emitted through an acoustic megaphone (speaking trumpet – the old-fashioned vamp-horn was thus sung through, and Wagner specified a powerful speaking-trumpet for the voice of Fafner); or it may be electrically amplified with or without much or little modification of the sound.

When these resources are employed by a solo singer, they provide means of expression of which the variety is extraordinarily wide, though the sensuous beauty suffers correspondingly. The same danger of monotony paradoxically arises; only an inspired composer can take care of this, and then, perhaps, only if he is willing to bring back, in some new form, the traditional resources of *bel canto*, which rest on the unchangeable nature of the vocal instrument, and exploit everything exploitable within the possibilities of voice training in the traditional sense. It is there that the chief variety as well as the chief beauty of the voice must be sought, whether for Monteverdi, for Bach, for Bellini, for Wagner or for the genius yet unfound who will one day do as much for modern music as those past geniuses did for their earlier styles and periods.

When the same techniques are employed, or partly employed, in vocal ensembles and choruses, a hair-raising battery of human utterances is at the composer's call. That smooth and disciplined art by which voices in ensemble or chorus drew equal lines of melodic counterpoint, and by these lines made regular progressions of harmony, the whole being made subject to a steady pulse or a subtle interplay of rhythms, seems very far off today, when each part goes its own way, perhaps in unrelated patterns, perhaps in unpredictable echoes as voice answers to voice in violent opposition or powerful juxtaposition. Even without electrical amplification or modification, there is bedlam to be raised by the new vocal idioms; with superimposed distortions and reverberations, there is all hell to be let loose at the touch of a switch.

One price to be paid for many of the new vocal resources is losing all possibility of understanding the words. But for purposes of the new music, this loss is not necessarily a hardship, and may even be a welcome gain; for it is often desired that the words shall not be understood. It is often desired that the sounds and the syllables shall be caught as fragments, and not the words as wholes. Not the semantic sense but the suggestive verbal sonorities are meant to penetrate; and although words in poetry, whether set to music or not, always do carry these suggestive sonorities, swift or slow, light or heavy, high or low, and all this much more so when combined with the like musical sonorities, nevertheless to remove all distraction arising from the semantic meaning can heighten this direct suggestiveness. It heightens it by taking it straight into the unconscious, which is well accustomed to emotive sounds devoid of intellectual logic, whereas words as logic require the lucid co-operation of consciousness.

A further variant, however, and a less restricted one for artistic use, is to allow words to penetrate as vivid entities, though with little or no thought to any grammar or syntax connecting them. Words by themselves are often very powerful emotional counters, charged with symbolism to which grammar and syntax may have little to add in certain contexts.

This obliteration or fragmentation or isolation of the words in some new vocal music is perhaps part of that general retreat from consciousness, and refuge in unconsciousness, which is the most paradoxical result of scientific obsession, and the least surprising in an age of such terrifying insecurity as our own. Autobiography once more, at bottom, but none the less good art on that account. No artist can do good work who is not true to his own times and his own inner state. Of all this he shows us more than he knows himself, and in so doing shows us something of ourselves.

New styles in opera

The new vocal idioms, and the new instrumental idioms too, are taking very interesting effect in opera. Words and music have run a perennial race in opera. Which comes first? Which really has the most importance? Can both be winners simultaneously? That has not often been supposed. It was Monteverdi's wish to make the words the mistress of the music and not the servant, but Handel's practice to let the words come off second best. It was Gluck's aspiration, and Wagner's achievement, to put them both in the service of the drama, though no one really doubts that Wagner was a better dramatist than poet, and a better musician than either.

But modern opera? Berg's *Wozzeck* (1925) still stands out as a classic, even as a classic of genius; and, of course, it is a masterpiece of craft and form, as well as of expressive force. The words are crucial, and they can be clearly heard, in a blend of arioso and speech-song which proved an influential source for later opera. Some of the newest developments in opera have moved much further from comprehensible drama and intelligible words, achieving an expressionistic, even a surrealistic power for which it is rightly thought better to find some other term than opera (for example, Music Theatre or Musical Theatre): for the meaning of opera is surely what it always was, *dramma per musica*, drama in music; and for drama to unfold, words and a plot are needed, and both of a lucid kind not of necessity intellectually, but of necessity symbolically.

One of the best achievements of recent music has been to evolve new variants of recitative and ariosos capable of carrying, as the declamatory parts of opera have always contrived to carry, a natural flow of words in an expressive flow of music. But here the words are meant to be clearly understood.

Electronic music

Of all the new music, the newest in scope and kind is probably the electronic music which by-passes all conventional instruments of music, electrophones included, and emerges from the deliberate synthesis of wave-forms in any desired shapes, frequencies, amplitudes and combinations.

It is now quite out of the question to dismiss electronic music as

a false turning in the history of the art. There are no false turnings
in the history of art. There are only turnings which have or have not
in fact been taken.

There are, it is true, detours, when the straight path for some
reason does not lie open, and a roundabout route is of necessity the
only way forward: straight on from Strauss, for example, would
have been no way forward at all for the succeeding generation.
There are even dead-ends, from which the only escape is by just
getting out again: Scriabin's idiosyncratic harmony and melody, his
near-theosophy and his colour music could be regarded as such;
so, perhaps, could Harry Partch's weird but beautiful orchestra
and 43-note octave, since no school seems to be leading on from it.

But electronic music is certainly no dead-end, and probably no
detour. It is so obviously going on in the work of a substantial school.
This school is not a passing deviation or a trivial aberration. Electronic music is by now a fact of history.

There is already in existence a very substantial amount of electronic music. Its novelty has begun to wear off; its quality is beginning to show through its initial strangeness. The situation as it
thus reveals itself is by no means altogether satisfactory: technical
achievement has so far exceeded artistic accomplishment, as was
perhaps only to be expected. But there has been enough accomplished
to hold out the promise of more and better things to come.

Of a very high proportion of electronic music so far, the best
that can be said is that it evidently forwarded some indispensable
experimentation in the new techniques. This kind of electronic
music was and remains all very ingenious, laborious and expensive
to produce; but when you have got there, what have you got?

What you have got includes a dry, brittle virtuosity, capable of
attaining, and of making perceptible, a degree of velocity hitherto
unprecedented; a moderate extension of available sonorities and
envelopes, but not so great as might have been thought since
traditional instruments already cover a surprisingly high proportion
of the acoustic possibilities, and other sound-producers (such as
telephone bells and slamming doors) fill in many of the remaining
gaps; and a quantity of imperfectly audible algebra, of which the
complexity as mathematics far exceeds the mental capacity even of
the experienced listener to take in as aural patterns. No hidden depths
of beauty and significance being revealed by repeated hearings,

a sufficient artistic criticism of this kind of electronic music, and of all that other *avant-garde* music which, while not electronic, could not be more wearisome if it were, is: so what?

There is also a surprising amount of electronic and other *avant-garde* music in existence, and continuing to be brought into existence, of which the unremarkable truth is that it is very conventional indeed. Beneath the electronic finery or the *avant-garde* gimmickry of such aural sheep in wolf's clothing, there is certainly a musical content to be discerned; but it is a content of such drab banality and old-fashioned triteness, that no seriously conventional composer, not even a self-respecting film composer, would either dare or want to put it forward. Here the *avant-garde* is merely the *arrière-garde* in thin disguise.

There is a pleasanter variety of unimportant electronic music which contrives naïvely to remind us of what Donald Duck or Mr Magoo have been offering us as background music for a good many enjoyable years past. So innocuous a use of new means to old ends does nobody much harm, or much good either; and whatever it may contribute to an advancing technique, it does nothing in particular to advance the art of music.

But then there are the fewer, the inevitably far fewer electronic compositions into which more has gone than technical ingenuity and high (or not so high) aspirations. Then indeed a new land of shimmering forms and shifting meanings is sensed opening up to far horizons and unfamiliar distances. Then indeed new beauty and new significance waits to be uncovered more clearly by repeated hearings. Every so often, a vision of authentic clarity and originality glows out at us in some electronic passage; and it is then that we know, beyond a doubt, that this road does not just lead nowhere. How far it leads, and how rewardingly, are matters which can only depend upon the travellers.

Computer music

When the Northwest Passage, at fearful cost, was at last discovered, it was found to be so foggy, icy and in every way treacherous that it was given up as impracticable. Until just recently. It is still foggy, icy and treacherous; but it is now being pioneered all over again as a promising short sea route for specially equipped oil tankers from

Alaska. So little do we know, ahead of time, what the price and what the rewards of exploration are going to be.

Consider all that expensive mechanical and electronic complexity which constitutes an advanced computer. Consider the elaborate arrangements for coding into numbers, at immense speed, all the relevant physical factors of a series of musical events, for storing them, recalling them, combining them and processing them in any mathematical or random manner desired. Consider the system for digital-to-analogue conversion by which the numerical information is translated into meticulously matching electrical impulses. Consider the apparatus for amplifying the impulses and transmitting them to loud-speakers which convert them to mechanical impulses setting up acoustic vibrations in the air, or for recording them on magnetic tape to be subsequently fed into amplifiers and loud-speakers.

All this may seem, on the face of it, a very roundabout and above all costly method (costly in computer time) of producing music. But in certain respects it is, like the Northwest Passage, a short route. The machinery is complicated and costly; but it dispenses once and for all with the necessity for an orchestra, which is not altogether cheap to assemble nor always altogether easy to rehearse; and it can produce results more certainly and consistently as the composer proposes them than any orchestra.

Computer music can be controlled with a minute accuracy of detail such as human performers cannot approach. Composers who want very finely calculated and proportioned relationships of pitch, rhythm, duration, amplitude, tone-colouring (harmonic spectrum), envelope (attack, steady-state, decay), vibrato, inversion, retrogression, etc., such as human performers can only approximate, are likely to be well served by computer technique.

This very possibility of minute control, however, conceals a danger, or at least a temptation. So finely can the details be calculated, and so closely can they be linked and organized one with another, that the composer may take this linking and this organizing for the sufficient substance of his composition. His own predisposed and experienced ears may detect the fine distinctions and the fine connections; but they may not seem very evident or very important to most other people.

It is already a tendency on the part of the *avant-garde* to dismiss as irrelevant the broader properties of music, and instead of them to make an organized structure out of minuter ingredients of timbre or vibrato or volume-change or speed-change such as are a mere play upon the surface in traditional performances. The temptation is really, of course, in the composer's psyche rather than in the machine's technology. With or without the computer, composers of that inclination have been and will go on falling into it. Interestingly enough, it has been much the same for some time in certain schools of painting. Some of the distinctions have got too fine, or too unplanned, to make much difference. When refinement goes too far, there is not enough substance left to be refined. It may be exquisite, but it is not interesting.

Or rather, it is interesting to those who are enthralled in following it up, and to others likewise engaged. But it is not interesting to those broader audiences to whom traditional music, and some contemporary music, is so profoundly moving. It is not obliged to be; and artists are always entitled to follow up their own preoccupations. Indeed, they must. But narrowness of appeal is a limitation none the less. Great artists get in touch on a wider scale and a deeper level.

Great music will come out whenever there is great genius to produce it; and some of it may come out through the computer. So long as we have only great talent, we cannot be sure. To underestimate genius, or to believe that it is out of date, is one sign that you have not got it; and the fashionable pretensions of not wanting to make great music, or widely accessible music, count for little against our plain need for it. The next genius may well be with us already, but if so he is not yet developed. When he is, he will probably answer our groping questions in no uncertain language.

Meanwhile, the probability today is that whether or not electronic music is on the main road to the future, computer music is going to represent the main future of electronic music. The complexity with which electronic sounds can be organized by means of a computer, and synthesized by means of a digital-to-analogue converting system, far exceeds the reach of any more direct method. The indirectness is to some extent the unavoidable price of the complexity. But methods of improving and accelerating the communication between the man and the machine, between the composer and the computer, are being more effectually developed all the time.

Computer music can itself be seen as a stage further, as quite a long stage further, in the same direction as serialized music at its most mathematical. There may well be going on, at the present time, something of a flight into mathematics, and from there a flight into machinery, in just the same sense although not with the same consequences as that flight into illness well known to modern psychology. At bottom, it is a flight from emotion.

Such a flight is always more or less unconscious, and it always tends more or less to be away from two things: from hard reality outside; and from alarming feeling inside. It is not necessarily unprofitable; on the contrary, it often carries an artist into an immense inner activity, of which his works of art are the outer products and gifts to the world.

But it is a flight none the less. It is perhaps the same at bottom with the random school as it is with the mathematical school; and indeed, computerized music combines elements of both. Avoid personal responsibility: leave it to the mathematics to work it out; leave it to the machinery; or just (if you believe in chance) leave it to chance.

Let not thy left hand know too much about what thy right hand doeth. But so long as your unconscious knows enough, and it generally does, your sureness of aim will not be diminished by a conscious preoccupation with seemingly safe and unemotional objectives. If anything, your aim will be improved, just as in Zen Buddhism you will never shoot your arrow so surely at the target as when you have learnt to take aim without looking at where you are taking aim.

Many of the more general aspects of the new music are extraordinarily reminiscent of what Picasso has long stood for in painting, or Henry Moore in sculpture. That ought not to seem revolutionary to anyone by now, but classical in a once revolutionary style. In these aspects, music, not for the first time, has lagged behind rather than pushed ahead of contemporary developments.

But computer music does not lag behind even the most recent of visual developments, which themselves are a long way from Picasso or Henry Moore. Computer music has invoked the extremely expensive aid of one of the most powerful new machine tools, perhaps the most powerful, of this powerful new age. How could it not depart from conventional aims, if it is to assert and develop its own identity in that formidable alliance? To use the computer conventionally is not merely a shocking waste of money; it gets the very worst of either world. Only a composer who finds his inspiration in and through his new unconventional medium can stand up to its enormous potency and draw out of it an individual work of art. But when this does happen, the results are interesting indeed.

The Natural Harmonic Series continues to provide an objective foundation deep beneath the structure of the most diverse musical organizations. Harmonic partials retain their acoustic symmetry and their emotional convincingness as of old. But they can be organized electronically in all sorts of unfamiliar bands and series, closely or widely gapped, with every variation of relative amplitude. They need press no fundamental upon our attention; yet neither need they build up into the structured intervals of a chord. They can simply reach us as a compound phenomenon of pitch and colouring in their own right.

These compounds can flex and melt before our very ears into other compounds. Their flexibility and their mobility are a large part of their fascination. It is the perpetual shifting of the sounds one into another which is so magical an ingredient. No scale need bind them; no temperament restrict them. Their envelopes, their rhythms, their durations, and their pitch ingredients are indefinitely and continuously variable and combinable. Their content of partials has no obligation even to remain harmonic; for though a harmonic partial is always a harmonic partial, carrying a certain natural smoothness and authority from its ubiquitousness in our objective universe, it has nothing to lose and everything to gain from being contrasted, in the new electronic music, with other partials which are inharmonic (we are quite used to some of these in bells).

Periodic wave-forms can be contrasted and combined with unperiodic wave-forms; related rhythms with unrelated rhythms; contrived events with averaged events and either with random events. There are remarkably few insuperable limits. Pandora's box is open with a vengeance: perhaps it takes a computer to bring all this electric harmony and disharmony under our human control again.

It may have become temporarily forgotten, but if so it will certainly be rediscovered in the not too distant future that art is human communication, and that conscious responsibility and unconscious inspiration have perhaps about equal shares to take in human culture.

Machinery is like fire: a good servant but a bad master. Therefore, use machinery to further but not dictate human ends. Mathematics and other sciences offer potent tools, but double-edged. Therefore, cut with them boldly but carefully, not to be cut down in the process. All roads may in principle lead to art, but some of them go a very long way round. Therefore, remember that a computer can take a composer for a ride just as easily as the other way about, and that music, like democratic government, can only be of people, by people, for people.

The computer as an instrument of music

Our machines are clever, but they are not people. Not even the enchanting song of the birds can really be music for people, though sentimental people in love with nature sometimes project their own feelings on to it, and though, in another sense of which we know little, the song of the birds may really be music – but that is for the birds. The song of the machines is not in itself music for anybody.

If somebody has rigged up a machine to work out music, this can only be that somebody's music at a more or less distant remove. If this is not the case, the machine is not working out music, but going through the motions of working out music; and what is worked out is going through the forms of being music without being music, since there is nothing in it excepting for the forms. This may be pattern-making, but it is not art.

A sentimental machine-minder, like a sentimental bird-lover, may indeed project his own mental contents on to the song of the machines. But then we are back with the sleepless passenger who hears a ghoulish music in the rhythm of the train wheels. For that music, if we wish to call it music, is only what he is mentally projecting. He is only listening to the echo of his own imagination. There is nothing else meaningful there to which he could be listening.

There are two quite different ideas of computer music to be distinguished here. One is computer composition: i.e., asking a computer to do the composing. The other is computer sound-generation: i.e., asking a computer to synthesize what a composer wants it to synthesize. The first cannot, but the second can be, in the human sense, music.

We might therefore put it that a computer which is instructed to work out aural patterns of its own devising is not an instrument of music. We might put it that the same computer when instructed to work out aural patterns derived, however indirectly, from a composer's specifications, is an instrument of music. On this definition, the human purpose is what makes the difference.

Can the same complex of machinery, then, both be and not be an instrument of music? Of course it can. Computers were not evolved to be instruments of music; they were evolved to be the instruments of any purposes within their ever-increasing range, among which purposes music was subsequently found to be a possibility when suitable digital-to-analogue converters are incorporated to transform numerical samplings into electrical impulses, in turn convertible into acoustic impulses. It is perfectly possible for a computer to be a part-time instrument of music. It is practically impossible for a composer, even quite a rich composer, to own a full-time computer.

The numerical stage is of the essence in computer music; for not until every aural phenomenon required is coded into numerical equivalents, sampled at the enormous rate of perhaps 40,000 for each second of resulting music, can the computer start operations in re-combining them and inter-relating them. The amount of computer storage capacity required for such a quantity of information is very great indeed; and the financial expense of this remains a limiting factor of the utmost practical importance. Nevertheless, herein lies the vast potentiality of the computer's aid.

For those composers who are interested, as many composers have for some time been interested, in a music of combinations and permutations, the use of computers as instruments of music has prodigiously increased the scope and subtlety of the operations over which they can exercise some more or less indirect control.

In such music, the degree of control is itself a deliberately variable element. It is, for example, possible to give general instructions of which the working out in detail is left, in any desired degree, to the computer. The details may be more or less at random, and thus quite unpredictable and out of the composer's control; or the details may be determined by previous weightings and averages, which the composer has himself originally controlled in whole or part, but the results of which he is still not altogether able to predict.

These results, therefore, may still surprise him considerably, either for better or for worse. But this is perhaps not very different in principle from the surprises sometimes in store for a conventional composer when his performers find aspects in his music which he himself was not aware of having put there. The composer is still the composer, even if he is not sure quite what is going to happen to his music in the actual outcome; and this outcome can still be music.

At the moment of writing (1970), this combining of the composer's deliberate choices with the computer's more or less random handling of those choices seems to be what most interests a majority of the composers who are using computer techniques. Enthusiasm on the whole seems to be shifting somewhat away from computer music and other synthesized music, back towards concrete music (*musique concrète*) processing outside sounds; but all of this is fair and open territory for composers who are prepared to remain sufficiently responsible for their own music.

It is one thing to co-operate with a machine or a performer; another thing to abdicate entirely from the proceedings, if such a thing is really possible. If it is possible, it is not desirable or probable.

Again, it is not at all a novelty in principle for a composer to find mechanical factors modifying his music in more or less unpredicted ways. The acoustic properties of different rooms, for example, may modify the tone-colouring, the envelope, the amplitude, the texture and the balance of his music to a significant extent. The long reverberation and distant spaciousness of a great cathedral are virtually elements in the scoring of a Renaissance motet by Josquin or Palestrina; and half their beauty is missing in a smaller or a less resonant hall. That was intuitively understood, though in detail neither controllable nor predictable.

Moreover, all instruments of music have their mechanical characteristics and their acoustic properties. Performers manipulate them, each performer differently and individually. Composers exploit them, each according to his purpose and his personality. But that they are neither totally controllable nor totally predictable is part of their artistic fascination. That, too, implies no sort of abdication by the composer.

The most difficult element to introduce into electronic music of every kind is an element corresponding to human fallibility and human waywardness. This is no problem at all with most conventional instruments, whose response to fluctuations of control is prompt and evident enough. All too prompt and evident at times. Machines themselves are not infallible; but when they are working properly they are not wayward; and it is quite hard, although not impossible, to give them a plausible semblance of being so.

As to who wants the plausible semblance rather than the living reality, perhaps it is just those whose psyche compels them to go the long way round. Perhaps they are like sculptors for whom none less than the hardest stone will do. The results may justify it; and certainly nothing else can. The results got by a composer with the aid of a computer may indeed be music. The results got by a computer without the aid of a composer cannot be music. A machine has no psyche. A person has.

A conventional performance of conventional music is not only wayward; it is wayward in close and immediate reflection of the performer's moods as they fluctuate in response to the composer's music. It is a living experience, happening here and now. The audience, too, is partaking in that living experience. There is a flow of sympathy backwards and forwards, in which every person present is both consciously and unconsciously involved.

No stereophonic equipment, no trickery with lights and film projections, no blending and shifting from channel to channel is going to take the place of that. Either the music is happening before your eyes and ears, so that your empathy reaches out to the musicians as they go through their difficult and rewarding parts; or you are just getting the play-back from some previous event of which the risk and the excitement are safely in the past, and only the fixed and invariable record is being delivered to you in the present. The beauty, the significance, the intrinsic interest of an electronic composition must be excellent indeed to stand up to so disadvantageous a comparison.

As to that excellence, there are still plenty of different opinions. Is that surprising? On any calculation, to have achieved so much sheer newness in both music and the instruments of music as our electronic and our other *avant-garde* composers have done, in so relatively short a time, is a remarkable achievement. It would be too much to expect it to be an uncontroversial achievement in addition. Few significant innovations are. The critics, as usual, worry too much. It will all fall into place one way or another when the next genius comes along. As, whether the *avant-garde* expect it or not, he certainly will.

Q

It would seem, from our present standpoint, that the electronic composers might be best advised to cultivate their extraordinary new medium in its fullest and most unadulterated capacities, rather than in imitation of conventional instruments, or even in combination with them. It is quite common at present to mix live performers with recorded tapes. That has the understandable and valid motive of trying to retain an obviously human element. Tapes alone can be enjoyable in private, but they can scarcely make a concert situation (who is to be clapped, or to take a bow?). Yet the combination of tapes with live performers has not yet been certainly shown to be an acceptable working solution. Perhaps it is; but it has its own disadvantages.

So far from the live performers giving a sense of immediacy to the recorded tapes, the tapes seem rather to give an air of unreality to the live performers. It is a little as though the live performers were themselves reduced, if not to automatons, at least to prisoners in some existentialist limbo where humans can no longer be spontaneous, but can only underline the machine's lack of spontaneity. This may be appropriate for certain melancholy purposes; but perhaps not otherwise, since the two worlds, when mixed, may tend to take away each other's value.

The purely electronic world holds a magic of its own which neither needs nor altogether tolerates the intrusion of any live performer. What it does need is the unobtrusive presence of a genuine composer. The outer boundaries of music are strong and flexible enough to contain all that is strange and wonderful in electronic sound, so long as the explorer of that sound is a human explorer. No harm, perhaps, in sending up from time to time a few unmanned satellites to probe and pioneer; but it is when men commit themselves, head and heart, that music happens. They do; it does.

Music in our time

And so the fascinating chapter which is music in our time unfolds. It has its extremes of novelty, of harshness, of violence, of expressiveness, of poignancy, and every now and again of the most startling beauty. It has not yet settled to a steady course.

There may be no one settled course. It looks at present much more likely that there will be various and fluctuating courses, at least for some considerable time to come; but that there will be a way through, or ways through, I have not the smallest doubt. I have a great belief in the young generation, and in the power of life itself to take them forward along the paths they should be following. I have a great belief in life.

I have even a belief in the random music made by young disciples of that fearless adventurer, John Cage; perhaps more than I do in the mathematically oriented schools of which Milton Babbitt has been so dedicated a pioneer. But this is partly because I do not really believe that it is random music (and perhaps the other is not really mathematical music either).

When John Cage relies upon the Chinese I Ching (the Book of Changes) to supply him with seemingly random material, I am bound to point out that whatever it may be that the Book of Changes comes up with, it is certainly not chance. If the Book of Changes works at all, and I am sure that it does, it works by constellating some disposition already latent in the unconscious. You put a problem to it, and it gives you an answer which is relevant although it is not causally connected. Apparently it is connected in some other meaningful way, to which Jung attached the label of synchronicity. Two events can happen at the same time which relate to one another, although neither of them is the cause or the result of the other. If that is not what happens when the Book of Changes comes up with relevant answers, nothing can be happening except a series of remarkable and indeed quite incredible coincidences.

Random appearances cannot be meaningful unless they are connected in ways which are meaningful although they are not causal. The connections, since we are not aware of them, are evidently made in the unconscious; and the communication passes between the unconscious of those who take part in it, whether (for music) as composers, as performers, or as listeners.

If this were not the case, John Cage would be a non-composer making non-music for a non-audience. Perhaps he thinks he is; but the facts seem to be against him there. For then nothing would be happening at all; and the fact is that taken by and large something is happening; and the fact is that a very considerable interest is aroused by what is happening.

Non-music could be of no possible interest to a musician, nor presumably to a non-musician either. Music not made, or minimally

made, in the conscious, must be quite powerfully made in the unconscious to produce the effects it does. But then, it has long been
obvious that communication between one unconscious and another
is continually happening without necessarily surfacing at any point.
Much modern music seems unusually dependent upon such unconscious levels of communication, and of creation also. But there can
never have been any music which does not depend upon the unconscious in some degree.

What is called random or aleatory music could not be performed
at all if the performers were not picking up a great deal more than
is communicated to them either by the sketchy notation in front of
them, or by vague word of mouth from the composer. But they do
seem to pick up what it is all about, and the music does happen.
And many other kinds of modern music happen too, carrying us
forward, for the moment, somewhat unknowingly, but surely very
positively, into the future.

I am not convinced, though I may well be wrong, that the genius
is yet at work who will point our way with clearer knowledge into
the future. But I am convinced that as that future arrives, we shall
find our new instruments and instrumental usages, like our old ones,
serving purposes proper and natural to them. We shall go on valuing
them, as we always have and should, not as ends in themselves, but
for the sake of those musical ends to which they are the best-fitted
means: in short as, literally, the Instruments of Music.

GLOSSARY

A select glossary of technical terms used in this book, or commonly met with in discussions of this subject.

ACCIDENTAL. As adjective, foreign to the prevailing scale; as noun, any symbol or note implying an alteration in the prevailing scale. *Antonym*: Natural. (And see Diatonic, Flat, Sharp.)

ALEATORY. Resulting (more or less) from chance.

ANSWER. In Fugue (see), the second entry of the theme (see), usually a little modified from the first, or subject (see) proper. Subject and answer tend to alternate throughout the fugue.

ATONAL. The adjective of atonality.

ATONALITY. Strictly, 'no-tonality', i.e. absence of definite pitch. Loosely used of a system of composing known as the twelve-note (twelve-tone) technique, in which the twelve semitones of the tempered scale (see Temperament) are treated so far as possible on an equality, as all diatonic (see) and none chromatic (see).

ATTACK. The manner in which a tone, etc., initially builds up. Can be percussive, smooth, gradual, etc. (See Envelope.)

AUGMENTED. Of intervals (Interval, i): increased by a chromatic semitone; of chords: including such an interval. (See also Semitone.)

BAR. (i) A convenient unit (measure) of musical time, usually kept constant until the metre changes. (ii) The line of division drawn to demarcate each such unit: also known as bar-line.

BASS. (i) The lowest part. (ii) That note in a chord which is taken by the lowest part.

CANON. Literally, 'rule'; in effect, a composition proceeding on the rule that a melody appearing in one voice or part shall soon recur exactly (but sometimes transposed in pitch) in another voice or part ('two in one'); or in several other voices or parts ('three in one', 'four in one', etc.). Each entry, in short, imitates its predecessor: the result may be called a melody overlapping with itself.

CHORD. Two or more (some would say three or more) notes heard simultaneously and appreciated as harmony (see).

CHROMATIC. Literally, 'coloured'; in effect, introducing notes or intervals or chords such that they would not occur naturally (see Natural) in the prevailing scale (see). *Antonym*: Diatonic. (See also Semitone.)

COMPASS. Literally, 'boundary'; in effect, the maximum range of notes obtainable by a voice or instrument, or demanded by a part.

COMPOSER. Literally 'putter-together'; in effect, one who writes music.

COMPOSITION. A work of music.

CONCORD. A musically reposeful chord (see Chapter 1).

CONCRETE MUSIC. Music built from the deliberate use of casual sounds, arranged and modified electronically (Fr. *musique concrète*).

CONSONANCE. Relative smoothness of sound-vibration, due to a comparative absence of beats (see Chapter 1).

CONTRAPUNTAL. The adjective of counterpoint (see).

COUNTERPOINT. Literally 'counter-note'; in effect, (i) any reasonably independent melody set against another or others. (ii) More strictly, such a melody in fugue (see). (iii) A passage (or the structure of a passage, or the art of constructing a passage) thus constructed of reasonably independent melodies simultaneously heard: such a passage is said to be 'contrapuntal' or written 'in counterpoint', or 'linear'. *Synonyms*: Polyphony (see); (loosely) Part-writing (see). (iv) More strictly, such a passage (or the structure of such a passage, or the art of constructing such a passage) in fugue.

The antonym of counterpoint (iii) and (iv) is harmony (ii) (see): or melody unaccompanied; i.e. monophony (see): or melody accompanied by vertical harmony (see Vertical); i.e. monody (see). Homophony (see) is often composed as a somewhat restricted variety of counterpoint (iii). Polyphony (see) is virtually a synonym for counterpoint (iii) and even (iv). But it would be much more convenient and precise if we could restrict the word counterpoint to counterpoint (iv), and the word polyphony to counterpoint (iii); introducing some such term as counter-melody for counterpoint (i), and confining ourselves to the strict technical terms Subject, Answer and Countersubject (see Entry, Fugue), for counterpoint (ii).

CRESCENDO. Literally, 'growing'; in effect, increasing in loudness (volume, amplitude). *Antonyms*: Decrescendo. Diminuendo.

CROOK. An extra length of tubing inserted in some lip instruments to lower their pitch.

DAMPER. A device incorporated on some string keyboard instruments to check the vibrations of their strings at will.

DECAY. Manner in which a tone, etc. falls silent. Can be abrupt, gradual, etc. (See Envelope.)

DECRESCENDO. Synonym of Diminuendo. *Antonym*: Crescendo.

DEGREE. Step, note, tone of scale (see); e.g. the fifth degree of the scale is the dominant.

DIATONIC. Literally, 'through the tones'; in effect, introducing no note or interval such that it would not occur naturally (see Natural) in the prevailing scale (see). *Antonym*: Chromatic.

DIMINISHED. Of intervals (Interval, i): decreased by a chromatic semitone; of chords: including such an interval. (See also Semitone.)

DIMINUENDO. Literally, 'diminishing'; in effect, decreasing in loudness (volume, amplitude). *Synonym*: Decrescendo. *Antonym*: Crescendo.

DISCORD. A musically restless chord (see Chapter 1).

DISSONANCE. Relative harshness of sound-vibration, due to a comparative prevalence of beats (see Chapter 1).

DOMINANT. Fifth degree (now) of any scale; so called because, in classical Western harmony, this note, when employed or implied (see Root) in the bass, exerts a dominating tension in the direction of the tonic (see) of the same scale (and see Sub-dominant, Modulation).

DRONES. Notes held unchangingly while another part proceeds melodically; the whole not forming true harmony (see) in the normal sense. (And see Pedal, ii.)

ENHARMONIC. Differing as do, for example, G flat and F sharp, i.e. by a minute interval when justly tuned, but not at all, objectively, under Equal temperament. (See Just, Temperament, and Appendix IV.)

ENTRY. An appearance of a theme or subject; e.g. the second entry of a normal fugue is called the answer.

ENVELOPE. Manner in which a tone or other sound builds up to and falls away from its (more or less) steady state. (See Attack, Decay.)

FANTASY, or FANTASIA. (i) A free composition, not in any strict form. (ii) In the sixteenth and early seventeenth centuries, a loosely fugal (see Fugue) composition for instruments, constructed broadly in the form of a motet (see).

FIGURATION. Free melodic patterns ornamenting a progression (see) which could be less ornately traced.

FLAT. As adjective: (i) low in pitch: e.g. the singer is flat, i.e. out of tune (see Tune, ii) by being lower than the proper pitch, such as the pitch of an accompanying piano. *Antonym*: Sharp. (ii) Lowered by a semitone: e.g. B flat, the note a semitone below B natural (see Natural). As noun: (iii) the injunction to lower a given note or notes by a semitone: e.g. there are three flats in the key of C minor (see Key, ii; Mode; Minor). *Antonym*: Sharp. (iv) The symbol (♭) indicating that injunction: e.g. there are three flats in the signature (see) of C minor. Double flat (♭♭) indicates lowering by a further semitone: i.e. by a tone in all. (And see Accidental.)

FORM. (i) Any basic, more or less standard pattern to which a composer may choose to conform: e.g. sonata form, rondo form. Consult a text-book for such standard forms. (ii) The pattern taken by a given composition, whether standard or not. *Antonym*: Content.

FREQUENCY. In acoustics, the rate of vibration, measured by the number of complete vibrations (cycles) of a sounding body per second; c.p.s. (cycles per second) for short. (See Chapter I.)

FUGUE. Literally, 'flight'; in effect a species of modified canon (see) in which each entry of the main theme, after the first such entry, is normally accompanied by a second theme (a continuation of the first), known as the countersubject; and usually relieved from time to time by contrasting episodes in a freer style. Each entry imitates its predecessor, though not so rigidly and continuously as in canon proper. Towards the end, the entries often follow each other at shorter intervals (see Interval, ii), in what is called a stretto; but since the earlier entries never quite catch up with the later, the result is like a perpetual pursuit: whence the name fugue. (See Counterpoint, Answer.)

GLISSANDO. Literally, 'gliding'; in effect, rapidly rushing up and/or down a series of notes: e.g. a Glissando passage for the harp.

HARMONIC. (i) As noun, strictly speaking an element in a periodic vibration (see Chapter 1), but commonly used of the partial tone thereby produced. Also used as an adjective, to describe such partials. (ii) As adjective of harmony (see), composed primarily of chords. *Antonym*: Melodic (i). (iii) The name of one of the two basic forms of the minor scale. *Antonym*: Melodic (ii). (See Mode.)

HARMONIZE. To employ or add chords.

HARMONY. (i) Simultaneous notes heard and appreciated as chords. (ii) That aspect of harmonized music which consists, not in its melody or melodies, but in the harmonic progressions (see) which support that melody (where the music is monodic – see Monody), or which result from those melodies (where the music is polyphonic – see Polyphony). *Antonym*: Melody (ii); or Counterpoint (iii) or (iv).

HOMOPHONIC. The adjective of homophony (see).

HOMOPHONY. Literally 'like-voice'; in effect, harmonized music whose parts all move (more or less) in the same rhythm, producing block chords, and as it were speaking with one accord. (Also called Homorhythm. And see Monody, Monophony, Polyphony.)

HORIZONTAL. Composed of markedly independent melodies (appearing, in notation, *horizontally* across the page: see Score) from whose combination the desired chords result; i.e. more or less contrapuntal (see Counterpoint, iii). *Antonym*: Vertical.

INTERVAL. (i) The interval of pitch between two notes, whether heard successively or simultaneously. (ii) The interval of time between various entries of a fugal or quasi-fugal (see Fugue) composition.

INTONATION. (i) Pitch adjustment. (ii) Congruity of pitch (see Tune, ii).

INVERSION. (i) The act of transposing the notes of an interval (Interval, i) or a chord into a different order of pitch. (ii) An interval or chord so transposed: e.g. the chord *e, g, c'* is the first inversion of the triad, *c, e, g*; their common root (see) being *c*. (There are other important meanings in connection with the technique of fugue: but they can be ignored for the purpose of the present book.)

JUST. Of temperament, based on acoustically true intervals (Interval, i); of intonation, truly in tune. (See Temperament, and Appendix IV.)

KEY. (i) The lever operating the action of a note on a keyed or a keyboard instrument, when designed to be depressed by a finger. *Antonym*: Pedal. (ii) A selection of notes to which a composer chooses, basically, to confine himself for a time: these notes being called diatonic (see); and any alien notes which he may permit himself, being called chromatic (see). There are theoretically as many different keys as there are notes employed in our present musical system. However, in this system, notes very nearly identical, e.g. A flat and G sharp, can be treated as identical, by being tuned to a compromise between the two (see Temperament). Therefore, for example, the key of A flat and the key of G sharp can be treated as interchangeable, and may be notated as whichever is most convenient. A key such as B sharp would never be notated literally; it would always be set down as C major. Thus *in effect* there are only twelve distinct notes and twelve distinct keys in our present musical system. (See also Mode. Some reckon twenty-four keys, counting major and minor separately: but this is less accurate language, as the difference between major and minor is one of mode, not of key.)

There are seven notes diatonic to each key, and five chromatic. Of the seven diatonic notes, five are reached from the note below by the interval of a tone; two are reached by the interval of a semitone. The order in which the five notes and the two semitones are arranged is the same for every key: thus every key is alike except for its relative pitch. For this reason, it is easy to carry the music smoothly and continuously through the changing keys, returning eventually to the starting-point. (See Modulation.)

Keys may be used in a variety of modes, of which two only, the major mode and the minor mode, were in classical use.

LEADING-NOTE. The seventh degree of the scale (see: and see Subtonic for an explanation of its name and function).

LEGATO. Literally 'bound'; in effect, smooth in style because virtually devoid of minute silences between one note and the next. *Antonym*: Staccato.

LINEAR. Synonym of horizontal; but used in particular with reference to counterpoint conducted with unusual disregard for harsh harmonic consequences.

MADRIGAL. A moderately contrapuntal (see Counterpoint, iv) vocal piece, in the same general form as a motet (see).

MAJOR. Literally, 'greater'; in effect, an adjective indicating (i) that common mode (see) in which the third degree of the scale (see) is major (Major, ii); i.e. a tone above the second degree. *Antonym*: Minor. (ii) The wider variety of any interval (Interval, i) such that it has two basic varieties, one wider (by not more than a semitone) than the other. *Antonym*: Minor.

MEDIANT. The third degree of the scale (see: and see Progression). Only less useful as a harmonic pivot than the dominant (see) and sub-dominant (see). (And see Sub-mediant, Modulation.)

MELODIC. (i) The adjective of melody: composed primarily of melody. *Antonym*: Harmonic (ii). (ii) The name of one of the two basic forms of minor scale. *Antonym*: Harmonic (iii). (See Mode.)

MELODY. (i) Successive notes heard and appreciated as tuneful (Tune, i). (ii) That aspect of harmonized music which consists, not in its harmonic progressions (see) but in the melody or melodies (Melody, i) which those progressions support or are constructed from. *Antonym*: Harmony (ii).

MICROTONE. Literally, 'small-tone'; in effect, any interval (see Interval, i) smaller than a semitone.

MINOR. Literally, 'lesser'; in effect, (i) that common mode (see) in which the third degree of the scale (see) is minor (Minor, ii); i.e. a semitone above the second degree. *Antonym*: Major. (ii) The narrower variety of any interval (Interval, i) such that it has two basic varieties, one wider (by not more than a semitone) than the other. *Antonym*: Major.

MODE. Like key (Key, ii), a selection of notes to which a composer chooses basically to confine himself for a time. Medieval and Renaissance composers recognized up to eight (in the sixteenth century, up to twelve) modes: today, we usually, though not by all means always, confine ourselves to the two we call major and minor, using the latter, however, in two slightly varying versions. (Melodic minor and harmonic minor – the former slightly different, again, in its ascending and descending forms.)

Modes (unlike keys) differ in their distribution of the two semitone intervals and the five tone intervals (Interval, i) which each includes: thus no two modes are quite alike. Whereas the difference between different keys is relative and can only be sensed when they are juxtaposed, the difference between different modes is absolute, and can be sensed in itself. Hence, for example, major remains unmistakably major, and minor remains unmistakably minor, in whatever key. So too, in varying degrees, when any other distinct mode is introduced; with the important result that further modes than major and minor may also be exploited, given discretion, in music primarily based on key, as a number of successful experiments have shown. (See also Key, ii.)

MODULATION. A journey through diverse tonalities (see) so conducted that each stage is felt to be a logical continuation of the preceding stage.

MONODY. Literally, 'alone-song'; strictly, a kind of Italian vocal music c. 1580–1630; loosely, music in which a single melody has outstanding importance, while the accompanying harmonies have merely a supporting role. *Antonym*: Polyphony.

MONOPHONY. Literally, 'alone-voice'; in effect, unaccompanied melody. (See Homophony, Monody, Polyphony.)

MOTET. A more or less contrapuntal (see Counterpoint, iv) vocal composition, usually to sacred words, each sentence or phrase of which is set to a separate theme, a new musical section beginning with each new verbal sentence or phrase.

MUTE. A device designed to damp or check partially the vibrations of certain instruments, thus temporarily reducing both the volume and the brilliance of their tone.

NATURAL. As adjective: neither flat (see) nor sharp (see). As noun: the symbol (♮) cancelling an accidental (see). *Antonym*: Accidental. (And see Diatonic, Flat, Sharp.)

NOTATION. (i) Symbols by which music is set down in writing. (ii) The act of so doing.

NOTE. (i) A musical tone at its perceived pitch; ordinarily, the pitch of its fundamental harmonic (see Chapter 1). (ii) The written symbol for such a tone.

OCTAVE. (i) The eighth degree of a scale (see); i.e. the degree at which the scale is regarded as repeating itself, though at a pitch one octave (Octave, ii) higher. (ii) The interval thus spanned.

Consecutive octaves are a blemish in pure part-writing, owing to the fact that the ear perceives them, not as two parts, but as one part differently coloured (the same occurs, though in lesser degree, with fifths, and even, in certain circumstances, fourths). The reasons are physical (see Chapter 1).

PART. (i) In counterpoint, or part-writing (see) of any kind or degree, one of the more or less independent melodies which combine to produce the harmony. (ii) More loosely, the notes assigned to any instrument in a concerted composition: e.g. the piano part of a song.

PARTIAL. Any ingredient of a compound tone, whether its ingredients (partials) are harmonic (see Harmonic, i) or not (see Chapter 1).

PART-SONG. Vocal music written in parts (Part, i; Part-writing); it being generally implied that the highest voice has a more or less prominent tune, and the remainder more or less subordinate accompanying parts.

PART-WRITING. Roughly the synonym of counterpoint (iii); it being generally implied, however, that less independence in the several combined melodies, other than the highest melody (Tune, i), is required to justify the description part-writing, than to justify the description counterpoint (see). Some minimum degree of part-writing must result where there is even a melody with a passably independent bass.

PEDAL. (i) The lever operating the action of a note on an organ or other keyboard instrument, when designed to be depressed by a foot, not a finger (*Antonym*: Key); or operating the stops of such an instrument as the harpsichord, or operating the pitch-changing devices on the pedal harp, or the like. (ii) An effect in harmony produced (or like that produced) by keeping one's foot down on an organ pedal for a substantial time, during which the remainder of the harmony progresses with greater freedom, in relation to the held note, than would normally sound well. Somewhat like a temporary drone (see).

PERPENDICULAR. Synonym of vertical (see).

PISTON. (i) A tap or valve for introducing a permanently attached crook (see) into the effective length of certain lip instruments. (ii) A device on many organs for operating a quick change of stop, or other special effect.

PITCH. Acuteness or gravity. Acute, or high notes, are those associated with rapid frequencies; grave, or low notes, are those associated with slow frequencies. (See Appendix III.)

POLYPHONY. Literally, 'many-voice'; in effect, music in which every part has a melody of more or less equal importance, these melodies resulting in the desired harmony when combined. *Antonym*: Monody. (And see Counterpoint.)

PROGRESSION. In harmony (see), a succession of chords comprehensively related; i.e. in such a way that it is possible to grasp some genuine affinity between each neighbouring link in the succession. For example, the progression, common chord of G major to common chord of C major (G, B, D, to C, E, G), is easily comprehended, owing to the presence in each of the note G; the fact that the tonic of G major (G) is the dominant (see) of C major; and the ease with which the mediant (see) of G major (B) presents itself to the mind as the leading-note (see) of C major.

QUARTERTONE. A microtone (see); by definition, half a semitone (see). (See Scale.)

REGISTER. (i) A part of the whole compass (see); e.g. the bottom register of the clarinet is cadaverous in quality. (ii) A synonym for stop (i).

REGISTRATION. In connection with the organ or harpsichord, choice of stop or stops (Stop, i).

RHYTHM. (i) That aspect of music which most nearly corresponds to rhythm in poetry; i.e. more or less regularly recurring stress, or emphasis, or duration of sound. Where the rhythm is exceptionally free, as in recitative, the rhythm of prose would be a better analogy. (ii) Any specific variety of musical rhythm. (See Time.)

ROOT. That note, called the fundamental bass, which is either the bass (Bass, ii) of an uninverted chord (see Inversion); or which would be the bass of an inverted chord if this chord were not inverted; or which would be the bass of an incomplete chord nowhere including it, if this chord were both complete and uninverted. For example, in the key of C major, the root of the incomplete chord of the dominant ninth: *b*, *d′*, *f′*, *a′*, is *g*. (But there are certain objections to this latter theory of 'omitted roots', at least if pressed too far.)

SCALE. Literally, 'ladder'; in effect, all the notes diatonic (see) to a given tonality (see), arranged in ascending order of pitch under the following names: tonic, or key-note; super-tonic; mediant; sub-dominant; dominant; sub-mediant; leading-note or sub-tonic. Such a diatonic scale is simply a convenient rationalization of that choice of notes to which the composer proposes, *for the time being* (however short) basically to restrict himself (see Key, ii; Mode). The chromatic (see) scale is simply a similar rationalization of all the notes normally used by traditional Western composers *at any time*: i.e. a total of twelve semitones, which may, however, be notated, according to the context, in more ways than one (see Key, ii; Temperament). The octave (see) may be divided into more than twelve notes by using smaller intervals than the semitone: i.e. microtones. This is quite customary in purely monophonic music (see Monophony) such as many Eastern schools cultivate in great subtlety and perfection: but is not a possible basis for harmony, in the functional sense, though it can be used up to a point at the same time. It is now a common feature in Western music of the *avant-garde*.

SCORE. A notated copy of all the parts of a concerted composition, set out horizontally one above the other in such a way that a vertical line drawn from top to bottom would more or less accurately represent a synchronized moment in all the parts alike. *Avant-garde* scores are more pictorially suggestive.

SEMITONE. A twelfth part of an octave (see), given equal temperament (see Temperament); there are other sizes. The smallest normal interval of our traditional Western music.

SFORZANDO. Literally, 'forcing'; in effect, with a pronounced accent or stress.

SHARP. As adjective: (i) high in pitch: e.g. the singer is sharp, i.e. out of tune (Tune, ii) by being higher than the proper pitch, such as the pitch of an accompanying piano. *Antonym*: Flat. (ii) Raised by a semitone: e.g. C sharp, the note a semitone above C natural (see Natural). As noun: (iii) the injunction to raise a given note or notes by a semitone: e.g. there are three sharps in the key of A major (see Key, ii; Mode; Major). *Antonym*: Flat. (iv) The symbol (♯) indicating that injunction: e.g. there are three sharps in the signature (see) of A major. Double-sharp (×) indicates raising by a further semitone: i.e. by a tone in all. (And see Accidental.)

SIGNATURE. The symbol or symbols notated at the beginning of
each line of a composition to indicate which sharps and flats
(Sharp, iii; Flat, iii), if any, are diatonic (see) to that composition,
unless and until a change of signature occurs.

SPICCATO. Literally, 'cut-off'; in effect, (i) on bowed string instruments, rather detached in style, with a delicate separation of
each note from its successor, produced by causing the bow to
rebound slightly from the string between each stroke. (ii) More
generally, a style like that so produced.

STACCATO. Literally, 'separated'; in effect, markedly detached in
style, because prolonging unusually the minute silences between
one note and the next. *Antonym*: Legato.

STOP. (i) As noun: on organs, a device for bringing into operation
a rank (or ranks) of matched pipes similar in timbre but graded
in pitch, hence, such a rank (or combination of ranks) itself; on
harpsichords, the corresponding device for bringing in a set of
strings: hence such a set itself. (ii) As verb: on stringed instruments, to curtail the sounding length of string by pressing it with
the finger; or on wind instruments, to increase the sounding
length of tube by closing a hole with the finger; hence, to play a
note: e.g. a violinist playing in the first position stops *e"* with
his little finger.

SUB-DOMINANT. The fourth degree of the scale (see), exerting a
harmonic tension only second to that of the dominant (see) itself,
of which it is the inversion (Inversion, ii; and see Modulation).

SUBJECT. (i) Synonym of theme. (ii) A more formal and fully pro-
pounded section of musical material for subsequent development, especially in sonata form (see standard text-books). (iii)
The subject of a fugue.

SUB-MEDIANT. The sixth degree of the scale (see), scarcely less useful as a harmonic pivot than the mediant (see), of which it is the
inversion (Inversion, ii; and see Modulation).

SUB-TONIC. The seventh degree of the scale (see); always, in the
major mode (see Mode), and often, in the minor mode, leading
by the enticing step of a semitone to the tonic: whence its alternative name of 'leading-note'.

SUPER-TONIC. The second degree of the scale (see); particularly
useful in modulation (see) as the dominant of the dominant.

TEMPERAMENT. Such modification of the true acoustic intervals

(Interval, i) as is necessary in freely modulating music on instruments of fixed pitch. (See Appendix IV.)

TEMPO. Literally, 'time'; in effect, the speed at which a composition is performed.

TESSITURA. Literally, 'texture'; in effect, that part of a vocal compass on which a given voice part most continuously draws. For example, a soprano song with a high tessitura is one which demands unusually frequent use of the highest register of the soprano compass.

THEME. A musical fragment or short entity capable of extended subsequent development; in particular, the subject of a fugal work or passage.

TIMBRE. Quality of tone, in contradistinction to pitch, or to volume.

TIME. The nearest musical equivalent to metre in poetry; the grouping of rhythmic accents in more or less constant units known as bars (but the subject is complex, and has been more so in the past). (See Rhythm.)

TOCCATA. Literally, 'touch-piece'; in effect, originally a free and brilliant preluding in which the player warmed himself up and loosened his fingers: hence a standard Baroque form in which a certain element of bravura, reminiscent of a virtuoso improvising, remained.

TONALITY. All those consequences which arise for music from the combination (successive, simultaneous or both) of tones, i.e. sounds definite in pitch. These consequences arise from the acoustic properties of our objective universe, and are therefore essentially unalterable, although an unlimited variation can be brought into our manner of using them. Music organized in any manner by tones cannot, strictly speaking, be called atonal, although this term is often used loosely for twelve-note music (see Atonality). Schoenberg, the developer of twelve-note music, himself deplored this loose terminology, and did not like to have his music called 'atonal'; but the misuse has unfortunately become somewhat usual. Another misuse of the term 'tonality' is in the meaning of 'key tonality' as opposed to 'modality' (which in fact is also tonality, and can properly be called 'modal tonality'). Key tonality (i.e. what history and theory books frequently miscall 'tonality') was very thoroughly established indeed by about

R

the year 1600, as can be seen in much advanced music of the time (e.g. the keyboard music of John Bull, Sweelinck and others). The generation of Corelli and Alessandro Scarlatti did not (as still often misstated) establish key tonality, but refined it to a classic lucidity, less adventurous than the bold and far-reaching modulations of its earlier and more revolutionary period.

TONE. (i) A note. (ii) Any definitely pitched sound (see Chapter 1). (iii) A synonym for timbre. (iv) That interval (Interval, i) which, given equal temperament (see Temperament), is twice a semi-tone (see); sometimes called whole tone (there are other sizes).

TONIC. The first degree of the scale (see; and see Tonality); also known as the key-note or final (but this last term strictly refers to the tonic of a mode, which is its first degree if the mode is one of those called authentic, but its fourth degree if the mode is one of those called plagal: yet always with the same implication of representing the tonality around which the music centres, and to which it must return).

TRANSPOSE. Literally, 'carry across'; in effect, change to another pitch without otherwise altering.

TRIAD. Any three-note chord, in root (see) position, bounded by the interval of a fifth, and containing two intervals of a third; or any inversion (Inversion, ii) of such a chord.

When, in root position, the lower third is major and the higher third is minor, the triad is major. When the lower third is minor and the upper third is major, the triad is minor. These triads, and their inversions, are also known as common chords.

When both thirds are major, the triad is augmented. When both thirds are minor, the triad is diminished.

TUNE. (i) A succession of notes at various intervals (Interval, i), and usually of varying lengths, such that it is expressive of emotion in the manner hinted at in Chapter 2; a virtual synonym of melody (i), but carrying more of the implication of a *completed* melody. (ii) A synonym of intonation (ii), e.g. the singer is out of tune with the piano.

TWELVE-NOTE (TWELVE-TONE) MUSIC. See Atonality.

VALVE. (i) A synonym of piston (i). (ii) A device controlling the passage of air in sundry mechanisms on the organ.

VERTICAL. Composed of markedly unpolyphonic, block chords (appearing in notation *vertically* on the page: see Score), on which rests a more or less prominent melody, normally in the highest part; i.e. more or less monodic (see Monody). *Synonym*: Perpendicular. *Antonym*: Horizontal.

VIBRATO. Slight, fairly rapid but controlled variations of pitch and intensity for purposes of expression, almost indispensable for a lively effect in the voice, on bowed string instruments, and on the clavichord; used frequently though less continuously on many wind instruments, especially the oboe; and also imitated in the tremolo stop of many organs. Also produced electronically. It is possible to distinguish vibrato (as pitch fluctuation) from tremolo (as intensity fluctuation).

APPENDIX II

ALPHABETICAL NOTATION SYMBOLS USED IN THIS BOOK

Where it is not intended to specify any particular octave, plain Roman capitals are used: as in the phrase, the key of C. Whenever a specific octave is intended, the letter is italicized.

The specific octave beginning on the 32-foot organ bottom C is notated $C_{,,}$ to $B_{,,}$.

The next higher octave is notated $C_{,}$ to $B_{,}$.

The next, C (bottom note of violoncello) to B.

The next, c (tenor C, bottom note of viola) to b.

The next, c' (middle C) to b'.

The next, c'' to b''.

The next, c''' to b'''.

The next, leading to the top note of the piano (c^v), is notated c'^v to b^v.

To make all clear, the following is the staff notation and the short-hand notation of a complete diatonic octave, from c' (middle C) to c'':

Chromatic notes are indicated by the usual suffixes; for example:

In the system of tuning known as Equal Temperament (see Appendix IV), on which the modern keyboard is based, C sharp and B double-sharp are treated as the equivalent in pitch of D flat; D double-flat and B sharp are treated as the equivalent of C natural;

234

C double-sharp and E double-flat are treated as the equivalent of D natural. The same principle applies throughout the scale. The equivalence is strictly only a convenient compromise; but this need not concern us here. In practice, the complete chromatic scale in the octave shown above can most conveniently be notated, upwards, simply as *c', c' sharp, d', d' sharp, e', f', f' sharp, g', g' sharp, a', a' sharp, b', c"*; or downwards, as *c", b', b' flat, a', a' flat, g', g' flat, f', e', e' flat, d', d' flat, c'*.

STAFF NOTATION

'HELMHOLTZ' NOTATION as used in this book and by acousticians generally

$$(c'''' \quad b'''')$$

$C_{\prime\prime} \ B_{\prime\prime} \ C_{\prime} \ B_{\prime} \ C \ B \ c \ b \ c' \ b' \ c'' \ b'' \ c''' \ b''' \ c^{IV} \ b^{IV} \ c^{V}$

$$(c' \quad b' \quad c^2 \quad b^2 \quad c^3 \quad b^3 \quad c^4 \quad b^4 \quad c^5)$$

ENGLISH ORGAN-BUILDER'S NOTATION

CCCC BBBB CCC BBB CC BB C B c b c' b' c'' d'' c''' d'''' c''''

STANDARDS OF PITCH

Pitch can only be defined exactly by the frequency in vibration cycles per second (c.p.s.). Notated standards of pitch are a matter of arbitrary convention, and have varied widely and continually throughout musical history.[1] Today, some approach to a uniform agreement on the subject has at last been achieved. In England, our most usual standard in the decades before the war wrote a' for the note given by 439 c.p.s. (New Philharmonic pitch). In 1939 British Standard Concert Pitch was officially based on $a' = 440$ c.p.s. This is the present international standard, and any conductor who allows it to rise again is doing us a great disservice. Unfortunately, several such are at large.

Medieval, Renaissance and Baroque standards of pitch varied bewilderingly. Early, however, in the eighteenth century, a fairly usual practice had been deduced probably lasting till after the death of Beethoven. This is known as Classical pitch, standing at about $a' = 415$ c.p.s., or roughly a semitone below New Philharmonic pitch. During the nineteenth century, standards of pitch rose extravagantly, under the illusion that brilliance would be enhanced thereby; our present standard represents a reaction towards a more traditional level. (Old Philharmonic pitch put $a' = 452.5$; though this had been raised from 433·2, and that in turn from an earlier pitch, chosen in 1813, of 423·7.) Much music down to Beethoven's death ought perhaps to be dropped another semitone, to Classical pitch: what makes this impracticable is chiefly the fact that modern instruments are designed for modern pitch. Wind instruments in particular cannot change their pitch substantially without structural alteration.

---

[1] Thorough research in A. Mendel, 'Pitch in the 16th and Early 17th Centuries', Pts. I-IV, *Musical Quarterly*, xxxiv, 113 (January, April, July, Oct. 1948).

TEMPERAMENT

Where, and in what form, just intonation is attainable

We have seen in Appendix III that the pitch we indicate by a given note-name is arbitrary. But once that choice is made, the pitches indicated by other note-names, though they may be flexible, are no longer arbitrary. How were they arrived at?

By instinct and tradition. Eastern tradition, which made no essential use of harmony, allowed a freer choice of intervals than Western tradition since this became based on harmony, which does not sound well unless its main intervals are just or very nearly so.

By a just interval is meant one tuned to evince the least possible roughness due to beating. As we saw in Chapter I, the most consonant interval after the unison is the octave; for which very reason it is the most narrowly hedged about by dissonance, since the contrast between its beatlessness when perfectly tuned and its beating when imperfectly tuned is particularly marked. The remaining intervals are progressively less beatless; thus the augmented fourth, for example, beats so little the worse for being slightly mistuned that it is in practice difficult to give it an exact tuning at all.

In short, some intervals both can and need be tuned less exactly than others; and this is fortunate. For it is very doubtful whether our objective universe is such as to permit us to employ just intervals *consistently*.

Three musically paramount intervals are the octave, the fifth, and the major third, with ratios as $2 : 1$, as $3 : 2$ and as $5 : 4$. Now 2, 3 and 5 happen all to be prime numbers to one another: i.e. such as cannot be divided without remainder by any other number except unity. This means that if we calculate our intervals from a given note by octaves, by fifths and by major thirds, we can never hope to reach another note *exactly* the same by any two, still less by all three routes.

Start with a note $C_{\prime\prime}$. Now $\frac{2}{1} = 2$ and $\frac{3}{2} = 1\cdot5$, so that to reach the octave you multiply by 2 and to reach the fifth you multiply by 1·5. But 2^7, which gives the seventh octave, is 128, while $(1·5)^{12}$, which gives the twelfth fifth, is 129·75.

Thus the b'^v sharp reached by going up twelve fifths, though it is very nearly the same note as the c^v reached by going up seven octaves, is not quite the same; it is sharper by a vexatious little gap of almost a quarter of a semitone, known as the ditonic or Pythagorean comma. Conversely, the $D_{,,}$ double-flat reached by going down twelve fifths from c^v, though it is almost the same note as the $C_{,}'$ reached by going down seven octaves, is not quite the same; it is flatter by a ditonic comma. And likewise with all other notes, so that, if reached in this way by a series of fifths, B flat is not quite the same note as either A sharp or C double-flat, etc.

Or you can reach a quite different b'^v sharp by going up three major thirds from c'^v; this will be flatter than c^v by an even larger gap, known as the diesis. You can reach e'' by going up four fifths from c; this will be sharper than the e'' which is the major third above c'' by yet another gap (minutely smaller than the ditonic comma), known as the syntonic comma or merely as the comma. And likewise with all other notes, so that if we tune our fifths true, we necessarily mistune our major thirds, and if we tune our major thirds true, we necessarily mistune our fifths.

The pure scale

Now suppose we want a diatonic major scale starting on c'. We may take its octave c'', its fifth, g', its fourth, f', and its major third, e', all as just intervals to c'.

Next to the tonic triad C E G we shall most want its dominant G B D and its sub-dominant F A C. So we may add d' as the just fifth to g, b' as the just major third to g', and a' as the just major third to f'. This completes a scale which may fairly be called pure.

We shall find that our major seconds c' to d', f' to g' and a' to b' are 'major tones', while our major seconds d' to e' and g' to a' are 'minor tones', smaller by a comma. Our diatonic minor seconds e' to f' and b' to c'' are 'major semitones' (always different letters in their notation), slightly larger than chromatic minor seconds such as from c' to c' sharp, which are 'minor semitones' (always the same letter: *N.B.* these two kinds of semitone).

Now rise the major sixth from c', and you will reach a'. Rise the fifth from d', and you will reach, not the same a', but one sharper by a comma; for a major tone (c' to d') plus a perfect fifth (a' to d') is a comma wider than a major sixth. What is to be done?

Rather than sound your a' at two different pitches running (c' a', d' a'), you will instinctively flatten your d' instead, making it the minor instead of the major tone above c'. But if the major sixth d' to b' should chance to intervene (c' a', d' b', d' a'), you will instinctively keep your d' unchanged and sharpen your a' at its second appearance.

In yet other contexts, you may instinctively modify each note a little. The circumstances in ordinary music are usually far more complicated, and demand a very subtle interplay of pitch, involving several notes at a time and a continual subconscious vigilance on the performer's part.

The notes thus liable to be modified are called mutable notes; and clearly all notes must become mutable as a result of modulation through all the keys.

For G major the tone g' to a' must become major instead of minor, the tone a' to b' must become minor instead of major, and f' must be replaced by a new note, f' sharp. For A minor the tones c' to d' and f' to g' must become minor instead of major, the tones d' to e' and g' to a' must become major instead of minor, and f' and g' must be supplemented by two new notes, f' sharp and g' sharp. And so on.

The pitch at which a note is taken, particularly when not essential to the harmony, is also modified by the melody. In an ascending phrase such as c', d', e', f', g', in which the second and fourth notes are not part of the prevailing harmony, these two notes will probably be made sharper than they would be in the same phrase descending, as g', f', e', d', c'. A leading note, such as b', leading up enticingly to the tonic c'', would almost invariably be taken decidedly sharp. A returning semitone, such as d' flat reached from but falling back upon c', would usually be taken decidedly flat. Both are diatonic semitones, and should justly be wider than chromatic semitones such as c' to c' sharp; but in these circumstances they are likely to be taken narrower, and will sound much better if they are.

In a word, good intonation is not fixed, but flexible; and so too, therefore, must our *pure* scale be *flexible* in practice.

For if it were fixed, the mutable notes could not be brought into tune, nor the melodic line humoured, as they are instinctively by all good singers, string and wind players.

But being thus flexible, good intonation, approximating to the pure scale, can properly be called just intonation.[1] In practice, however, the term is apt to be misleading, and is therefore best avoided. The point is that in practice *good intonation is always a compromise*. It is never 'exact' and to some extent is even a matter of taste.

Where, and for what reasons, temperament is required

There are certain instruments, such as the piano and the organ, which cannot employ 'just intonation', because their notes are fixed. They have therefore to be tuned to some compromise, which we call a temperament.

All just scales are flexible; but all tunings are fixed. Hence all fixed scales are tempered scales; and all tunings are temperaments.

It might be thought that by providing enough alternative notes within each octave, an untempered tuning could be achieved; but this is not the case. For fixed notes, however close, are not continuous. Each time you took a mutable alternative you would commit yourself to a slight but general change of pitch which you could not recover, as you do on flexible instruments, by edging imperceptibly back. Nor could you slide imperceptibly to an enharmonic neighbour.

Even Bosanquet's celebrated harmonium with fifty-three subdivisions to the octave gave faintly tempered major thirds. It was, however, a near enough approximation to sound untempered to normal listeners, and was described as smooth and sweet but quickly cloying.

Our present keyboard with five black and seven white notes, making a total of twelve (semitone) subdivisions to the octave, possesses two overwhelming advantages. It has a feasible and familiar technique. And it affords us the now indispensable ability to modulate enharmonically by at least imagining the same note, e.g. as B natural when striking it but as A double-sharp or C flat when leaving it.

Untempered tuning is thus as undesirable as it is unattainable. And the only temperaments of practical value are those adapted to our standard keyboard.

[1] American usage seems a little different: cf. J. Murray Barbour, *Music and Letters*, January 1938; Ll. S. Lloyd, ibid., October 1939 and July 1943. By just intonation American writers mean what I shall call just temperament, following Ll. S. Lloyd, for this term is now so defined in the British Standard Glossary of Associated Terms.

Just temperament

This name can fairly be applied to a tuning similar to the normal position of the pure scale except in being made rigid instead of flexible. Now we saw that the major sixth (as c' to a') less the major tone (as c' to d') gives a comma short of a perfect fifth; and likewise the perfect fourth (as c' to f') less the major tone (as c' to d') gives a comma short of a minor third (as d' to f').

That gives a supertonic minor third and fifth each tempered by almost a quarter of a semitone, which makes supertonic harmony unendurable, and renders just temperament useless save as an arbitrary but convenient reference tuning with which to compare the mistuning implied in other temperaments.

Mean-tone temperament

Here you tune your major thirds just, and you abolish the distinction between major and minor tones by splitting the difference (whence the name 'mean-tone'), which makes all your tones the half of the just major third.

Your fifths you make a little narrow (flat), so that by going up four of them from c you arrive exactly at the e'' which is the major third above c'', instead of overshooting it; while by going up twelve of them you would arrive at your b'^v sharp actually about two syntonic commas short of c^v, instead of a ditonic comma beyond.

That reconciles your major thirds (which being just, sound wonderfully well) with your fifths (which being only slightly tempered, sound very tolerable); but at the price of positively aggravating the discrepancy between C, B sharp and D double-flat, etc.

The result is exceptionally good in the keys (usually B flat, F, C, G, D, and A major, and G, D, and A minor) which need no notes beyond those provided (usually E flat, B flat, F, C, G, D, A, E, B, F sharp, C sharp, G sharp). You can, in short, modulate through a sequence of eleven fifths; *but there your cycle breaks*, because, on a twelve-note keyboard, you have now run out of new notes with which to continue it. Thus if you want, for example, A flat which is not provided, you must make do with G sharp, which is: but that will be nearly three-fifths of a semitone off the just major third with C, and nearly one-third of a semitone off the just fifth with E flat. It was this horrible gap which earned the name of 'wolf'.

You could move the wolf round a little by providing A flat at the sacrifice of G sharp, or D sharp at the sacrifice of E flat. You could drive the wolf a short way back by inserting divided finger-keys for striking both G sharp and A flat, both D sharp and E flat. You could cook the position of your 'black' notes, bringing G sharp midway between G and A, so as to serve rather better as A flat at the cost of serving much worse as G sharp (sometimes called unequal temperament, a term also used of non-cyclic temperaments in general).

But no modification will make mean-tone temperament, which is the best of all temperaments where remote sharps and flats are excluded, suitable where modulation is carried to extremes.

Equal temperament

This is a cyclic temperament using twelve subdivisions (there have been others using 19, 31 or 53) to the octave, and is our present system. You cut the Gordian knot by making every semitone equal (whence the name) as the twelfth part of the octave; your tones twice your semitones; your major thirds four times your semitones; your fifths seven times, etc.

That leaves no interval just save the octave. Every chord is decidedly worse out of tune than the best chords in mean-tone temperament; but no chord is as painfully out of tune as the worst chords in mean-tone temperament. You have slain the wolf; amalgamated your enharmonic neighbours C, B sharp, D double-flat, etc.; and reconciled your thirds, fifths and octaves.

You can go up or down twelve fifths and reach a B sharp or a D double-flat which is the same as C. You can go up and down three major thirds and reach a B sharp or a D double-flat which is the same as C. You can go up or down four fifths and reach an E or an A flat which is the same as the major third above or below C. You can strike a note as G sharp and leave the same note enharmonically, as A flat. You can modulate without restriction, either sharpwards or flatwards. For you have brought the infinite spiral of non-cyclic temperament into a closed cycle of the requisite twelve notes, neither more nor less.

Equal temperament imposes a certain hardness due to no single chord ever ringing perfectly in tune. (Choral or string music can never be judged properly at the piano, which harshens some of it and deadens the rest.) Most Renaissance and Baroque keyboard music would sound better in mean-tone temperament (the exact choice of notes to be made available being determined by the remotest accidentals chiefly needed).

Bach's keyboard music probably calls, not for equal temperament (despite the legend that he sponsored it) but for a mean-tone temperament brought very near to equal temperament by sharpening (widening) its major thirds; and the same may be true of earlier experiments in unrestricted modulation, though the principles and perhaps the practice of equal temperament were familiar to the Renaissance, if not to ancient Greece and still more ancient China.[1]

Equal temperament, despite its very appreciable imperfection, is a necessary condition of keyboard music as we now practise it, and is also (though not necessarily) the most usual basis at present of our electronic music. And for obvious reasons of convenience, it underlies the greater part of our Western music, both traditional and *avant-garde*. But it is habitually modified in practice by all performers whose instrument is flexible enough to permit of this: a fact both natural and desirable.

---

[1] J. Murray Barbour, 'Bach and the Art of Temperament', *Mus. Quart.*, January 1947. See also Percy A. Scholes, *Oxford Companion to Music*, 1938, etc., s.v. 'Temperament'; and consult Ll. S. Lloyd's articles on Temperaments in the fifth edition (1954) of Grove's *Dictionary of Music and Musicians*. This article is a most important recent treatment of the subject, and is a classic of its kind.

Bach's celebrated Forty-eight Preludes and Fugues in all twenty-four keys major and minor, of which the first volume was published in 1722 under the title *Das wohltemperierte Clavier* (which may as correctly be translated 'well-tuned' as 'well-tempered' keyboard), may have had a partial model in J. C. F. Fischer's *Ariadne musica neo-organoedum* of 1702, in nineteen different keys major and minor. Mattheson used all the keys in his *Organistenprobe* of 1719. Some extreme enharmonic keyboard modulations by John Bull (c. 1562-1628) and others appear to imply completely equal temperament. But it is worth remembering that there is one Renaissance and Baroque keyboard instrument of which the tuning is not fixed rigidly, but is flexible enough to permit just intonation in theory, and with skill perhaps in practice: namely the clavichord, Bach's reputed favourite.

READING LIST

APEL, WILLI. *Harvard Dictionary of Music*. Cambridge, Mass., 1944. 2nd ed. Cambridge, Mass., 1969 (much expanded editorially and by further contributors, but less reliable).

BACHMANN, WERNER. *Die Anfänge des Streichinstrumentenspiels*. Leipzig, 1964. Trans. by Norma Deane as *The Origins of Bowing and the Development of Bowed Instruments up to the Thirteenth Century*. London, 1969. (Important, and has valuable illustrations – photographs of early depictions.)

BACKUS, JOHN. *The Acoustical Foundations of Music*. New York, 1969. (A most valuable introduction, on a fairly detailed scale.)

BAINES, ANTHONY. *Bagpipes*. Oxford, 1960. (A specialist of the best kind.)

BAINES, ANTHONY. *European and American Musical Instruments*. London, 1966. (A most valuable illustrated introduction, excellent both in its pictures and in its text.)

BAINES, ANTHONY. *Victoria and Albert Museum: Catalogue of Musical Instruments. Volume II. Non-Keyboard Instruments*. London, 1968. (A model of its kind.)

BAINES, ANTHONY. *Woodwind Instruments and Their History*. Foreword by Sir Adrian Boult. London, 1957. 3rd ed. London, 1967. (The standard work in English, and full of human interest into the bargain.)

BAINES, ANTHONY. ed. *Musical Instruments Through the Ages*. Harmondsworth, 1961.

> *Contributors:* Klaus P. Wachsmann, Cecil Clutton, Thurston Dart, Raymond Russell, David D. Boyden, Kenneth Skeaping, Christopher Bunting, Eric Halfpenny, Michael W. Prynne, Albert Birch, Anthony Baines, James A. Macgillivray, Christopher W. Monk, R. Morley Pegge, James Howarth and James Blades.

(Weak in parts, but mainly excellent and very well edited; and as a whole a fascinating and reliable popular account.)

BARBOUR, J. MURRAY. *Trumpets, Horns and Music.* [East Lansing, Michigan], 1964. (Not uniformly reliable, but much excellent matter, especially on clarino techniques.)

BARBOUR, J. MURRAY. *Tuning and Temperament: A Historical Survey.* East Lansing, Michigan, 1951. 2nd ed. East Lansing, Michigan, 1953. (Important.)

BARTOLOZZI, BRUNO. *New Sounds for Woodwind.* Trans. with added notes by Reginald Smith Brindle. London, 1967. (Lucid account – with many music examples and a record of illustrations – of new techniques for producing forced sounds, including microtones and chords, from flute, oboe, clarinet and bassoon. Many fingering charts are included, and some recorded illustrations.)

BATE, PHILIP. *The Flute: A Study of Its History, Development and Construction.* London and New York, 1969. (Valuable and up-to-date general account.)

BATE, PHILIP. *The Oboe: An Outline of Its History, Development and Construction.* London and New York, 1956. (Excellent general account.)

BATE, PHILIP. *The Trumpet and Trombone: An Outline of Their History, Development and Construction.* London and New York, 1966. (Excellent study.)

BECK, SYDNEY and ELIZABETH E. ROTH. *Music in Prints.* New York, 1965. (A very pleasant collection.)

BÉKÉSY, GEORG VON. *Experiments in Hearing.* Trans. and ed. by E. G. Wever. New York, Toronto, and London, 1960. (Not designed for lay readers, but a scientific treatise on the frontiers of research, and as such highly interesting and important.)

BESSARABOFF, NICHOLAS. *Ancient European Musical Instruments: An Organological Study of the Musical Instruments in the Leslie Lindsey Mason Collection at the Museums of Fine Art, Boston.* Preface by Edwin J. Hipkiss and Foreword by Canon Francis W. Galpin. Boston, 1941. (Confusingly arranged, but immensely informative.)

BLADES, JAMES. *Percussion Instruments and Their History.* London, in preparation. (A fine performer's thoughts and descriptions, largely from first-hand experience.)

BOYDEN, DAVID D. *Catalogue of The Hill Collection of Musical Instruments in the Ashmolean Museum, Oxford.* London, 1969. (Very well described.)

BOYDEN, DAVID D. *The History of Violin Playing from Its Origins to 1761 and Its Relationship to the Violin and Violin Music.* London, 1965. (A classic of modern musicology. Indispensable for all students of early violin music and its proper performance.)

BRAGARD, ROGER and FERDINAND J. DE HEN. *Musical Instruments in Art and History.* Trans. by Bill Hopkins. Preface by G. Thibault. London, 1968. (Text unreliable, pictures magnificent.)

BRINDLE, REGINALD SMITH. *Contemporary Percussion.* London, 1970. (Very thorough, up to date and admirable.)

CARSE, ADAM. *Musical Wind Instruments: A History of the Wind Instruments Used in European Orchestras and Wind-Bands from the Later Middle Ages up to the Present Time.* London, 1939. Reprinted New York, 1965, with Introd. by Himie Voxman. (Still a most concise survey of this very tricky and important field. Some judgements are outdated now; but Himie Voxman's excellent introduction warns the reader and specifies and evaluates the main subsequent literature.)

CARSE, ADAM. *The Orchestra in the XVIIIth Century.* Cambridge, 1940. (No longer up to date, but still valuable if used with caution.)

CLEMENCIC, RÉNÉ. *Old Musical Instruments.* Trans. by David Hermges. London, 1968. (Excellent pictures and a pleasantly informative text.)

CLUTTON, CECIL and AUSTIN NILAND. *The British Organ.* London, 1963. (Excellent: the standard work.)

CLUTTON, CECIL and GEORGE DIXON. *The Organ.* London, 1950. (Particularly recommended.)

DART, THURSTON. *The Interpretation of Music.* London, 1954. 4th ed. [same as the 1st ed. except for an updated bibliography and a few changes in minor details] London, 1967. (A most readable and suggestive introduction.)

DOLMETSCH, ARNOLD. *The Interpretation of the Music of the XVIIth and XVIIIth Centuries Revealed by Contemporary Evidence.* London [1915]. New ed., London [1944]. Reprint of the 1946 [*sic*] ed., with good Introd. by R. Alec Harman. Seattle and London, 1969. (A pioneering classic, still of value.)

DONINGTON, ROBERT. Articles in *Grove's Dictionary of Music and Musicians*, 5th ed., ed. Eric Blom (London and New York, 1954), especially on Baroque Interpretation; Bow; Chamber Organ; Chest of Viols; Consort of Viols; Dolmetsch; Fingering; Frets; Harpsichord playing; Harpsichord stops; Instruments (an attempt at a general classification); Phrasing; Pianoforte playing; Violin playing; Violoncello playing.

DONINGTON, ROBERT. *The Interpretation of Early Music*. London, 1963; New York, 1964. 2nd ed. London, 1965; New York, 1966. (A detailed investigation, based on contemporary evidence, into the most authentic and effective ways of performing music of the Baroque period from Monteverdi to J. S. Bach.)

DORF, RICHARD H. *Electronic Musical Instruments*. New York, 1954. 3rd ed. New York, 1968. (Full, detailed and excellent. Third ed. is wholly re-written and replaces the earlier eds.)

DOUGLAS, ALAN L. M. *The Electrical Production of Music*. London and New York, 1957. (Still useful, though considerably dated in a rapidly developing field.)

EBY, ROBERT L. *Electronic Organs: A Complete Catalogue, Textbook and Manual*. Wheaton, Illinois, 1953. (Solid though no longer up to date.)

EIMERT, HERBERT and KARLHEINZ STOCKHAUSEN, eds. *Electronic Music*. Anon. trans. of *Die Reihe*, vol. I. Bryn Mawr, Pa., 1958. (A series of authoritative statements of aim by electronic composers; propagandist and tendentious, but valuable as such.)

FOERSTER, HEINZ VON and JAMES W. BEAUCHAMP, eds. *Music by Computers*. New York etc., 1969. (A little bad history and worse aesthetics; otherwise informative, excellent, and not too difficult for readers who have mastered Max V. Mathews' symposium – see below. Includes recorded examples, of which Side I, by J. K. Randall, is particularly recommended for repeated hearings.)

FORSYTH, CECIL. *Orchestration*. London, 1914. 2nd ed. London, 1935. (Though badly outdated in parts, this continues to be an outstandingly practical and valuable book.)

GALPIN, FRANCIS W. *Old English Instruments of Music: Their History and Character*. London, 1910. 4th ed., rev. Thurston Dart. London, 1965. (A pioneering classic, conservatively revised, and now more interesting historically than practically.)

GALPIN, FRANCIS W. *A Textbook of European Musical Instruments:*
S

Their Origin, History and Character. London, 1937. (Now out of date, but still worth consulting for its fine blend of scholarship with musicianship.)

Galpin Society Journal. Approximately yearly, from 1948. (Full of articles of detailed interest with regard to musical instruments from many different points of view.)

GEIRINGER, KARL. *Musical Instruments: Their History in Western Culture from the Stone Age to the Present.* Trans. by Bernard Miall. London, 1943. (Uneven, but there is much of value, and a fine musical mind behind it.)

GREGORY, ROBIN. *The Horn: A Guide to the Modern Instrument.* London, 1961. 2nd ed. London and New York, 1969. (A valuable and detailed study, a little defective on early history and technique.)

Grove's Dictionary of Music and Musicians. 5th ed., ed. Eric Blom. London and New York, 1954. Supplementary vol., ed. Eric Blom and Denis Stevens. London and New York, 1961. (Though still extremely uneven, this tremendous compendium is quite indispensable for serious work, but it is less essential for the average layman.) 6th ed. by Stanley Sadie now in preparation.

HALFPENNY, ERIC. Articles in *Grove's Dictionary of Music and Musicians,* 5th ed., ed. Eric Blom (London and New York, 1954), on Bow; Soundhole.

HARDING, ROSAMUND E. M. *The Piano-forte: Its History Traced to the Great Exhibition of 1851.* Cambridge, 1933. (Now a little out of date with regard to the origins of the piano, but in other respects this book is definitive.)

HARRISON, FRANK and JOAN RIMMER. *European Musical Instruments.* London, 1964. (A most attractive and well-described picture book.)

HAYES, GERALD R. *Musical Instruments and Their Music, 1500–1750.* Vol. II. *The Viols, and Other Bowed Instruments.* Introd. by Arnold Dolmetsch. London, 1930. (An important study of all the bowed string instruments, including the violins, now partly but not wholly superseded. There is also a polemical Vol. I, *The Treatment of Instrumental Music,* London, 1928. Subsequent volumes were planned but did not appear.)

HELMHOLTZ, HERMANN L. F. VON. *On the Sensations of Tone as a Physiological Basis for the Theory of Music.* Trans. by Alexander

J. Ellis from the 3rd German ed. of 1870 [1st German ed. 1862]. London, 1875. 2nd English ed. Trans. and ed. by A. J. Ellis from the 4th German ed. of 1877, with Introd. by Henry Margenau. New York, 1954. (Long, detailed and stiff, but the indispensable starting-point for the serious student of musical acoustics, and the foundation of all subsequent research, which has confirmed an astoundingly high proportion of its conclusions. Helmholtz used simple apparatus and was in most ways a pioneer; but he was guided by a very wise philosophical understanding and his whole attitude was exactly right.)

HOWES, FRANK S. *Full Orchestra*. London, 1942. 2nd ed. London, 1942. 3rd [unrevised] ed. 1943. (A very readable general survey which pays due regard to the underlying principles.)

HUBBARD, FRANK. *Three Centuries of Harpsichord Making*. Foreword by Ralph Kirkpatrick. Cambridge, Mass., 1965. (Excellent and invaluable.)

HUNT, EDGAR. *The Recorder and Its Music*. London, 1962. (Widely informative and valuable, including an excellent survey of the current situation at that date.)

HUTCHINS, CARLEEN MALEY. 'The Physics of Violins', *Scientific American*, vol. 207 (Nov. 1962), pp. 78–93. (Typical of the new researches of the past decade, and extremely interesting.)

JEANS, SIR JAMES. *Science & Music*. Cambridge and New York, 1937. (Extremely clear and readable, always a little over-simplified, and now substantially out of date.)

JUDD, FREDERICK CHARLES. *Electronic Music and Musique Concrète*. London, 1961. (Still a useful short introduction.)

KELSEY, FRANKLYN. 'Voice-Training', in *Grove's Dictionary of Music and Musicians*, 5th ed., ed. Eric Blom (London and New York, 1954), IX, pp. 43–66. (Detailed, perceptive and – except for some very fallacious music history – mainly very good.)

KENNAN, KENT WHEELER. *The Technique of Orchestration*. Englewood Cliffs, N.J., 1952. (Useful.)

KINSKY, GEORG, ed. *A History of Music in Pictures*. Introd. by Eric Blom. London, Toronto, and New York, 1930. (Still an invaluable work of reference for pictorial matter; the captions must be taken with considerable caution.)

LANGWILL, LYNDESAY G. *The Bassoon and Contrabassoon*. London and New York, 1965. (Excellent.)

LEIPP, ÉMILE. *Le Violon: Histoire, esthétique, facture et acoustique*. Paris, 1965. Trans. by Hildegarde W. Parry, *The Violin: History, Aesthetics, Manufacture and Acoustics*. Toronto, 1969. (A valuable supplement to Boyden's *History* – see above – especially on structure and acoustics.)

LLOYD, LL. S. *Music and Sound*. Foreword by Sir William Bragg. London, New York, and Toronto, 1937. (Now inevitably dated; but Lloyd's approach combined the highest scientific skill and integrity with the understanding of a good musician, and his work remains outstanding and important.)

LLOYD, LL. S. *The Musical Ear*. London, New York, and Toronto, 1940. (An invaluable companion volume to the above.)

LLOYD, LL. S. Articles in *Grove's Dictionary of Music and Musicians*, 5th ed., ed. Eric Blom (London and New York, 1954), on Acoustics; Intervals; Just Intonation; Pitch, absolute; Pitch notation; Pitch, standard; Sound; Temperaments; Theory; Tuning; Tuning-fork. (A series of linked studies which together form one of the most important contributions to the subject. Highly recommended both to specialists and non-specialists.)

LLOYD, LL. S. and HUGH BOYLE. *Intervals, Scales and Temperaments*. London and New York, 1963. (Reprinted articles by Lloyd with excellent supporting matter by Boyle.)

MARCUSE, SIBYL. *Musical Instruments: A Comprehensive Dictionary*. New York, 1964. (Inevitably a little uneven, but useful.)

MATHEWS, MAX V. *et al. The Technology of Computer Music*. Cambridge, Mass., and London, 1969. (Important and valuable.)

MILLER, DAYTON C. *Sound Waves: Their Shape and Speed*. New York, 1937. (The fascinating report of a piece of primary research.)

MORLEY-PEGGE, R. *The French Horn*. London, 1960. (A fine study.)

NEWMAN, SIDNEY and PETER WILLIAMS, eds. *The Russell Collection and Other Early Keyboard Instruments in Saint Cecilia's Hall, Edinburgh*. Edinburgh, 1968. (Very well done.)

PERLE, GEORGE. *Serial Composition and Atonality: An Introduction to the Music of Schoenberg, Berg and Webern*. London, 1962. 2nd ed. Berkeley, Los Angeles and London, 1968. (A thorough, important and very competent analysis. Shows the extremes to which mathematical calculation has been carried by post-Webernites. The author is himself a very good composer.)

PISTON, WALTER. *Orchestration*. New York, 1955. (Does not replace Forsyth – see above – but is imaginative.)

RENDALL, GEOFFREY. *The Clarinet: Some Notes upon Its History and Construction*. London and New York, 1954. (Corrects many previous misapprehensions. A most important and valuable study.)

RUSSELL, RAYMOND. *The Harpsichord and Clavichord: An Introductory Study*. London, 1959. (A most important and informative study.)

RUSSELL, RAYMOND. *Victoria and Albert Museum: Catalogue of Musical Instruments. Volume I. Keyboard Instruments*. London, 1968. (Admirable.)

SACHS, CURT. *The History of Musical Instruments*. New York, 1940. (A concise narrative account, against a background of musical and social history. Highly unreliable, but also valuably suggestive.)

SCHOLES, PERCY A. *The Oxford Companion to Music*. London, New York, and Toronto, 1938. 9th ed. London, New York, and Toronto, 1955. (This admirable volume will sit side by side with Grove on the specialist's shelf; but it is still more valuable to the lay reader, being at the same time genuinely popular and on the whole unusually dependable.)

SEASHORE, CARL E. *Psychology of Music*. New York and London, 1938. (An ambitious and uneven but important book, covering more physiology than psychology.)

STUCKENSCHMIDT, H. H. 'Contemporary Techniques in Music', *The Musical Quarterly*, XLIX (Jan. 1963), pp. 1–16. (A lucid account of fairly recent *avant-garde* views.)

SUMNER, WILLIAM LESLIE. *The Organ: Its Evolution, Principles of Construction and Use*. London and New York, 1952. 3rd ed. London, 1962. (A standard work of reference, full and valuable.)

SUMNER, WILLIAM LESLIE. *The Pianoforte*. London, 1966. (A very solid and interesting piece of work.)

TAYLOR, HENRY W. *The Art and Science of the Timpani*. London, 1964. (Not always scientifically tenable, but of much practical value and interest.)

TERRY, CHARLES SANFORD. *Bach's Orchestra*. London, 1932. (A quite excellent study, not much out of date, but caution is needed.)

VETTER, MICHAEL. *Il flauto dolce ed acerbo. I. Instructions and Exercises for Players of New Recorder Music*. Celle, 1969. (Parallel German and English texts. Does for the modern technique of the recorder what Bartolozzi – see above – does for the flute etc., and does it extremely well.)

VICTORIA AND ALBERT MUSEUM. *Musical Instruments as Works of Art*. Foreword by John Pope-Hennessy. London, 1968. (Excellent pictures, with good annotations, of instruments from this important collection.)

WHITWORTH, REGINALD. *The Electric Organ: A Historical Introduction and a Comprehensive Description of Modern Usage of Electricity in Organ Building*. London, 1930. 3rd ed. London, 1948. (Still useful.)

WILLIAMS, PETER. *The European Organ 1450–1850*. London, 1966. (Valuable for its detailed descriptions.)

WILSON, MICHAEL. *The English Chamber Organ: History and Development 1650–1850*. Foreword by W. L. Sumner. Oxford and Columbia, South Carolina, 1968. (Historically amateurish, but descriptively of great value.)

WINTERNITZ, EMANUEL. *Musical Instruments and Their Symbolism in Western Art*. New York, 1968. (A cultural historian's thoughtful approach.)

WINTERNITZ, EMANUEL. *Musical Instruments of the Western World*. New York and Toronto, n.d. [1966 ?]. (Magnificently chosen and photographed instruments of unusual beauty.)

WOOD, ALEXANDER. *The Physics of Music*. London, 1944. 6th ed., rev. J. M. Bowsher. London, 1962. (A stiffish but very useful text-book, though by now a little out of date.)

INDEX

(Reference is not made to entries in the Glossary or the Reading List, since these are themselves alphabetically arranged. Varieties of an instrument distinguished by such prefixes as 'treble', 'alto', 'bass', etc., are not indexed under these prefixes but under the name of the instrument itself. Bold numbers refer to plates.)